Adventure Tourism

This book is dedicated to:

Susan Horner and John Michael Richard Swarbrooke, two great companions on the ultimate tourism trip . . . life.

Gill's partner, Pete Oates – someone who has inspired me to write, through his continuous encouragement and the many great adventures that we have shared.

Ceri and Sam Beard for their continual source of youthful inspiration.

Steve Elliott, who Suzanne would like to thank for his constant understanding and support.

Our students, past and present, for their inspiration and good company.

Past and present friends at the University of Bethlehem, in the hope of a better future for all of them and for the people of Palestine.

Adventure Tourism

The new frontier

John Swarbrooke
Colin Beard
Suzanne Leckie
Gill Pomfret

BUTTERWORTH
HEINEMANN

OXFORD   AMSTERDAM   BOSTON   LONDON   NEW YORK   PARIS
SAN DIEGO   SAN FRANCISCO   SINGAPORE   SYDNEY   TOKYO

Butterworth-Heinemann is an imprint of Elsevier
Linacre House, Jordan Hill, Oxford OX2 8DP, UK
30 Corporate Drive, Suite 400, Burlington, MA 01803, USA

First edition 2003
Reprinted 2005, 2006

Notice
No responsibility is assumed by the publisher for any injury and/or damage to persons
or property as a matter of products liability, negligence or otherwise, or from any use
or operation of any methods, products, instructions or ideas contained in the material
herein. Because of rapid advances in the medical sciences, in particular, independent
verification of diagnoses and drug dosages should be made

British Library Cataloguing in Publication Data
A catalogue record for this book is available from the British Library

Library of Congress Cataloging-in-Publication Data
A catalog record for this book is available from the Library of Congress

ISBN–13: 978-0-7506-5186-8
ISBN–10: 0-7506-5186-5

For information on all Butterworth-Heinemann publications
visit our website at books.elsevier.com

Transferred to Digital Printing in 2009

Working together to grow
libraries in developing countries

www.elsevier.com | www.bookaid.org | www.sabre.org

ELSEVIER   BOOK AID
International   Sabre Foundation

Contents

Acknowledgements

In writing this book, the authors have been greatly helped by the following people:

Judy Mitchell, who showed great patience in typing and compiling the manuscript, and in working with four very different authors.

Friends who have given us the opportunity to see adventure tourism and adventurous destinations at first hand, including Marina Sukueva in Siberia, Adriano Piazzi in Brazil, and Dimitrios Skalkos in the Epirus region of Greece.

Sue Norbury and Julian Harlow, who shared with us the exciting experiences that they had whilst working for GREENFORCE.

Chris Craggs, a renowned rock climber and author of several climbing guidebooks, who gave such an interesting account of this sport and its growing importance in Spain.

Frank Hibbert, who provided cutting-edge research on risk management in mountain adventure tourism from his high quality Master's dissertation.

Brad and Keith Pearse, who supplied some very useful information about the South African-based company, 180° Adventures.

Joni Ong and family, and all staff at Outward Bound Singapore.

Todd Hesket, who generously supplied information and ideas about his company 'Active Family Vacations'.

List of case studies

Additional case studies are available online at
www.bh.com/companions/0750651865

Preface

This book represents a very ambitious project! It is an attempt to explore the growing, but broad and ill-defined, phenomenon of adventure tourism.

At the same time, the sub-headings of the book reflect the authors' view that adventure tourism represents a 'new frontier' in tourism in several ways.

First, in many ways the changes that have taken place in adventure tourism in recent years appear to illustrate and support the idea that we are seeing the transition from 'old tourism' to 'new tourism'.

Second, in terms of the geographical dimension of tourism adventure tourists are pushing back the frontiers, making destinations of the last wildernesses on earth, and even of space!

Third, in many types of adventure tourism we are seeing new forms and variations on a theme, which are shifting 'the frontier' in the different sectors of tourism.

Finally, we are living in a time where 'classic' natural wilderness adventure travel is being complemented by adventure experiences in man-made artificial environments, often in urban areas.

The authors are determined to try to present as holistic a view as possible of adventure tourism. In most texts adventure tourism is seen as a physical phenomenon, involving tourists undertaking physical activities in unfamiliar and often inhospitable environments. However, it is our contention that there is also a non-physical dimension to adventure tourism in two ways. In the first place, physical adventure activities have a strong non-physical element in the emotion of fear and, taking mountaineering as an example, in the almost spiritual feeling experienced when standing alone on one of the highest points on earth.

More fundamentally, though, there are forms of adventure tourism that are largely or wholly non-physical in nature. Non-physical adventure tourism can, perhaps, be divided into different types, namely:

- Intellectual adventure, such as travelling for mental self-development
- Emotional adventure, for example gambling or hedonism
- Spiritual adventure, where people travel in search of spiritual enlightenment.

The inclusion of non-physical adventure tourism in this book has made it almost unbearably difficult to write, because non-physical adventure has received much less attention from academics than its physical counterpart. As a result, there is little theoretical literature in this field, and very few data exist for many forms of non-physical adventure tourism. For this reason, non-physical adventure tourism receives less coverage in this book than the more traditional physical forms. However, the authors wish to stress that this imbalance is mainly as a result of the lack of data and theoretical literature, and it in no way reflects their view of the respective importance of the two forms of adventure tourism.

It became clear to the authors very early on that adventure tourism is a diverse field. Even physical adventure is highly heterogeneous. The breadth of physical adventure tourism today was clearly illustrated in a small book given away free in 2002 with *Global* magazine in the UK. This listed 'Great Adventures for 2002', including:

- Trekking holidays in Morocco and Asia
- Bike-riding adventures in South Africa
- Diving trips to the Red Sea
- Whale-watching in Norway
- Swimming amongst sharks in South Africa
- Cheetah-watching in Namibia
- Dog-sledding and reindeer expeditions in Lapland
- Sailing tall ships across the Atlantic
- White-water rafting in Turkey
- Surfing in Cornwall, UK
- Riding the full length of the Trans-Siberian railway
- Taking part in charity challenge adventures, including the 'Vietnam Life-Cycle Challenge' and the '2002 UK Challenge Series'
- Going on a polar cruise to either the Arctic or Antarctica
- Going on holiday and paying to work on conservation projects in the UK

- Micro-light flying in the UK
- Taking part in the 'running of the bulls' in Pamplona, Spain
- Sky-diving in Spain and Florida
- Driving a Formula 1 racing car in the UK
- Practising falconry in the UK
- Taking a motorcycle tour of the South Island, New Zealand
- Training with Thai boxers in Thailand
- Horse-trekking in Kyrgystan
- Participating in the Outward Bound 2002 Expedition.

Non-physical adventure tourism is also a very diverse field, encompassing everything from gambling trips to hedonistic sun, sand, sea and sex vacations to journeys in search of spiritual enlightenment.

What is clear is that adventure is not an absolute concept that is the same for everyone. The concept of adventure is highly personal, and means different things to different people. Something that is quite everyday or mundane for one person can be a rare adventure for another, depending on experience and personality.

Sadly, this is just one of the areas in which the writing of this book was constrained by the lack of empirical data on many aspects of adventure tourism. Hence in Chapter 12 we have made an impassioned plea for more research to be conducted in adventure tourism.

Having talked a little about the aims of the book, and the problems experienced in writing it, it is time to tell the reader a little about its structure.

Part A sets the scene. Chapter 1 makes a brave attempt to introduce the concept of adventure tourism and offers some key definitions and typologies, while Chapter 2 puts adventure tourism into its historical context.

The adventure tourist is the focus of Part B. Chapter 3 concentrates on individual tourists and their characteristics and motives, while Chapter 4 analyses the scope and nature of the global adventure tourism market.

In Part C we turn our attention to the supply side of adventure tourism. Chapter 5 looks at destinations and views, while Chapter 6 looks at the structure of the adventure tourism industry.

Part D explores three key aspects of the management of adventure tourism. Chapter 7 concentrates on the marketing of adventure tourism, while Chapter 8 covers the crucial subject of risk management. In Chapter 9, the highly topical issue of ethics is examined.

Part E features two chapters on important and rapidly developing sectors of adventure tourism; wildlife tourism (Chapter 10) and artificial environment tourism (Chapter 11).

In Part F, the authors endeavour to look into the future and predict how adventure tourism is going to develop over time.

Part G is a very important section because it consists of real case studies, drawn from many different countries, which illustrate many of the points made in the text.

Finally, there is a detailed bibliography to help those who want to do further reading.

We hope that all kinds of people will find this book of interest, from students to policy makers, practitioners to academics.

We have tried, however imperfectly, to produce a book without geographical boundaries – one that explores the phenomenon of adventure tourism in different parts of the world.

This is not a book that is polished, nor does it provide comprehensive coverage of the subject, and it offers very few answers. Instead it is in many ways untidy and selective, and it raises far more questions than answers. This may well be due to our inadequacies as authors, but it also reflects the complexity of the field, its rapidly changing nature, and the very ambitious goals we set for ourselves. It is a classic case of 'work in progress', and we hope that this book will be a catalyst for other, more gifted, people to become interested in researching aspects of adventure tourism. If this happens, then the time taken writing this book will have been well spent.

John Swarbrooke, Colin Beard,
Suzanne Leckie and Gill Pomfret
Summer 2002

Part
A

Setting the context

1

Introduction, definitions and typologies

Introduction

This chapter endeavours to introduce the reader to the field of adventure tourism from the perspective of the authors. It analyses the fundamental components of adventure tourism, offers key definitions, examines the relationship between adventure tourism and other established niche tourism sectors, and puts forward various typologies to help the reader understand the nature and scope of adventure tourism.

Adventure tourism is a much-heralded phenomenon, but what exactly is it? To begin, we would like you to consider the five scenarios below and ask yourself, which ones encompass 'adventure tourism'?

1 A 30-year-old British man, an experienced mountain walker and climber, booking onto a specialist operator's package for a four-week

expedition to the Karakoram range of the Himalayas, including a summit attempt of Spantik, a 7000-m peak. The expedition is led by one of the tour operator's guides, and group sizes are no larger than eight.

2 An Afro-Caribbean couple from Miami, booking a cheap flight to Shanghai, who aim to explore the Yangtze River region of China. They have no specific plans or itinerary and intend to make transport and accommodation arrangements once they arrive, when they will 'see where things take them'. They have never been to China before.

3 A group of four UK award-winning mountain athletes entering a 48-hour adventure race (involving fell-running, canoeing and cycling) in Scotland. They form a team sponsored by a well-known outdoor clothing manufacturer.

4 A 45-year-old woman going abroad for first time, on her own, to attend a 'discover your inner voice' course in self-development at an alternative therapy centre in the foothills of the Sierra Nevada in Spain.

5 A family visiting the Lake District for the day, who book onto a 'family thrills and spills' day where they can try kayaking, climbing or canyoning.

Not sure where to draw the line? Neither were we when we started this book. Players in the tourism industry have enthusiastically adopted the term 'adventure tourism', but it has no readily agreed definition. It can be used to describe anything from taking a walk in the countryside to taking a flight in space! Most commentators concur that adventure tourism is a niche sector of the tourism industry, but there are plenty of other niche sectors – such as ecotourism and activity tourism – which have characteristics that overlap with those of adventure tourism. There are also many related phrases, such as 'adventure travel', 'adventure recreation' and 'hard and soft adventure', which on one hand can confuse but on the other can also contribute to understanding the potential breadth of adventure tourism. Adventure tourism is a complicated and somewhat ambiguous topic!

The study of any type of tourism typically involves breaking down the complexities of real life into distinct and separate components or disciplines, such as supply and demand, tourism marketing, or operations management. The tourism industry is complex, and so this process of deconstructing it into bite-sized pieces can help us begin to understand it. However, this can also create its own problems, as many of the phenomena that are involved in tourism are intertwined and interrelated in such a way that they cannot sensibly be separated.

Roberts and Hall (2001: 18) observe that the study of tourism is suffused with 'paradox and irony', incorporating apparently binary opposites such as continuity and change, sustainability and unsustainability, and even good and bad. They note it is also full of terms that 'imply the existence of qualities which may be more apparent than real', such as *niche*, *industry* and *product*. It is against this backdrop that we tackle our investigation into adventure tourism. It will inevitably involve deconstruction and its associated problems, as well as the use of those widely accepted but nebulous terms. However, in doing so it will also highlight paradoxes and allow readers to reconstruct their own understanding of adventure tourism.

Our analysis of what adventure tourism means begins with a review of the term *tourism* and is followed by an analysis of the nature of *adventure*, as obviously adventure tourism must in some way combine both concepts. The latter part of this chapter analyses the relationships between the different niche sectors that overlap with adventure tourism, such as ecotourism and activity tourism, as this will help set the context for the rest of the book.

Tourism

The leisure, recreation and travel elements of tourism

Although tourism is said to be one of the world's largest industries, it is difficult to define its limits and decide what counts as tourism and what doesn't. Many definitions of tourism lie within a leisure and recreational context, such as Pearce's (1987: 1) conceptualization that 'tourism may be thought of as the relationships and phenomena arising out of journeys and temporary stays of people travelling primarily for leisure or recreation purposes', or Leiper's (1995: 20) suggestion that 'tourism can be defined as the theories and practice of travelling and visiting places for leisure related purposes'.

In this sense, tourism shares strong fundamental characteristics and theoretical foundations with the recreation and leisure studies field. The terms *leisure*, *recreation* and *tourism* represent a type of loose unity that is focused on experiences and activities. Although there are many conceptualizations of leisure, commonly agreed characteristics include the following:

■ It provides opportunities for enjoyment, self expression and satisfaction, which makes it intrinsically motivating
■ It takes place in time set aside from obligations such as employment and family care
■ It is perceived as being freely chosen and entered into by the participant.

'Recreation' is often used interchangeably with 'leisure'. Recreation is also voluntarily undertaken, primarily for pleasure and satisfaction, during leisure time. The simplest distinction between leisure and recreation is one that identifies leisure with time and recreation with activity. Pigram and Jenkin (1999: 6) draw together the ideas of many authors, saying: 'Leisure has now become viewed as a process and recreation an experience which is goal oriented, with participation expected to yield satisfactions, and therefore physical and emotional rewards'.

Whilst there is a strong argument for the fact that tourism is undertaken for leisure or recreation purposes, the World Tourism Organization has also taken a slightly broader view of the purposes of tourism. It describes tourism as 'the activities of persons travelling to and staying in places outside their usual environment for not more than one consecutive year for leisure, business and other purposes' (WTO, 1994; see Pigram, 1996: 227).

This is very similar to the widespread understanding of the term *travel*. Indeed, the term *adventure travel* is often used both in the literature and in the industry as an alternative to adventure tourism. Addison (1999: 417) defines adventure travel as 'any activity trip close to nature that is undertaken by someone who departs from known surroundings to encounter unfamiliar places and people, with the purpose of exploration, study, business, communication, recreation, sport, or sightseeing and tourism'. This suggests that adventure travel is somewhat more extensive than tourism or leisure, by including goals that might be related to, for example, professional activity.

The concept of tourism generally involves the act of travel or journeying. Putting aside any debate over the length of the journey, tourists are expected to travel from their home to another destination. The reliance of tourism on travel is one of the reasons the two are so intertwined. Perhaps virtual reality will grey this one characteristic of tourism upon which most people agree!

The tricky question of the duration of a tourism experience usually crops up in discussions that attempt to define tourism. The most convenient 'rule' is that tourism involves an overnight stay. Leisure activities that do not involve an overnight stay may variously be defined as recreational activities or excursioning. However, these have an important role within the tourism industry. In the context of adventure tourism, many adventures are sought and provided near to home and therefore do not involve overnight stays. Although these may fall outside this conventional and narrow definition of tourism they will be explored further in this book, as these experiences often form the basis of trends in adventure tourism or support the development and growth of adventure tourism activities. An example of this is the use and development of climbing walls. These facilities are often used on a day-visit basis by people developing their technical climbing skills, and this skill development could be part of the preparation or build-up to an adventure trip. The operator running the climbing wall facility may also offer adventure holiday packages, using the wall to promote and advertise these potential adventure tours.

What does tourism mean in an 'adventure tourism' context?

So, although the most prevalent perception of tourism is that it is a form of leisure that incorporates an element of travel and an overnight stay, we think there is a justification for investigating activities and products that sit outside these boundaries – such as adventure recreation, adventure education and adventure competition. Adventure tourism is at the cutting edge of world tourism, and its newness merits a comprehensive examination, unhindered by the confines of traditional delineations. The frontiers that adventure tourism is forging make us re-assess the value of conventional definitions.

Adventure

We need to get to the heart of what we mean by adventure if we are to understand both what makes adventure tourism distinctive and where it overlaps with other tourism sectors. The term 'adventure' is evocative for many people – images and associations flood into the mind at the mention of the word. Imagination and emotion are very much part and parcel of the adventure experience, as we will see.

Below is a range of words frequently used in magazines and brochures purveying adventure products. Do these reflect your own associations with the word adventure?

Thrill	Challenge	Awe-inspiring
Adrenaline	Ultimate	Risk
Excitement	Elation	Conquer
Fear	Terror	Success
Journey	Expedition	Daring
Roughing it		

It is interesting to look at some of the ways that we develop our understanding of the term 'adventure'.

Even before we are old enough to encounter a dictionary definition of adventure, most of us have acquired an idea of what adventure is about. Adventure stories often play a role in forming our early images of the constituents of adventure. Classic adventure stories by authors such as Conrad, Stevenson and Rider-Haggard, and more modern stories such as *The Famous Five* series by Enid Blyton, have captivated many youngsters in the English-speaking world. Fisher (1986) analyses the characteristics of classic adventures stories and notes: 'The reader . . . is to be taken away from normal concerns by events of an exaggerated, heightened nature, often taking place in exotic, distant surroundings . . . they offer surprise rather than confirmation, strangeness rather than familiarity . . .'. These stories often promote a romantic view of the world, where heroism abounds and everything ends happily ever after. Nowadays these types of yarn are often translated into film for modern audiences, as in the case of *Indiana Jones and the Temple of Doom*. This kind of literature was sometimes referred to as 'escapism', and whilst any form of tourism can provide an escape from the humdrum ordinariness of everyday life, adventure tourism might be expected to capitalize on this escapist and fantasy element. Price (1974) talks of the link between adventure and romanticism, and notes that both can be illusionary and false on the one hand but visionary and idealistic on the other.

An analysis of adventure stories quickly shows that there is undoubtedly an element of contrivance in much of this genre – typically, good overcomes evil and there are happy endings. This has implications for the tourism industry, and for the commodification of adventure.

In contrast with romanticized adventure stories, there are grittier versions of adventure. Real-life experiences provide us with another influence on our perception of adventure. These experiences may have happened to other people or may be personal. Quests have been undertaken throughout history, where the dangers and the consequences were very real. Arctic explorers pushing the limits of endurance, climbers pushing the limits of skill and astronauts pushing the limits of technology have all died in their attempts. On a personal (and hopefully less tragic) level, many of us will have had an experience we would describe as an adventure. People commonly describe real-life adventures that involve challenges entailing a certain amount of discomfort or anxiety. Feeling scared, exhausted and thoroughly tested is sometimes part of the deal. In many ways, there is an expectation and acceptance that adventure might involve a certain amount of hardship and unpleasantness. Addison (1999: 417) reflects this when he suggests that adventure travel implies 'launching into the unknown with the expectation that it could turn out to be an ordeal'.

Initial reactions to the word 'adventure' are a good starting point for analysing its meaning, because they have unconsciously permeated our understanding of the concept. Some of these ideas will be enlarged upon in the next section, which attempts to identify the core or essential qualities of adventure.

Core characteristics of adventure

We do not believe there is a single characteristic that effectively sums up the nature of adventure; what follows is an attempt to draw out the key qualities of adventure. The focus is on the nature of adventure at this stage, rather than adventure tourism. We will discuss the ways on which tourism and adventure have been partnered together in the following section. However, occasionally we will pre-empt our discussion of adventure tourism by highlighting instances where other writers have relied on one of these core characteristics in their attempts to define adventure tourism.

The points below summarize the core characteristics or qualities of adventure that form the basis of the following analysis:

- Uncertain outcomes
- Danger and risk
- Challenge
- Anticipated rewards
- Novelty
- Stimulation and excitement
- Escapism and separation
- Exploration and discovery
- Absorption and focus
- Contrasting emotions.

Many of these qualities are inter-related and interdependent – for example, novelty contributes to both the sense of challenge and the degree of stimulation. Any of these qualities taken alone do not make an adventure. However, when they are all present, we believe an adventure is more or less guaranteed.

Uncertain outcomes

One of the most fundamental characteristics of adventure is that the outcome is uncertain. The absence of a guaranteed conclusion to the experience helps stimulate excitement and commitment in the participant. Uncertainty is one of the factors that sets up a challenge, and it can be created in a number of ways. The presence of danger, which in turn creates risk, ensures the outcome is not predictable. Uncertainty can also be created by novelty – by doing something that is new and unfamiliar. It is not surprising that adventurers might feel a little bit of trepidation as part of the complex array of emotions that adventure conjures up.

Danger and risk

Danger and risk are closely associated with uncertainty, in a 'chicken and egg' type of way! Uncertainty itself creates a sense of risk, and risk bolsters uncertainty. Risk involves people exposing themselves to danger. The risks could be damage to physical well-being (in the form of injury, pain, or death) or to psychological well-being (through humiliation, embarrassment, loss of confidence or loss of friendships). Danger resides in many situations, and not always in such obvious forms as a strong undercurrent or an icy ridge.

The ability to tolerate (or perhaps even enjoy) risk varies between individuals. The same set of circumstances produce excitement in one individual but fear in another. The perception of the likelihood of a risk being realized, and assessment of its consequences, also varies between individuals. The extremely personal nature of risk perception affects an individual's perception of what constitutes an adventurous experience.

As might be expected, given its association with uncertainty of outcome, there is a general consensus that adventure involves risk, and risk is frequently identified as one of the defining characteristics of adventure.

Challenge

Factors such as uncertainty of outcome, danger and the expectation of having to cope with difficult circumstances all combine to create a challenge. This challenge can be of an intellectual, moral, spiritual, emotional or physical nature.

The degree of challenge affects the intensity of the adventure experience, creating a continuum from extremely adventurous to mildly adventurous. Challenge is not only dependent upon the level of danger, but also upon the skills and abilities of the participant. The skills could be physical or technical skills, or personal attributes such as self-reliance. Mortlock (1984) explored this relationship between risks and competence in an adventure context, and produced a useful typology of stages of adventure (Figure 1.1). If the level of danger is low and the level of technical and personal skills is high, then the experience might be described as play – easy and enjoyable.

At the other end of the scale, where the nature of the activity far exceeds the skills of the participants, the experience is straying into the realm of misadventure, or even disaster and tragedy.

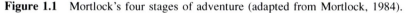

Figure 1.1 Mortlock's four stages of adventure (adapted from Mortlock, 1984).

Mortlock's model alludes to a crucial facet of challenge in an adventure context. Not only must the challenge be within the capacity of the participants but, just as importantly, there must also be some expectation (on the part of the participants themselves) that they can meet or overcome the challenge. If an experience is to be anticipated as an adventure, there has to be a glimmer of optimism and a feeling that success is possible. This proposal illustrates the authors' view that the concept of adventure is heavily dependent on mental and psychological factors.

Anticipated rewards

There is an expectation among adventurers that they will benefit from their experience, and that there will be some intrinsic reward. Adventure is entered into freely, without coercion, and in this respect shares some of the characteristics of leisure. Also, like leisure, adventures are to a large degree inner-directed and self-motivated. Sometimes there is a specific goal or driving imperative associated with adventure, but failure to achieve the original goal or mission is not necessarily an obstacle to achieving a sense of reward – the sense of satisfaction that comes from 'giving it a good try' will be enough for many participants. The achievement may also be something intangible, such as a sense of fulfilment or a 'peak experience'. On the other hand, the reward might well be a 'trophy' of some kind – an ethnic artefact, a sunken marine relic, or a tale to top all others! Stories, photographs, journals, logs and letters help commemorate the experience and provide lasting, tangible evidence of the event.

The anticipated benefit may not, in fact, be consciously articulated, but without it the sense of adventure is compromised. It is perhaps easier to understand the importance of perceived reward by considering what the experience would be like without it. Without some element of personal benefit, an adventure would turn out to be more of a trial or obligation.

It is an interesting paradox that 'uncertainty of outcome' has to live alongside expectation of reward or benefit. Indeed professionals such as outdoor education providers, who orchestrate adventurous experiences for clients, have been debating for some time how adventurous these experiences really are. Price (1974) suggests that as soon as one becomes a deliberate purveyor of adventure, one is in danger of losing much that is fundamental to it. He suggests it becomes a package deal, with something false and synthetic about it. This adventure paradox creates a certain tension for the adventure tourism industry. Tourism shares with romanticized adventure stories an element of contrivance, given that tourism providers generally seek to fulfil clients' dreams and expectations. It will be interesting to see how tourism businesses accommodate these conflicting attributes of adventure.

Novelty

Returning to the other major contributor to uncertainty, namely novelty, we find that most adventure involves an element of doing or experiencing something new. Novelty can be a major part of the adventure experience in cases where almost everything is new and fresh, or it may be a subtle twist, perhaps involving extension or development of previous experiences. An experience that is a straightforward and predictable repeat of a previous experience is never going to be an adventure!

Travel offers plentiful opportunities for exposure to new things. This is one of the reasons why travel or tourism makes an excellent vehicle for an adventurous experience. Looking at the other side of the coin, Voase (1995: 45) proposes that the motive for travel is the attractiveness of exposure to 'otherness' and 'abnormality'. If this is the case, it means most travellers are seeking an element of adventure in their travel experience.

A significant proportion of tourists who seek adventure, with its frisson of uncertainty, can be expected to seek it primarily through novel rather than physically dangerous experiences.

Stimulation and excitement

Adventure is a stimulating and intense experience. During an adventure people are exposed to environments and situations that stimulate the senses, the emotions, the intellect and the body's physiology.

Many adventurers report that adventure brings with it heightened awareness and a sense of immediacy and aliveness. Sometimes this heightened sense of awareness is brought on by the adrenaline rush that accompanies moments of fear, but equally it can accompany transcendent moments of great absorption and calm.

High levels of stimulation create excitement, but the exact level of stimulation required to reach a state of excitement varies from individual to individual. What creates excitement in one person creates agitation in another. This is another example of the subjective nature of adventure.

Muller and Cleaver (2000: 156) have identified stimulation as one of the main distinguishing features of adventure tourism, saying that adventure tourism is 'characterized by its ability to provide the tourist with relatively high levels of sensory stimulation . . .'.

Escapism and separation

The stimulation and intensity associated with adventure also contributes to removing the experience a step or two from the routine of everyday life, and giving it special significance that allows it to be identified as a specific and significant event. As described earlier in this chapter, the element of novelty also contributes to a sense of escapism. Exotic surroundings, new activities or unconventional social norms give an opportunity to enter into a parallel universe, where priorities can be different. Adventure is something apart. The ordinary world and everyday concerns are left behind.

Exploration and discovery

Exploration and discovery are core components of the adventure process. The increased knowledge and self-awareness that accompanies the discovery of new places, cultures and skills forms one of the rewards referred to earlier. Addison (1999) argues that education and the hunger to learn from new situations are key motivations for both travel and adventure.

The 'journey of discovery' that is associated with adventure works in a number of different contexts. Many adventure tourism experiences incorporate a physical journey over time and distance, echoing the journeys of early explorers. However, the journey of discovery could just as well refer to the mental, emotional or spiritual progress derived from an experience. Addison (1999: 418) notes the opportunities for discovery offered by the inner journey undertaken by adventure travellers:

> Since most of the world has been mapped and studied, true adventure has become more deliberate, specialized and technically demanding, as well

as being somewhat arbitrary in its selection of targets for conquest. There is little geographical need to 'discover' places on earth (satellites can do the job), so what remains is the pure brutality of the elements and the interest of the 'inner journey' made by the explorer.

Absorption and focus

There are a number of mental and emotional states that are induced during an adventure, and these include absorption and concentration. A challenge requires concentrated application of skills or effort. There are generally periods of intense focus during an adventure.

Contrasting emotions

Adventure is an emotional experience. Often people have invested a certain amount of emotional and mental energy before the active part of the experience begins – for example, in dreaming, worrying, hoping, or building confidence. This pre-event part of the adventure process helps develop its committing nature. The uncertainty and risks, and the sheer difficulty of some parts of the experience, mean that most people go through waves of contrasting emotions – for example, terror and elation, joy and despair, anxiety and pleasure. Adventure can be a bit of a roller-coaster ride, and this is to be expected. Again, the absence of contrasting emotions is telling – could an experience that was simply pure fun and joy be a true adventure?

Adventure summary – a process and a state of mind

Adventure, then, is where participants are voluntarily putting themselves in a position where they believe they are taking a step into the unknown, where they will face challenges, and where they will discover or gain something valuable from the experience.

This state of affairs is based on the individual's perception of the situation and of themselves, and therefore 'adventure' is subjective and unique to each person. It is quite apparent that what is an adventure for one person – say a solo sailing trip around the Mediterranean – may not be regarded as an adventure by another. Adventure is a personal construct, based more on individual mental and emotional perceptions than physical capacities. Like beauty, which is in the eye of the beholder, adventure is in the mind and heart of the participant.

It is clear from this examination that adventure is not determined by specific activities, but by the state of mind and approach of the participant. This analysis supports Hopkins and Putnam's (1993) assertion that 'Adventure can be of the mind and spirit as much as a physical challenge'. Spending time living in a different religious community or attending a self-development course can be just as much an adventure as trekking up Kilimanjaro.

Although specific activities don't define adventure, it is apparent that adventure entails action. Adventure is not a passive experience; it's engaging. This engagement can be on a physical, intellectual, emotional or spiritual level. Cater (2000) comments that 'adventure tourism is fundamentally about active recreation participation, and it demands new metaphors based more on "being, doing, touching and seeing" rather than just seeing'. We propose that 'feeling' could be added to this list as well. Adventure involves effort and commitment, and often mental and physical preparation or training are necessary.

Most of the characteristics of adventure that have been discussed so far are interdependent, or overlap with one or more of the others. They work together to create that state of affairs which leads someone to describe an experience as an

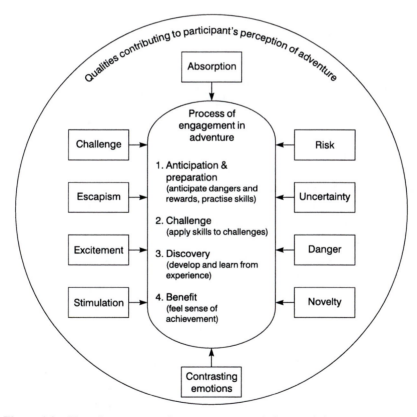

Figure 1.2 The adventure experience – process and characteristics.

adventure. Some of these core qualities relate to the main stages in the adventure process (see Figure 1.2); others describe the perceptions and feelings of the participant. These basic 'ingredients' of adventure can be combined in different proportions, giving a different flavour to the adventure experience.

So, to draw some preliminary conclusions on how the concepts of adventure and tourism combine to give us adventure tourism, in our view adventure tourism involves travel and leisure activities that are bought into (not simply financially, but as we are talking about tourism an exchange of money is often involved somewhere along the line!) in the hope that they will produce a rewarding adventure experience. Crucially, an adventure tourism experience will:

- Be of a heightened nature – a stimulating context will induce a range of emotions (of which excitement will be key), and separate it from everyday life
- Entail intellectual, physical or emotional risks and challenges – these will be absorbing
- Be intrinsically rewarding, providing opportunities for enjoyment, learning and self-development.

Manifestations of adventure in a tourism context

All of this discussion brings us to the question of how adventure manifests itself in a tourism context. If the core ingredients of adventure are applied to tourism activities, then a very broad range of activities that can take place in a wide range of settings results. This situation is exacerbated by the fact that any tourism experience that a participant thinks is an adventure, *is* an adventure! This, we suggest, is valid. However, it is also unwieldy. In addition, the tourist's point of view is only one half of the equation. The supply side of the tourism industry should also be considered, and for adventure tourism to be a saleable commodity it has to be parcelled into something that is 'suppliable'. So it seems that this idea of adventure tourism needs grounding in the practicalities of real life, and we need to divide it into manageable entities. We can begin this task by asking ourselves, 'How does adventure manifest itself in terms of what people do and where they do it?'

Certain settings and activities are strongly associated with adventure experiences, and for very good reasons. They facilitate the emotions, thoughts and sensations that define adventure. The most traditional and perhaps stereotypical associations with adventure experiences include those displayed in Table 1.1.

Table 1.1 Activities and settings typically associated with adventure

Activities associated with adventure	Settings associated with adventure
Physical activity, i.e. activities involving physical exertion or psychomotor skills	Outdoors, wilderness
Contact with nature, i.e. activities bringing contact with the natural world in general, or with specific wildlife	Outdoors, wilderness
Contact with different cultures, i.e. people, faith, lifestyles	Remote, unusual or exotic locations
Journeys, i.e. vehicle-, animal-, or human-powered voyages over land, sea or in the air	Remote, unusual or exotic locations

As it happens, the activities and settings that are commonly associated with adventure also form the basis of existing and well-recognized niche tourism sectors, as indicated in Table 1.2. When people refer to the 'adventure tourism industry', they are often referring to consumers and suppliers who focus on the adventure-oriented elements of these niche sectors.

These existing tourism niches clearly have the potential to offer opportunities for adventure tourism, given their strong relationship with activities and settings commonly associated with adventure experiences. This potential will be explained in the following sections. Many authors have concerned themselves with trying to identify the degree of similarity and difference between these niche forms of tourism and 'adventure tourism'. This debate has also resulted in the proposal of 'typologies' of adventure tourism. Whilst we have not always been able to align these ideas completely to our own analysis of adventure tourism, they have helped raise awareness of the adventure tourism phenomenon and made a useful contribution to the debate,

Table 1.2 Relationship between activities traditionally associated with adventure and existing forms of niche tourism

Activities associated with adventure		Existing niche forms of tourism
Physical activity	→	Activity tourism
Contact with nature	→	Nature-based tourism
Contact with other cultures	→	Discovery and cultural tourism
Journey	→	Expedition tourism

and so they have been noted in the discussion that immediately follows and throughout the book. The next section of this chapter addresses the four established tourism niches identified in Table 1.2 and their relationship with adventure tourism.

Activity tourism and adventure tourism

The association of physical activity with adventure is perhaps one of the most commonly held perceptions. The environment in which this most frequently happens, the outdoors, sits well with adventure because the natural world provides us with the resources for many of the activities that provide risk, challenge, sensory stimulus, novelty, discovery and so on. The outdoors incorporates a huge variety of elemental phenomena, such as tornadoes, polar ice caps, mountains, oceans and deserts, which, even if revisited, offer infinite novelty and many ready-made challenges.

The potential rewards that come from engaging in physically challenging activities are well known, relatively easy to achieve, and sometimes addictive. Challenges involving physical exertion are stimulating and absorbing. Coping with tough physical conditions tests and develops mental and emotional skills as well as physical prowess. The success of any venture that is so personally testing on all fronts can produce an incredible 'high' and a boost to self-esteem. Creating circumstances where people can push themselves to their physical limits is a convenient way to facilitate these benefits, and this is one of the reasons why 'physical activities' are so attractive to purveyors of adventure – including tourism providers. Another reason for their attractiveness to tourism providers is that engaging in activities generally involves the development of physical and technical skills, such as ice climbing or navigation. These help reduce the levels of risk. As competence levels change they modify the play-off between skills and danger, supplying endless opportunities to get out of the 'play zone' and into the 'adventure zone'.

Not surprisingly, the 'activity tourism' sector is perceived by many authors as having a high degree of overlap with adventure tourism. In order to position adventure tourism in relation to it, the characteristics and distinguishing features of activity tourism are examined briefly here.

The activity holiday market can simply be described as holidays that involve sport or a form of physical activity (Mintel, 1999), though others note that it can also include special interest and theme or hobby holidays (Roberts and Hall, 2001). It is therefore very broad, and includes activities ranging from sky-diving to landscape painting to learning a language.

The amount of physical exertion induced by these activities varies greatly. Of the range of activity holidays, those that involve outdoor recreation, outdoor pursuits and outdoor education sectors of the activity holiday market are particularly associated with adventure tourism, because the outdoors is such a good provider of challenging and stimulating situations, and because these holidays generally involve high levels of exertion or skill. However, not all physical activities – even those that take place outdoors – are adventurous. For example, many people would view a golfing or fishing holiday as relaxing and pleasurable rather than adventurous. The segments of the activity tourism market that do brand themselves as 'adventure activities' tend to involve activities that have high degrees of perceived or real risk. This is often created by the activities being based on elemental aspects of the environment that seem (or indeed are) dangerous – scaling high mountains, rafting fast rivers or diving deep caves would be included among adventure activities.

So it seems clear that some elements of the activity tourism market fit all of the requirements of adventure tourism, whereas other elements don't. The separation of those activities that do not fit the requirements of adventure tourism from those that do is hindered by the subjective nature of adventure. Different people will put different types of activity at either end of this continuum.

This is demonstrated in Figure 1.3, where we consider a hypothetical character, Pete, who is a 20-year-old student studying an Environmental

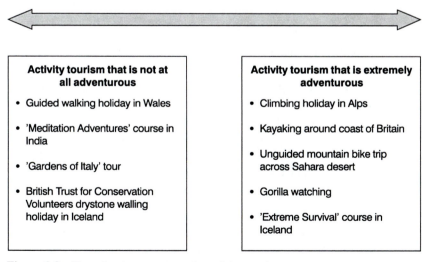

Figure 1.3 The adventure spectrum in activity tourism.

Conservation degree at Sheffield Hallam University. He undertakes voluntary conservation work with the National Trust at weekends. Pete keeps fit by hiking and mountain biking in the Peak District countryside. He has just started to learn to climb with the Student Union club at the local indoor climbing wall, despite his fear of heights. He has been abroad with his family and on school trips a couple of times. He hopes to become a National Park ranger when he finishes his degree.

Pete does not view the activities at the left-hand end of the continuum in Figure 1.3 as adventurous for various reasons; for example, he doesn't perceive them as exciting, having self-development potential or any element of risk or challenge. Other people might list different activities at each end.

It is apparent that activity tourism has a major role to play in adventure tourism. Millington *et al.* (2001) reached the same conclusion, and suggested that adventure tourism could be divided into two basic types – activity-driven and destination-driven. Interestingly, they also suggested that there still needs to be an exploration element for activity tourism to be classified as adventure travel, reflecting one of the core qualities of the adventure experience identified earlier in this chapter.

Despite the contribution that physical exertion and activity can make to adventure, these are not necessarily ingredients of adventure holidays. Adventures can be had without them. We now move on to discuss some of the other niche sectors of tourism that rely on associations with adventure that are not purely predicated upon physical effort and skill.

Nature-based tourism and adventure tourism

Table 1.1 identified contact with nature as an important ingredient in many adventures. Contact with wildlife has its dangers. The perceived and real risks associated with big cats, gorillas, elephants or sharks add a certain frisson to proceedings. However, as well as the danger there is the stimulation, the excitement and the transcendence of connection with wildlife. Pitting oneself against nature is but one approach to adventure; developing affinity with nature and pursuing a feeling of 'oneness' with nature is an equally challenging goal. Contact with nature 'in general' provides an escape from everyday life, especially the hectic and materialistic aspects.

Like many forms of activity tourism, nature-based tourism is associated with the 'great outdoors', which contains ecosystems that form the basis of wildlife tourism. The outdoors also provides a good setting for contemplation and self-development activities. The wilderness shares some of the qualities of 'remote' settings, which facilitate adventure in their own way and are discussed later.

Nature-based tourism is a generic term that covers tourism based on the 'use of natural resources in a wild and undeveloped form' (Goodwin, 1996: 287). Ecotourism and wildlife tourism are forms of nature-based tourism. Of these, ecotourism is the most well-known and frequently used in-phrase. Although it has a particular meaning in academic circles, it worth noting that it is often used when 'nature-based tourism' would in fact be a more accurate term. The development of the ecotourism concept has resulted in a plethora of definitions. A more thorough overview of ecotourism is provided in Chapters 3 and 10, but for the purposes of this discussion Fennell's (1999) definition will suffice:

> . . . ecotourism is a sustainable form of natural resource-based tourism that focuses primarily on experiencing and learning about nature, and which is ethically managed to be of low impact, non-consumptive, and locally oriented (control, benefits, and scale). It typically occurs in natural areas, and should contribute to the conservation or preservation of such areas.

Grant (2001) suggests that there is an overlap between adventure tourism and ecotourism. An activity such as whale watching could be described as either an adventure tourism experience or an ecotourism experience, depending on the emphasis and value the describer wishes to convey. Exactly the same argument applies to activity tourism, and the way it can overlap with both adventure tourism and ecotourism. A trip to see birdlife and butterflies in Costa Rica could be described using any of these three terms!

Fennell and Eagles (1990) created a 'tourism activity spectrum', illustrated in Table 1.3, which they use to explain the similarities and differences they perceive between adventure tourism and ecotourism. The three types of tourism that are included in the spectrum – adventure travel, ecotourism and tour travel – are associated with differing degrees of certain variables (risks, known and unknown results, certainty/safety, preparation/training). The unique character of adventure travel is based on the high degree of preparation and training needed prior to the experience, the high levels of uncertainty of outcome and high degrees of risk. This analysis supports some of our key 'ingredients' of adventure, outlined earlier in this chapter.

Some authors reason that ecotourism and adventure tourism are distinct entities, as adventure travel is primarily concerned with risk confrontation

Table 1.3 Tourism activity spectrum (adapted from Fennell and Eagles, 1990)

Increasing certainty/safety and known results ⟶

Adventure travel ⟷ (e.g. mountain climbing)	Ecotourism ⟷ (e.g. birdwatching)	Tour travel (e.g. package holiday)
■ Lack of certainty/ safety in adventure experience ■ Motivated by self-learning and personal fulfilment ■ Personal responsibility and mental/physical preparation are important	■ Covers adventure and tour travel ■ Combines educational pursuits and physical activities ■ Personal responsibility and mental/physical preparation are important ■ Highly personal experience; individuals benefit at different levels	■ Low level of personal preparation ■ High degree of safety ■ Group organization undertaken for the traveller

⟵ *Increasing degree of preparation/training/unknown results and risks*

whilst ecotourism's intrinsic component is nature appreciation. Whilst we are not altogether convinced about the practicality or realism of this type of differentiation, the analysis it is based upon does support our fundamental assertion that the interpretation of the nature of any activity is determined in the minds of the stakeholders, rather by the activity itself.

Preparation and training, which have been mentioned by both Fennel and Eagle (1990) and Grant (2001), highlight the importance of the pre-trip part of the whole adventure experience, especially in a tourism context. A tourism experience is not normally an accidental occurrence; there is usually a period of anticipation, even in a 'spur of the moment' decision.

Discovery/cultural tourism and adventure tourism

Our third tourism niche is associated with another set of characteristics that are strongly associated with adventure; namely contact with other cultures and remote, unusual or exotic settings. There are numerous destinations that fit the bill, especially as 'unusual' or 'exotic' is different from 'remote'. Smith and Jenner (1999: 45) note that 'the essential ingredients of an adventure holiday seem to include a remote, under-populated region with a traditional culture, where facilities are extremely limited'.

'Cultural tourism' is, like activity tourism, a very broad concept. Culture in this tourism sense includes 'high art' (opera, classical music, ballet, modern dance, painting and sculpture etc.), youth and alternative cultures (revolving around the music, dance and drugs scene), heritage and history (based on buildings and architecture, folk museums etc.), and anthropological/ethnographic interest in people and regions.

Anthropological investigations have formed the basis of a bout of recent publications by writers who have used their travels to 'strange' places as the source of inspiration. Living as a local and partaking of local customs, whether this involves hallucinatory drugs and voodoo trance or imbibing large amounts of dodgy alcohol before attempting some 'rite of passage' challenge, usually forms the premise of the tale. Many of these publications are purposefully written for popular consumption, often in a humorous style, and with a feeling for the adventurous elements of the experience, such as Hawkes (2000). 'Otherness', novelty, uncertainty, risk, exploration, discovery and revelation and many other facets of adventure are readily apparent in this type of adventure travel.

A tourism sector termed 'discovery travel' (Muller and Cleaver, 2000) is also largely based on contact with other cultures and visiting unusual destinations. As the term suggests, discovery travel also incorporates elements of exploration and learning. Muller and Cleaver (2000) choose to bind adventure tourism and discovery tourism together in what they term the 'adventurer and explorer' segment of the tourism market – adventure tourism is undertaken by adventurers, and discovery tourism by explorers. Although they differentiate between adventure tourism and discovery travel, the differences are a matter of degree and emphasis rather than the presence or absence of unique characteristics. This enables them to address the needs of the two groups at once in terms of the market analysis they undertake. They describe discovery travel as having more emphasis on mental stimulation and mind-broadening experiences, and less on physical thrill and challenge. The key characteristics of discovery travel are that opportunities for learning, discovery and personal growth are provided. They describe discovery travel in the following way (Muller and Cleaver, 2000; 156):

> Typically the travel experience is somewhat lengthier than in adventure travel and contains elements that offer self enrichment via exposure to novel places, novel cultures, novel activities and a requirement for the traveller to immerse him/herself in a learning environment provided by the tourism product.

23

Addison (2001) supports the role that learning has to play in adventure tourism, and also notes the value of detachment from everyday life in this process:

> The wilderness and travel to foreign societies may temporarily distance us from ourselves. Eventually we return to home base to reconsider who and what we are. Adventure travel should be an educative experience . . .

Examples of discovery travel include educational retreats, study holidays, archaeological digs, and trips to observe and interact with radically different cultures. Muller and Cleaver also note that participants can actually contribute to the experience. Wildlife survey expeditions also fit into this category. Again it is obvious that discovery and adventure travel are not completely distinct, and that there are considerable areas of overlap.

Expedition tourism and adventure tourism

Finally, if we return to Table 1.1, we find that journeys are frequently associated with adventure. Journeys to destinations that are remote or unusual, or that pass through difficult and dangerous terrain, are particularly reminiscent of adventure or travel stories.

Expedition travel is an established niche sector of the tourism industry that is based on journeys and voyages. These particularly pick up on the exploration aspect of adventure. Those adventurers who do not wish to engage in outdoor pursuits and sport challenges often favour this type of tourism. Expeditions can still be gruelling, and require both physical and mental endurance. They often take place in remote settings, where lack of infrastructure means the journey takes time, and thus often comprises the main 'activity'. Remote or unusual locations provide the conditions whereby challenge, novelty, 'otherness' and discovery can be almost guaranteed, simply by the nature of the location. In remote locations the risk element is enhanced by the lack of support services and rescue options should anything go wrong. Self-reliance can be an important attribute in these circumstances.

Overland expeditions are an obvious sub-sector of this niche. These may be motor vehicle-based (e.g. four-wheel drive or train), especially where distances are large. However, walking or trekking is sometimes the only way to see remote destinations. Animals such as horses, camels or sled dogs are sometimes used. Not all expeditions are strictly 'overland' – air- and water-based journeys are equally part of this sector, and might be marketed as sailing or canoeing voyages, or micro-light or hot-air ballooning expeditions. The method of transport often provides some of the novelty that contributes to an adventurous experience, and group travel is also frequently part of the deal with these kinds of trips. Social interaction adds stimulation, support and its own kind of challenge. Journeys also offer time to reflect, and the physical journey is often accompanied by an inner journey. Journeys, with various themes, are the basis of travel writing, and this has inspired many people to try this type of adventure tourism for themselves. The long duration and the physical and mental distance from home also contributes to the sense of separateness from everyday life, and enhance the adventurous quality of this type of tourism.

Clarifying the relationship between existing forms of tourism and adventure tourism

There has been a lot of debate about the differences between these established forms of tourism and adventure tourism. This analysis has led some authors to propose distinguishing features of adventure tourism, and some of these are embodied in the phrases contained in Table 1.2. Even a cursory examination of the niche forms of tourism discussed above makes it apparent that there is a considerable amount of overlap with adventure tourism. This in itself is not necessarily an unhelpful thing. In fact we suggest quite the opposite; it can be used to help highlight sub-sectors, or micro-niches, of adventure tourism.

Seductive though it is, we have not found the 'divisionist' approach (see Figure 1.4), where one tourism niche (e.g. activity tourism) is severed from another (e.g. adventure tourism), to be the most helpful or realistic approach

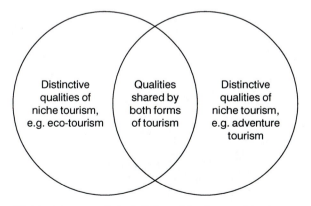

Figure 1.4 Divisionist approach to defining niche forms of tourism.

for the burgeoning adventure tourism industry. This is principally because the differences between any two forms of tourism are in the minds of the stakeholders and are not necessarily manifested in the products. Consumers' interests can also span two or more niche sectors, which contributes to the difficulty of drawing lines between them – for example, a person may be motivated by both adventure and fascination in wildlife. The impracticality of this divisionist approach is reflected by the fact that in the USA and Canada adventure, culture and ecological tourism are often amalgamated together as ACE travel (an acronym) for practical and business reasons, supporting the notion that there is a considerable amount of crossover between the three.

We prefer a more inclusive approach for adventure tourism, where some products in almost any niche sector of tourism can be regarded as adventure tourism (see Figure 1.5). We propose that adventure tourism could include

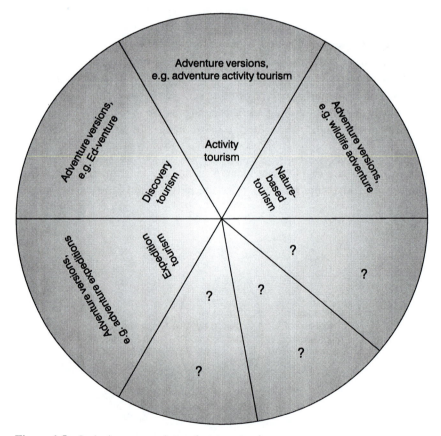

Figure 1.5 Inclusive approach to adventure tourism.

products that are currently seen as belonging to other tourism niches, as well as products that are designed from the outset to be mainstream adventure tourism.

Defining adventure tourism

As we conclude the discussion of how the concepts of adventure and tourism combine to give us adventure tourism, some definitions regarding adventure and adventure tourism have been provided in Table 1.4. It can be seen that they reflect some of the points discussed throughout this chapter.

Adventure tourism products

To recap, in our view adventure tourism involves travel and leisure activities that are contracted into in the hope that they will produce a rewarding adventure experience. An adventure experience will be of a heightened nature and involve a range of emotions, of which excitement will be key. It will entail intellectual, spiritual, physical or emotional risks and challenges. The 'vehicle' or 'product' that encompasses the adventure tourism experience will be constructed from the basic constituents of a tourism experience – environmental setting, core activities and transportation – and some or all of these may contribute the stimulus for adventure.

Adventure tourism can, theoretically, exist independently of the supply side of the tourism industry, because the consumer/participant decides whether any given tourism experience is an adventure or not. However, a pluralistic view of adventure tourism acknowledges that the supply side of the tourism industry creates products that fit the requirements of adventure tourism, and markets these as adventure tourism. The range of activities and settings that facilitate or encompass the adventure tourism experience are infinite due to the subjective nature of adventure. Also, the intensity of adventure can be varied. Hunt (1989), when focusing on the role of outdoor education in providing adventure for young people, suggested that adventure can be adjusted according to:

- The degree of remoteness
- The levels of skills required
- The levels of effort required
- The opportunity for responsibility
- The level of contrivance.

Table 1.4   Adventure and adventure tourism definitions

Definition	Source
Adventure (noun) an unusual, exciting and caring experience > excitement arising from this . . . Origin . . . based on L. *adventurus* 'about to happen', from *advenire* 'arrive'	*The Concise Oxford Dictionary*, 1999
'. . . to qualify as adventure . . . the outcome must be uncertain.'	Priest, 2001: 112
Adventure comprises 'freedom of choice; intrinsic rewards; and an element of uncertainty, for instance when the experience outcome is uncertain, or its risks are unpredictable.'	McArthur, 1989: 3, cited in Fluker and Turner, 2000
'The essential ingredients of an adventure holiday seem to include a remote, under-populated region with a traditional culture, where facilities are extremely limited.'	Smith and Jenner, 1999: 45
An essential component of adventure tourism is travel to 'an unusual, exotic, remote or wilderness destination'	Canadian Tourism Commission (cited in Loverseed, 1997)
Adventure travel is 'a leisure activity that takes place in an unusual, exotic, remote or wilderness destination. It tends to be associated with high levels of activity by the participant, most of it outdoors. Adventure travellers expect to experience various levels of risk, excitement and tranquillity, and be personally tested. In particular they are explorers of unspoilt, exotic parts of the planet and also seek personal challenges.	Millington *et al.*, 2001: 67
'. . . the main factor distinguishing adventure tourism from all other forms of tourism is the planning and preparation involved. While something of this characteristic may be present in all forms of travel and tourism, it is essential in the adventure tourism setting. The "journey of the mind" (*The Times*, 2000) refers not to the administrative planning of all trips but to that part of planning and preparation which allows for dreaming of the passion, excitement and fear that might be experienced, and the risks that may be encountered, much of this framed by accounts of journeys of past explorers. Essentially each person's mind journey is unique; importantly, it is a strong enough element to characterize the product.'	Grant, 2001: 167

Table 1.4 continued

Definition	*Source*
Adventure tourism is 'characterized by its ability to provide the tourist with relatively high levels of sensory stimulation, usually achieved by including physically challenging experiential components with the (typically short) tourist experience.'	Muller and Cleaver, 2000: 156
Adventure tourism is 'an outdoor leisure activity that takes place in an unusual, exotic, remote or wilderness destination, involves some form of unconventional means of transportation, and tends to be associated with low or high levels of activity'	Canadian Tourism Commission, 1995: 5, in Fennell, 1999: 49
'Perhaps the key distinguishing feature of an adventure holiday is that it must have a quality of exploration or of an expedition about it – for the entire length of the trip, not just for one or two days.'	Smith and Jenner, 1999: 44
'The threefold combination of activity, nature and culture marks adventure travel as an all round challenge.'	Addison, 1999: 416
Adventure tourism is 'the sum of the phenomena and relationships arising from the interactions of adventure touristic activities with the natural environment away from the participant's usual place of residence area and containing elements of risk in which the outcome is influenced by the participation, setting, and the organizer of the tourist's experience.'	Sung *et al.*, 1997: 57

The two factors of subjectivity and intensity give rise to a vast number of tourism 'products' that could fit the bill. To date the tourism industry has used products that involve activities and settings traditionally associated with a stereotypical view of adventure, such as physically challenging activities or journeys in remote, exotic or natural settings. No doubt this is because these associations are perceived to communicate 'adventure' to the customer instantly, and therefore involve less risk to the supplier. Figure 1.6 shows how current products are perceived in relation to conventional conceptions of both adventure and tourism.

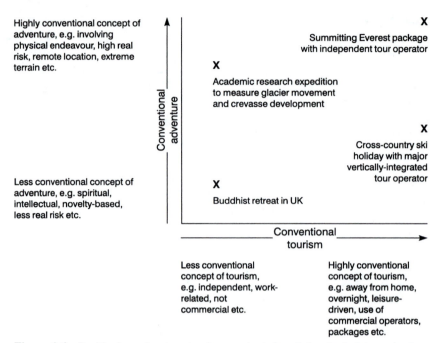

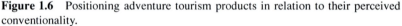

Figure 1.6 Positioning adventure tourism products in relation to their perceived conventionality.

However, it is our contention that this conventional view of adventure tourism is limiting and will change. Our own interpretation of adventure tourism leads us to suggest that new classifications of adventure tourism will emerge, and include elements such as:

- Artificial environments
- Urban exploration
- Charity challenges
- Conservation expeditions
- Hedonistic tourism
- Spiritual enlightenment
- Virtual reality
- Sex tourism
- Round the world travel.

Tourists are becoming ever more experienced and are increasingly able to identify their tourism needs and seek out activities that meet them. Their awareness of the adventure alternative is being stimulated by exposure to escalating media coverage of this fashionable topic. Meanwhile, suppliers, who are searching for a competitive edge, will create and market a range of innovative products to entice the adventurous tourist. New products will be created by reconsidering opportunities in terms of locations and settings, transport and other 'core' activities (see Figure 1.7). Refinements to existing products will create highly targeted products – for example, the amount of guiding and support offered 'on location' will be tempered to suit the competence levels of particular groups of customers.

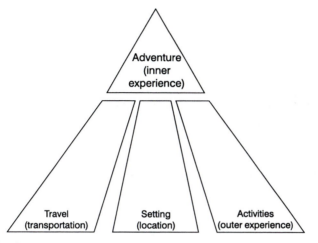

Figure 1.7   Components of adventure tourism.

This expansion and diversification is already beginning and, as Addison (1999) notes, 'It is misleading to speak about adventure without recognizing that the "industry" has diversified greatly to appeal to different segments of humanity'. In fact, in our view suppliers are augmenting the work of the media by articulating the 'adventure' theme in their marketing material and stirring up a dormant desire in the sleepier sectors of the market! Consequently adventure tourism, no matter how nebulous a term, is something the tourism industry cannot afford to ignore.

Typologies of adventure tourism

Adventure tourism is so broad a concept, involving such a wide range of products and people, that a number of authors have endeavoured to create categories or typologies of adventure tourism. Here we will briefly introduce three attempts.

Adventure and independence

Addison (1999), in writing about adventure travel, produces a typology of adventure. He creates a grid based on two axes. Along one we have the level of adventure. For Addison this is determined by 'the danger element and the technical skills needed', and thus could be interpreted as the degree of challenge. The other axis is based on the level of independence – i.e. the degree to which participants rely on others to organize the experience for them. This is particularly relevant and apposite for the tourism industry, as it reflects the degree to which tourists are reliant on suppliers to organize and manage the experience. Each axis is a continuum, going from low to high.

Addison uses recognizable terms for certain types of activity to indicate the nature of each quadrant, namely high adventure, adventure competition, recreation, and leisure. This typology works most easily with the 'adventure activity' element of adventure tourism, but could perhaps be adapted to be applied more widely. Figure 1.8 shows the four categories, plus some proposals as to the type of activity or product that might sit in each quadrant.

'Hard' and 'soft' adventure

These oft-used terms have been developed by researchers who devised a continuum to explain the diversity of behaviour, beginning with mild

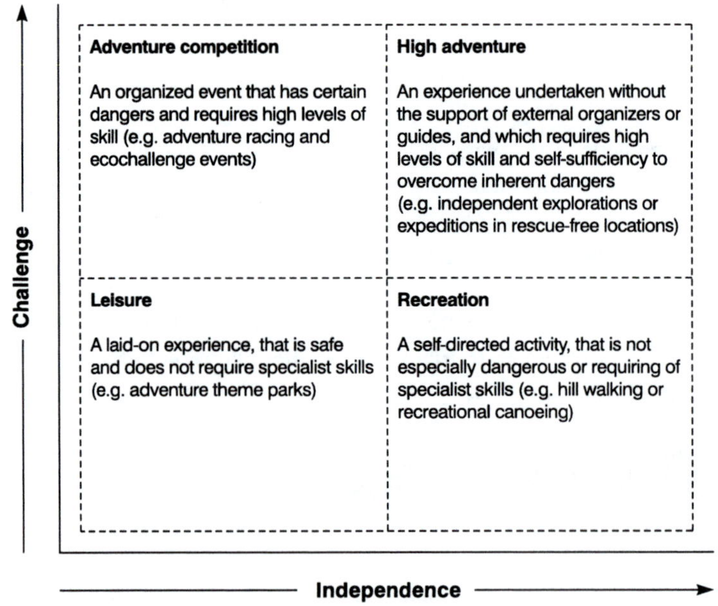

Challenge →		
	Adventure competition An organized event that has certain dangers and requires high levels of skill (e.g. adventure racing and ecochallenge events)	**High adventure** An experience undertaken without the support of external organizers or guides, and which requires high levels of skill and self-sufficiency to overcome inherent dangers (e.g. independent explorations or expeditions in rescue-free locations)
	Leisure A laid-on experience, that is safe and does not require specialist skills (e.g. adventure theme parks)	**Recreation** A self-directed activity, that is not especially dangerous or requiring of specialist skills (e.g. hill walking or recreational canoeing)

Independence ⟶

Figure 1.8   Adventure quadrants.

adventure (termed 'soft adventure') at one end of the scale and progressing to 'hard adventure' at the other extreme. This continuum, which is illustrated in Figure 1.9, involves differing degrees of 'challenge, uncertainty, setting familiarity, personal abilities, intensity, duration and perceptions of control' (Lipscombe, 1995: 42).

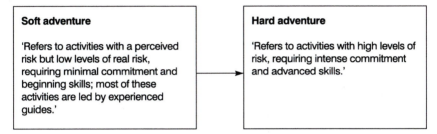

Soft adventure

'Refers to activities with a perceived risk but low levels of real risk, requiring minimal commitment and beginning skills; most of these activities are led by experienced guides.'

Hard adventure

'Refers to activities with high levels of risk, requiring intense commitment and advanced skills.'

Figure 1.9 The continuum of soft and hard adventure (source: Hill, 1995).

Millington *et al.* (2001) opt for a simpler way to differentiate between hard and soft adventure – hard adventure requires some experience and proficiency in the activity prior to the tourism experience, whereas soft adventure does not necessarily require previous experience. A Travel Industry Association of America (1997) survey included camping, hiking, cycling, animal watching, canoeing, water skiing, photo safari and a number of other activities in soft adventure, and climbing, caving, backpacking in rugged terrain, kayaking and others in hard adventure. Although many of the activities that would fall into the soft category are physically demanding, some (for example, hot-air ballooning) are not. The employment of mechanized transport is often associated with soft adventure. Sometimes the type of accommodation also influences the perception of a product's position on the hard/soft continuum, and it is generally thought that soft adventurers enjoy their home comforts. A safari with plush accommodation, hot showers, and sundowners served before a luxurious dinner would give the impression of a much 'softer' adventure holiday than a safari that involved finding your own firewood to cook dinner and pitching a roof-tent on top of the jeep. The characteristics and personalities of hard and soft adventurers are explored in Chapter 3.

Explore Worldwide, a large UK adventure tour operator, offers 200 trips throughout the globe. Their products are categorized as indicated in Box 1.1. Whilst some of their holidays clearly target the hard adventurer within the 'major treks' and 'wilderness experience' categories, others would appeal to the soft adventure market – for instance, 'easy to moderate hikes'.

Box 1.1 Explore Worldwide's adventure holiday categories

Culture/ adventure	Trips that explore exciting places but do not necessarily involve any particular physical activity, usually focusing on local cultures, historic sites or dramatic locations
Ethnic or tribal encounters	Trips that offer the opportunity to meet, and sometimes stay with, traditional local people or tribal groups
Easy to moderate hikes	Hikes involve a few days easy or moderate walking, usually in open countryside, based in hotel or tented accommodation. Most people in good health should find no problem with this level of walking
Major treks	This type of trip is recommended for strong mountain walkers who enjoy a challenge. Participants should be physically fit. Walking may be at high elevations (over 3500 m). Normally there's no backpacking, and the main luggage is transported by vehicles, porters or pack animals
Wildlife and natural history	Trips have a particular emphasis on wildlife or natural wonders – perhaps visiting some of the world's greatest game reserves. Explore's unique styles will make the experience memorable
Wilderness experience	Perhaps the ultimate travel adventure, this involves trips that venture into areas where man's influence is limited. The rewards of reaching such remote settings more than outweigh the fact that participants may have to 'rough it' for a few days
Sailtrek/ seatrek	Some of our most original adventures involve the use of sailboats, ships, ferries or even tall ships
Raft or river journeys	Journeys last anything from a few hours to several days. This category includes a wide range of activity types, from exhilarating white-water rafting to easygoing cruising and river exploration

Destination- and activity-driven adventure tourism

Millington *et al.* (2001) make a basic division within the adventure tourism market between adventure travel that is destination driven and that which is activity driven. Each of these basic divisions is then subdivided once more (see Table 1.5).

Table 1.5   Subdivisions of destination- and activity-driven adventure tourism

Destination-driven	*Activity-driven*
(a).By vehicle	(a) Hard
(b) Non-vehicularized	(b) Soft

In destination-driven adventure travel the destination is the most important aspect of the trip, with the traveller being interested in the landscape and scenery, the ecosystems, the people or the history of the place. The location will often be somewhere unusual, remote or exotic, providing novelty, stimulation, discovery and challenge for the traveller. In activity-driven travel, it is the activity rather than the destination that is crucial. The destination could be a remote or wilderness area if the activity demands it, but could just as easily be near home as abroad. As the choice of terms suggests, the division used by Millington *et al.* (2001) is based on tourist drive and motivation. However, this means the same experience, say an overland trip in a four-wheel drive vehicle, could either be regarded as an activity-driven trip if the participant finds the driving activity adventurous, or as a destination-driven trip if the transport is used merely as a means to access a destination that would otherwise be inaccessible.

So a number of approaches can be taken to categorizing adventure tourism. It can be based on product categorization, or consumer categorization. In fact, creating a typology of adventure tourism will always be a frustrating task, as consumers and suppliers do not always confine themselves to one category. Crossover is common – for example, research conducted by the Travel Industry Association of America found a substantial sector of respondents had participated in both hard adventure and soft adventure in the five years up to 1997 (Millington *et al.* 2001: 78.)

A quick examination of the dichotomies that exist within adventure tourism demonstrate the complexity of the subject (see Table 1.6).

Table 1.6   Dichotomies within adventure tourism

Hard	⟷	Soft
Remote	⟷	Local
Physical	⟷	Spiritual
Organized	⟷	Independent
Group adventure	⟷	Solo adventure
Domestic	⟷	International
Artificial environment	⟷	Natural environment
Commercial adventure	⟷	Voluntary adventure
Wilderness	⟷	Urban
Low cost	⟷	High cost
Planned	⟷	Unplanned
Set itinerary	⟷	'Go as you please'
Altruistic	⟷	Hedonistic
Long trips	⟷	Short breaks
100 per cent adventure	⟷	Intermittent adventure
Reliance on tourist facilities	⟷	Limited use of tourist facilities
Politically stable destination	⟷	Politically unstable destinations
New adventure tourist	⟷	Experienced adventure tourists
High-risk exerience	⟷	Low-risk experience
Real	⟷	Fantasy
Work	⟷	Play

It seems to us that no matter how much fun academics might have creating product-based typologies of adventure tourism, typologies based on psychographic segmentation of the consumers will be of most use to the tourism industry. This is an area that needs considerably more research before proposals can be made, and an introduction to the possibilities is contained in Chapter 3.

The development of the adventure tourism industry

The adventure tourism phenomenon is currently receiving a lot of attention. Despite difficulties in defining it, it is frequently lauded as one of the fastest growing segments in the tourism industry, especially in many of the developed regions of the world. For instance, it is '. . . the fastest growing sector of the tourism industry in North America' (Loverseed, 1997: 90), and 'the annual growth rate of adventure travel in Europe is estimated at 13–15 per cent' (Smith and Jenner, 1999).

No doubt the growth in adventure tourism is partly a result of re-packaging existing activities and re-branding them as 'adventure'. Nonetheless, the emergence of adventure tourism as a label that appeals to both the providers and consumers in the tourism industry means that it has hit a resonant chord and is likely to continue expanding in the near future. This resonance has been recognized by the World Tourism Organization (1997: 28), who note in their *Vision 2020* study that a polarization of tourist tastes is developing; the comfort based and the adventure orientated. They also expect tourism to develop around the 'three Es' – entertainment, education and excitement. Adventure tourism is well placed to supply these qualities.

It seems undeniable that appreciation of the significance of adventure tourism is growing. Because of this sudden increase in awareness, many people perceive it to be a new form of tourism. However, this is not the case. The themes that appear in the current adventure tourism industry have a long and distinguished past, and Chapter 2 explores the historical roots of adventure tourism.

Discussion points and exercises

1 What are the differences between adventure tourism and sport tourism and ecotourism?
2 Develop your own typology of adventure tourism and explain the rationale behind your typology.
3 Review one of the books or papers mentioned in Chapter 1 and discuss the contribution it makes to the adventure tourism literature.

2

Historical themes in adventure tourism

Introduction

It is clear from Chapter 1 that adventure travel and tourism is a complex field, with great diversity within it and no clear, tidy boundaries. This complexity and diversity is partly explained by the fact that adventure tourism today is the result of a number of streams of thinking, or themes, some of which are hundreds and even thousands of years old. An understanding of these streams is vital if we are to understand the present scope and nature of adventure tourism and predict its future, because the sector appears to follow the process shown in Figure 2.1.

Some of these themes (such as hedonism) are as powerful today as they were in previous times, while others (such as colonization) may appear less prevalent today. However, in general, these themes seem resilient to change. Figure 2.2 identifies a number of themes that are prevalent

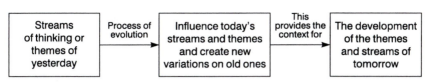

Figure 2.1 Streams of thinking.

in UK thinking about adventure travel and tourism. It does not claim to be a comprehensive list of themes in adventure tourism, but is instead designed to illustrate the diversity of themes and the fact that some are very old, while new ones are emerging all the time.

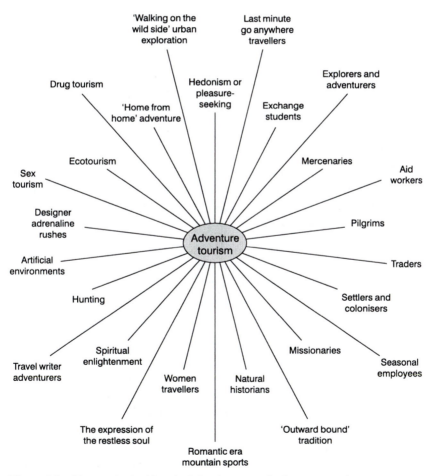

Figure 2.2 Themes in the historical development of adventure tourism.

All of these themes are clearly encompassed within the definition of adventure tourism set out earlier in this book.

It is important to recognize that this view is an Anglo-centric one. As we will see later in the chapter, the concept of adventure tourism, and its historic development, varies between different countries and cultures.

In this chapter we will look at some of the themes identified in Figure 2.2 in more detail.

Themes

Hedonism

Hedonism, or pleasure seeking, has a particularly long history. The desire for sensual pleasures and the willingness to travel for such purposes is age-old.

Often travel has been necessary for those wishing to pursue hedonism, as their activities would not have been socially acceptable in their home communities. Hedonistic travel has often involved a journey away from the social constraints of everyday life in pursuit of pleasures such as sex, heavy drinking and 'serious' partying.

Affluent Romans were distinctly hedonistic, and experimented widely with different sensual pleasures ... but usually away from their homes at the 'resorts' of the time. These people took part in group sex orgies and gambling, and made use of hallucinogenic substances – always searching for new experiences.

In the twentieth century, a number of destinations developed a reputation as places where would-be hedonists could enjoy the sensual pleasures denied them at home. Such places included Amsterdam and its red light district, Hong Kong with its Suzie Wong image, Shanghai, Las Vegas and Rio de Janeiro.

Today's young hedonists apparently have many opportunities to express themselves on holiday, including for example Club 18–30 type vacations and the party culture of Ibiza. However, these people are no longer going away to experience pleasures denied them at home; instead they are doing the same things on holiday as they do at home on Friday and Saturday nights. Social change now permits them to drink and have casual sex in their own community, so perhaps this form of hedonistic tourism is no longer truly adventure tourism.

Explorers and adventurers

European schoolchildren grow up with images of bold explorers fearlessly searching for new lands, charting previously unknown places. Such explorers include Columbus, Cook, Da Gama, Magellan and Raleigh. These people often suffered privations and even death in pursuit of new territories. At the same time, they often became rich as a result of their discoveries.

By the early twentieth century most lands and seas had been discovered by explorers, so new challenges had to be found for those seeking such adventure.

Once the North and South Poles had been conquered the spirit of exploration turned to the skies, with intrepid adventurers seeking to conquer the air. Pioneers such as Blériot, Alcock and Brown, and Lindbergh pushed back the boundaries of flying. Later aviators passed the milestone of breaking the 'sound barrier'. Aerial adventurers also experimented with airships and helicopters.

The exploration of the air went further with man travelling in space, landing on the moon in 1969, and launching orbiting space stations.

Adventurers such as Cousteau have also sought to explore under the sea through submarines and deep-sea diving.

The question now is, where else is left to explore? What can challenge tomorrow's explorers and adventurers?

Mercenaries

The twin motivators of money and adrenaline have, for centuries, inspired some men – and a few women – to offer their services as soldiers of fortune. Apart from the dangers faced in battle, such mercenaries have also faced cultural adventures, working for kings and governments in countries with very different traditions and customs to their own. For example, Vikings were employed as soldiers in the medieval period in Istanbul, while German mercenaries were employed around Europe in the Middle Ages. Yet the mercenary is not just a figure from history, for in our own times former members of the armed forces of the UK have fought as mercenaries in countries such as Bosnia, for instance.

Pilgrims

Pilgrimages to religious sites are perhaps the oldest form of tourism, and could also be seen as an early form of adventure tourism, involving two types of adventure. First, a pilgrimage has always been an emotional adventure, a journey to an unknown spiritual destination. Lives have often been changed irrevocably by these journeys. Second, these pilgrimages could be risky, dangerous undertakings. Robbers preyed on the pilgrimage routes such as those in the wilderness of the Massif Central in France, which pilgrims crossed from Northern Europe on their way to St Jacques de Compostella in the medieval period.

Over time, the pilgrimage has evolved and the physical danger has declined. Previously, pilgrimages involved individual people with religious beliefs visiting sites that were important to their religion. Today, however, two other types of pilgrims can be seen:

1 'Western' travellers who are not adherents of any particular religion travelling 'east' in the hope of spiritual enlightenment
2 People living stressful lives who see monasteries or religious retreats as places offering a relaxing lifestyle that will reduce their stress levels. This is true of the Orthodox monasteries on Mount Athos in Greece, for example.

Traders

Traders have been around as long as pilgrims, and can be seen as adventure tourists in that:

- They often went to places that were new to them in order to sell goods
- They regularly suffered from criminal attacks on themselves and their goods
- They could lose all their wealth if they could not sell their goods at their destination.

'Trading' can still be risky today, with robberies of business travellers being a common occurrence in many cities.

Settlers and colonizers

Generally, settlers and colonizers were not adventure 'tourists' in that their stays in their destination tended to be permanent rather than temporary. However, they could be tourists if they did not like their new 'home' and left it after a short period.

Colonization also created tourism in its own right, with visits to the colonists by their friends and relatives.

Seasonal migrants

For centuries people in different parts of the world have practised seasonal migration for employment, particularly in rural communities. In areas where farming was poor many farmers had secondary jobs, often as skilled artisans. In quiet times on the farm they would become itinerant craftsmen, taking their skills to the nearest town, to other regions, or even to other countries. In the nineteenth century, for example, many mountain villages in France had strong reputations for their stonemasons, knife grinders and woodcarvers, amongst other trades.

For these seasonal migrants the trip was an adventure, because often they were travelling to different regions with different traditions, dialects, and even languages. They often came from a parochial background, but were forced to travel and sell their services to 'foreign' communities for months at a time. It was also something of an adventure for the families left behind, because they had to look after themselves and could never be sure that the men would return at the end of the migration season.

Women too have been seasonal work migrants in many countries, particularly in spending time in towns and cities as maids or wet nurses. It is easy to imagine the sense of risk and adventure for a young woman from a closed village community travelling to a major city.

Seasonal labour migration is still an important phenomenon today, including everything from fruit pickers in France or California to employees in tourist resorts.

Missionaries

Over the centuries most religions have had their missionaries – people with religious zeal travelling far and wide to try to convert people to their point of view. In the past their travel is an adventure in a number of ways, because:

- Their travels and tribulations often tested their own faith severely
- They often chose to live amongst the poorest people in their chosen destination, whereas most settlers or residents avoid such areas wherever possible
- They often faced the threat of robbery, disease and violence, particularly when they wandered off the beaten track.

Missionaries, particularly those who are also involved in various aid activities in developing countries, are still an important phenomenon today. Their travels can also still be adventures, as they are sometimes singled out as targets by terrorists and repressive governments.

The 'Outward Bound' tradition'

In the UK particularly there is a long tradition, perhaps best exemplified by the successful Outward Bound organization, of the idea that pitting yourself against nature and your own fears is character building and can make you a better person. This tradition also has an almost puritanical dimension, eschewing comforts and convenience in favour of discomfort and taking the hard rather than the easy way.

This 'Outward Bound' tradition underpins much of the modern outdoor management development and survival course 'industry'. Companies believe that putting staff in unfamiliar, uncomfortable situations will help to achieve team building as well as the personal development of individuals.

Romantic era mountain sports

In the nineteenth century, the upper classes of developed countries started to 'test' themselves through mountain sports like rock climbing and skiing. Pioneers such as the Briton Edward Whymper were at the forefront of developing both sports in the Alps, for example.

This form of adventure tourism was linked to the Romantic movement in Europe in the eighteenth and nineteenth centuries. This movement emphasized nature, and endowed mountains with a spiritual, almost mystical quality. The nineteenth century mountain sport enthusiasts were often clearly influenced by these ideas.

Today the Romantic era is a thing of the past, but people still seek adventure in the mountains, and many mountaineers still talk about the spiritual dimension of their activity, echoing the ideas of the romantics of yesteryear.

Natural historians

For several centuries natural historians have indulged in their own form of adventure tourism, travelling in search of new species of flora and fauna. Often their motivation to make such discoveries encouraged them to undertake dangerous journeys to little known places. However, the main adventure for these natural historians was intellectual, pushing back the boundaries of scientific knowledge. Charles Darwin is an excellent example of this type of adventurer.

Today, with so much more being known about the earth's natural history, it is perhaps more difficult for modern natural historians to undertake similar adventures. However, from time to time new species are still being discovered on both land and sea.

Now ordinary people are able to follow in the footsteps of the early pioneers, using well-trodden, much safer steps to discover for themselves the natural treasures of the planet.

Wildlife-watching tourism has grown enormously in recent years, from orang-utan viewing in Borneo (Kallimantan) to whale watching off New England in the USA, from giant turtle watching in the Galapagos Islands to outback tours of Australia. For each of these tourists the vacations are a personal adventure, a journey into the unknown.

Women travellers

In recent centuries, particularly in Europe and the USA, women travellers have played a major role in the development of adventure tourism.

The UK has a long tradition of intrepid women from the upper classes travelling to places that were dangerous and very different from their own country. These women were not only experiencing physical adventure; they were also challenging the ideas of their time about the role of women in society. By strength of character they became accepted in many countries and cultures where women were rarely seen in public by outsiders.

One such traveller early in the twentieth century was Gertrude Bell, whose diaries have given a vivid picture of her travels – particularly in the Middle East – talking to tyrannical rulers and bandits and risking disease.

Often these women seem to have been successful travellers because they were prepared to try to assimilate some of their host's culture. Gertrude Bell, for instance, became an accomplished Arabic speaker. Many of these women travellers clearly were probably motivated by a desire to escape the conventions of their home environment, but some may also have had erotic, or at least romantic, motivations. The idea of meeting rich and powerful desert sheikhs could obviously be a powerful motivator for some women, just as the thought of nubile South Sea maidens may well have been a motivator for many male travellers.

The role of women today is clearly different to that in previous centuries, and today's woman adventure traveller is no longer an unusual phenomenon, but women still face particular challenges when visiting some parts of the world where indigenous male attitudes to them are very different from those they are used to at home.

Travel writer adventurers

In recent decades, as the travel-related media has grown, we have seen the development of a breed of travel writer adventurers. These people travel off the beaten track and then share their experiences with the less adventurous armchair traveller through their writings. Such writers include Newby and Thesiger. However, today new forms of travel writer adventurer are being seen. First, women are entering this previously male-dominated profession, notably Dervla Murphy. Second, such writers are often now looking for a new angle or fresh approach. This may involve travelling around the world on a bicycle or following a particular theme, such as retracing the footsteps of previous generations of adventure travellers. Third, they are becoming notably less serious and 'worthy' in tone, and more humorous and 'tongue-in-cheek!' in character. Finally, the adventure in the travel writing does not always come from the physical environment any more – it can also come from human beings, as with writers who record their travels with young hedonistic party animals and soccer hooligans, for example.

The expression of the restless soul

For a small number of people, adventure tourism or travel is an outlet for the restless spirit unable to fit in to conventional society. We saw earlier that this was the case for many women travellers in previous centuries. However, it is also a phenomenon that has affected many men, including Lawrence of Arabia in the Middle East and Matisse in the South Sea Islands, for example.

Hunting

Hunting is a form of adventure travel that is deeply embedded in many cultures. For some communities it is a way of getting food, while in others it is a leisure activity. However, often it involves adventure in that:

- It may take place in inhospitable places
- It may involve contact with dangerous animals
- It can be highly competitive, and the life and reputation of the hunter may be harmed if he or she fails to perform satisfactorily.

Today, when hunting is becoming less and less socially acceptable in many countries, it presents a new adventure – namely the ethical dilemma of whether to hunt or not. In countries where hunting is illegal, promoting it can be an adventure in itself! Whereas in general adventure tourism is viewed positively by societies, hunting is a form of adventure tourism that is increasingly frowned upon by many societies.

Spiritual enlightenment

The search for spiritual enlightenment has been a constant theme throughout history. In the past it manifested itself in the formal pilgrimages that were discussed earlier. However, in developed countries in recent decades we have seen the growth of a new form of spiritual enlightenment tourism. Increasingly people from materialistic cultures and rich countries have been rejecting the original religions of their own countries and turning to the religions and spiritual beliefs of other cultures for inspiration.

This has led to the growth of tourism to countries such as India, Nepal and Thailand, for example. These trips often combine spiritual adventure with physical risk such as disease.

At the same time, we have seen the rise of religious cults and sects in places like California and Europe, where the adventure is purely spiritual. This new phenomenon of spiritual adventure travel seems destined to last for as long as there are people who are dissatisfied with materialism and consumerism.

Artificial environment adventures

Traditionally, adventure tourism meant pitting yourself against nature in an outdoor environment in some way. However, today many people are facing new challenges in environments that are artificially created and indoors – for example, climbing walls in places like Sheffield attract those wanting to test their technical skills.

However, we are also seeing the growth of other artificial adventure environments such as dry ski slopes, water sports facilities and virtual reality simulators. This divorcing of adventures from natural environments is a major trend currently, but it is also controversial. For instance, some traditional climbers find it impossible to recognize the legitimacy of artificial climbing walls because there is not the key element of nature in terms of weather conditions, views, fresh air and so on.

Designer adrenaline risks

Since the 1980s we have witnessed the rise, in reality or in hype, of the so-called 'designer consumers' – those driven by the desire to be seen to be at the cutting edge of fashion. Such people have, not surprisingly, also sought to develop their own 'cool' adventure activities.

For this market it is vital that the activities have features that are new, and that participants can develop their own social mores, specialist clothing and 'patois'.

Early designer adrenaline risks were mountain biking and bungee jumping, and then came the rise of snowboarding. Now we see the development of variations on these themes.

This type of tourist is an interesting phenomenon in the field of adventure tourism, because activities integrate physical activity with clothing, language, and the clear trappings of a distinct sub-culture. Furthermore, these people are not wedded to any particular type of environment. They are keen to experience all types of adventure-risk activity, in different environments.

Sex tourism

Sex tourism is far from new, but it has now reached new levels – or perhaps we should say it has plumbed new depths. Sex tourism was once largely a matter for adults, but now there is a developing growth in child sex tourism.

The risk element in sex tourism comes from three sources, notably:

1 The danger of contracting sexually transmitted diseases, including HIV
2 The possibility of facing criminal prosecution because sex tourism is not legal in a number of countries
3 The chance that sex tourists may be targeted by criminals for either robbery or blackmail.

Some destinations rely heavily on sex tourism, and this reputation makes it hard for the destination to attract other forms of tourism. Sex tourism is a form of adventure tourism that has victims; it is built on the misery of those forced to take part in the trade because they have few options. Yet this is a form of adventure tourism that shows no signs of declining.

Ecotourism

Ecotourism is not necessarily adventure tourism, for it can involve travelling in comfort, on fairly well-trodden routes, to see wildlife and people 'in their natural habitat'. It can have an element of adventure when it takes travellers into an environment or situation with which they are not familiar; however, sometimes it appears that some tour operators emphasize the adventurous nature of their market to help them sell more vacations.

'Walk on the wild side' urban explorers

Since Orwell explored London and Paris in the guise of a 'down and out' over half a century ago, there has been a clear 'walk on the wild side' school of adventure tourism based on cities. This is totally in contrast to those forms of adventure tourism that take place in wilderness areas. Yet no-one can deny that this is adventure tourism, for it puts people in environments that are very different to those of their everyday lives.

New York today, for instance, offers tours to neighbourhoods that seem strange and extraordinary to most visitors.

We should not be surprised by this phenomenon, for over a century ago young English men went to Paris to live amongst artists and the working classes of Pigalle and Montmartre. Was not this the same phenomenon in reality, appealing to those with conventional backgrounds and everyday lives, because they represented a contrast with their ordinary lives?

Drug tourism – the ultimate adventure 'trip'?

Drug tourism is adventure tourism in two ways:

1 The drug-induced 'trip' takes the person on a journey to an unknown destination, without even a guarantee that he or she will survive the experience
2 The risks associated with buying drugs including criminal prosecution, and robbery and violence.

Drug tourism has become a significant attraction for destinations as diverse as Morocco and Amsterdam.

Many travellers also indulge in 'adventure tourism' when, often short of money after backpacking, they try trafficking drugs in return for cash. They face risks from the law and from some of the ways in which they transport the drugs . . . inside their bodies!

'Home from home' adventurers

These are the people who want to do adventurous things in places off the beaten track, but who do not want to make any real sacrifices. These are the people who are literally hauled up Everest by porters, with all the comforts of their everyday lives. This shows that, for these people, the motivation is the desire to be able to say they have been to such places. They are not motivated by the nature of the experience itself.

This market is growing, and there appear to be enough operators who are prepared to meet this demand, even if it endangers porters' lives and leads to waste being left on mountains.

'Last minute go anywhere' tourists

Here the adventure is nothing to do with the destination or the activities undertaken; it is based on the risk of people not knowing where they will be going, or even if they will be able to find a vacation. This group is growing because along with the element of risk goes, often, the benefit of low prices. Such vacations are particularly popular with those just looking for an escape, any escape, from their everyday lives.

Aid workers

In recent decades it has become quite common for people from one country to go to do voluntary work in other countries. Organizations such as Voluntary Service Overseas have almost institutionalized this phenomenon. However, such activity can carry risks, and in recent years a number of aid workers – not VSO volunteers – have been kidnapped and even murdered by terrorist groups.

Even if they do not face this extreme risk, all aid workers face the fear that they may not be up to the job they are taking on.

Student exchanges

The growth of higher education world-wide has led to an increase in cross-border student exchanges. This is a form of adventure tourism in that the students are taking a risk that they may fail when studying in a different culture or language. School pupil exchanges have also been growing, and here the risk is that young people at a vulnerable age may feel that they will be unable to cope in a different country, with a family of strangers.

Summary

This section has suggested that each of this selection of well over 20 types of tourism meets our definition of adventure travel and tourism. They all involve doing things that are out of the ordinary, in new environments, with some element of risk, either real or perceived. We will now conclude by looking at two separate interesting aspects of adventure tourism.

Old themes, new manifestations

Many themes in adventure tourism are old ones that are being constantly updated and modified, while the basic motivation remains the same. Hedonism is an excellent example of this phenomenon. The Romans went to spas for orgies, while the rich young English men went to Paris for their hedonistic pleasures in the Belle Époque period. Today, the hedonist has Club 18–30, Ibiza, and various adult resorts in the Caribbean to meet their needs. Perhaps hedonistic tourism has just become more democratic over time!

Cultural differences in the concept of adventure tourism

The themes we have been discussing are largely based on the evolution of thinking about adventure tourism in the UK and a handful of other early urbanized and industrialized countries, which are generally former colonial powers. However, the concept of adventure tourism varies between countries and cultures in a number of ways:

1 Adventure tourism is just another form of tourism in that it requires people with the money, time and inclination to travel. In many developing countries, most of the population clearly does not have the money to take part in any form of tourism, let alone adventure tourism. Most adventure tourism is therefore restricted to the residents of the so-called developed countries, and particularly to the more affluent residents of these countries.

2 The adventure tourism market develops differently in different countries based on the pace and nature of political, economic and social changes. For example, the pilgrimage market in Western Europe was at its peak in the Middle Ages. Since then the market in Europe has declined in spite of the wealth of these countries because of a reduction in religious devotion. However, today pilgrimage is a rapidly growing market in countries like Indonesia, Malaysia and Nigeria, where religious devotion to Islam is strong and incomes are rising.

3 The concept of adventure varies between cultures based on their history, traditions and geography. For example, adventure travel in the USA, Australia and Russia is often envisaged in terms of participants travelling to wilderness areas, retracing the steps of pioneers, and pitting their strength and wits against nature. Taming the wilderness, albeit temporarily, is a constant theme in such countries. By contrast, leisure travel in many Asian countries has often been concerned with the search for spiritual enlightenment. However, maybe as a result of globalization and the rise of the global consumer, we are seeing these differences slowly breaking down. Today Japanese people may be seen in the Alaskan wilderness, pitting themselves against nature, and American youngsters looking for new spiritual pathways in India and Thailand.

It is always important to be aware of these cultural differences in the concept of adventure tourism. However, it is often difficult for us to recognize other ways of viewing adventure tourism because each of us is strongly conditioned to recognize only our own culture's concepts of adventure travel.

Summary

This chapter has tried to set the scene for the rest of the text by looking at how adventure tourism arrived at where it is today, in one country at least. It is important that we understand the evolution of adventure tourism if, in this book, we are going to focus on where it might go from here. In the rest of the book we will explore many of the types of tourism and issues raised above.

Discussion points and exercises

1 Discuss the extent to which Club 18–30 type hedonistic vacations are just a modern version of the Roman orgy.
2 Compare and contrast the history of adventure tourism in Western Europe and the USA.
3 Discuss the evolution of religious tourism from pre-history to the twenty-first century.

Part
B

The demand side

3

The adventure tourist

Introduction

Adventure tourism is an increasingly widespread phenomenon in the new millennium, and appeals to an expanding proportion of the population who are seeking self-fulfilment and excitement through participating in physically and mentally stimulating activities, travelling to remote destinations or engaging in 'adrenaline-rush' experiences as part of their tourist experience. Patterns of consumer behaviour in tourism are in a constant state of flux, and as the 'new tourist' (Poon, 1993) emerges as a more experienced traveller, demanding unique and enticing holiday experiences, adventure tourism has begun to carve a niche market for itself.

Tourism organizations have facilitated the growth of adventure holidays through promoting and selling a vast array of organized adventure experiences to a diverse range of markets as novel and exclusive experiences, from whale watching to white-water rafting, bungee jumping to self-discovery holidays. Moreover, the independent travel market has triggered a growth in adventure tourism, with an increasing number of people tailor-making their own adventures to suit individual tastes and needs. Round the world travel (RTW), a form of independent adventure travel, has recently expanded in popularity amongst all age groups. Although some people follow the well-trodden RTW network of destinations in Asia and Australasia, meeting up with other fellow travellers *en route*, others visit more remote destinations – Siberia and Mongolia, for example. These are places where the tourism industry is not well established and other independent travellers are few and far between. Travelling to such countries, many kinds of adventure can be experienced – as the following extract from the book *Lonely Planet Unpacked* illustrates:

> Travelling independently can sometimes be tricky. The sacred mountain of Shiliin Bogd Uul is apparently closed to the disputed, undefined and unfenced Chinese border. After we spent several glorious hours exploring the mountain, our jeep was suddenly followed by a Mongolian army jeep, and then stopped by a machine-gun wielding soldier. He leaned into the driver's window, confiscated the keys and asked our reasons for being near the border. We obviously didn't say what he wanted to hear, so he forced us to detour to the military barracks and then questioned us for five hours. I was firstly accused of being a Chinese smuggler, and then, because I don't even remotely look Chinese, of being a Russian spy. The Mongolian soldier had never heard of Australia, and failed to comprehend my guide who constantly explained that I was 'from a lonely planet'.
>
> (Greenaway, 1999:21, cited in Wheeler, 1999).

This quotation sums up the experience of just one typology of adventure tourist who is seeking out an original and exciting holiday, with an opportunity to engage in self-discovery and cultural exchange, in a faraway place. A plethora of other 'adventurers' also exist whose motives, behaviour and experiences will differ from the example quoted above.

These different (yet sometimes overlapping) categories reflect the broad nature of the adventure tourism phenomenon and the many links it has with other forms of tourism. Some of these links will be explored from the adventure consumer's perspective throughout this chapter.

Although adventure tourism clearly overlaps with other tourism types, adventurers have a number of distinguishing attributes that set them apart from other tourist markets. They generally take risks and thrive from mental or physical challenge, they seek out novel and stimulating experiences, and they sometimes engage in adventure for personal development or reasons of self-esteem.

Before introducing the key topics covered within this chapter, it is important to point out that the subject of consumer behaviour in adventure tourism is not particularly well developed in terms of research. Indeed, there is a dearth of information on the characteristics of adventure tourists and their motives. This is due to the relatively recent recognition of adventure tourism as a unique market in its own right, coupled with the current evolution of this concept within academic circles. Most of the work carried out to date – based on the broad theme of 'adventure consumers' – originates from the fields of psychology and recreation. Many parallels can be drawn between these two subject areas and tourism, in relation to the consumer of adventure tourism. Without a doubt, psychology and recreation-based investigations have shaped the direction of research into the behavioural components of adventure tourists. Hence, in this chapter we have attempted to apply some of this work to the behaviour of adventure tourists.

The main themes of this chapter are as follows:

1 The changing patterns of consumer trends, and how newly evolving trends have instigated interest in adventure travel
2 The influence of consumer lifestyles and age groups on participation in adventure tourism
3 The behaviour of adventure tourists, including the following sections:
   ■ 'Soft' and 'hard' adventurers, their distinctive characteristics and behaviours
   ■ Tourist motivation, including key concepts that are relevant to adventure tourist motivation
   ■ Diverse motivational factors that influence people's decision to participate in adventure tourism, with particular emphasis on the role of risk as a primary motive
   ■ The characteristics and motives of other types of tourist that participate in similar forms of tourism to adventure tourism (i.e. ecotourism, wildlife tourism and expeditions).

Changing consumer trends

Over the last two decades, society has witnessed a number of changes in consumer behaviour. A move towards healthier lifestyles, a heightened sensitivity to green issues and a more quality-conscious consumer are just a few of the transformations taking place in contemporary society. Such changes are reflected in people's holiday-taking behaviour – for example, more people are taking activity holidays.

With regard to the British population, Mintel (1999) reports that between 1994 and 1999 the demand for domestic activity holidays grew by 5 per cent whilst the number of people participating in this type of holiday abroad increased by a dramatic 36 per cent. These statistics are a sure indicator of the rising popularity of activity-based holidays, and this growth can be attributed to lifestyle changes.

Another recently evolved trend concerns the role of leisure in people's lives. Undoubtedly leisure has become an increasingly important part of our daily existence, and has positively impacted on the demand for tourism in many different ways. Adventure tourism is no exception here. One line of thought, in relation to the growth of this form of tourism, is that modern-day living and work life lack clear meaning. This encourages people to search for meaning and fulfilment through active participation in leisure activities and tourism, seeking out '. . . a deep embodied experience unavailable in everyday life' (Cater, 2000: 51). Such an experience could result from any number of adventure activities, and at any levels of extreme. For instance, Shackley (1996: 63) comments on the ultimate visitor experience of being amongst silverback gorillas, a rare species, in the middle of a Rwandan rainforest. Seeing the gorillas in the wild after trekking through the jungle for eight hours is a deeply emotional experience for visitors, and this sensation arises from '. . . a sense of being completely alone in the wild with a magnificent and totally wild creature'.

Nowadays, tourists – otherwise known as 'new tourists' (Poon, 1993) – attribute more importance to the benefits that they can gain from their holidays, in particular the uniqueness of the experience. New tourists have a set of distinctive characteristics, and these are identified in Figure 3.1. Poon also suggests that we have moved away from being 'old tourists', who:

- Were homogeneous and predictable in their tastes
- Regarded travel as a novelty
- Were interested in warm destinations (destination choice was not important)
- Attributed little importance to the quality of tourist services
- Went on holiday to escape from work and home life
- Felt secure through travelling in numbers.

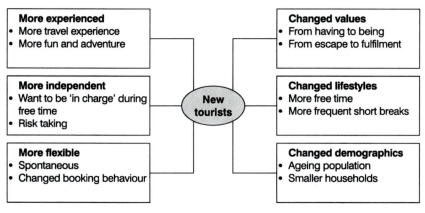

More experienced	Changed values
• More travel experience • More fun and adventure	• From having to being • From escape to fulfilment

More independent	Changed lifestyles
• Want to be 'in charge' during free time • Risk taking	• More free time • More frequent short breaks

More flexible	Changed demographics
• Spontaneous • Changed booking behaviour	• Ageing population • Smaller households

Source: adapted from Poon (1993)

Figure 3.1 The nature of 'new tourists'.

One of the key characteristics of new tourists is their need to escape from everyday routines in a bid to achieve some form of fulfilment. The majority of tourist experiences include some degree of escapism, and many people would express the need to 'get away from it all' as an important motive for taking a holiday. The need to escape may be triggered by a desire temporarily to take a break from home life so as to feel like you are really on holiday, or by a desire to escape from everyday life and its associated stresses. The reasons for escapism will depend on the type of experience and the typology of tourist. For instance, a person going on a beach holiday to Barbados to de-stress, laze around and socialize may feel the need to escape from city life and a very busy career for a couple of weeks. On the other hand, a different city dweller might take a short city break in Barcelona to escape the home environment and visit cultural tourist attractions in a city distinct from his or her own. It could be argued that the more distinct from everyday life the tourist experience is, the more the person is escaping and achieving some form of fulfilment.

Adventure tourism involves such active participation from individuals that it can result in the ultimate in escapism from daily life. Taking a river trip in the Amazon jungle, or a camel trip across the Gobi Desert, or swimming with dolphins in Australia, can all trigger sensations of total escapism. This feeling of escapism is inextricably linked to the 'peak experience' (Maslow, 1976) phenomenon that many adventure tourists thrive from and strive for. Pritchard (2000: 23), in describing the sensations that rock climbers feel towards the end of a challenging climb, sums up the 'peak experience' in the quotation below:

That moment between knowing that you've cracked it and topping out is the moment that climbers search for. That moment when the pulse begins to race and the joy overwhelms you and you slow down wishing that the feeling will never end. That is *the* moment.

To sum up, it is clear that these changing patterns of consumer behaviour are beneficial to the growth in demand for adventure tourism, as people adopt healthier lifestyles and seek out holiday experiences that dramatically contrast with their day-to-day lives.

Consumer lifestyles, age groups and adventure tourism

Contrary to the commonly held belief that adventure tourism stimulates only the interests of the youth market – exaggerated by images of Pepsi-Max™-type stereotypes promoted in brochures – there is a different viewpoint arguing that adventure tourists span a broad range of people. It is thought that these people make their holiday choices based on lifestyle rather than age. In referring to the UK adventure travel market, '. . .the characteristic quality is not age per se but attitude – a spirit of adventure and enthusiasm' (Economic Intelligence Unit, 1992: 45). Therefore a pensioner who is physically active in his or her everyday life may well successfully take part in a charity challenge that involves cycling through Iceland or white-water rafting in Nepal, for example. On the other hand, a recently graduated 22-year-old student may prefer a relaxing 'Medsun' holiday with a group of friends.

Various outbound tour operators also echo the idea that people's lifestyles are more influential in their holiday decision-making than their age. Explore Worldwide, the UK's leading adventure operator, offers an extensive range of holidays catering for diverse adventure markets. Interestingly, Explore's clients' average age is between 40 and 45 years. A number of other European adventure operators state the average age of their clients as around 40 years (Smith and Jenner, 1999). Details of High Places' clientele, as seen in Table 3.1, also serve to illustrate that the typical adventure traveller who books holidays through a tour operator spans most age groups.

High Places promote and sell trekking holidays in many different regions of the world, and takes care to match its clients with the appropriate level of trek according to their fitness levels and experience (see Box 3.1). Although age is not identified as a restricting factor in High Places' trek grades, it is apparent from Table 3.1 that although the company's holidays appeal to people of all ages, the majority of clients fall within the 31–40, 41–50 and 51–60 years age brackets. A much smaller proportion of customers are over the age of 60

Table 3.1   Age demographics of High Places' clients 1996–1999 (source: High Places, personal communication)

Year	Under 21 (%)	21–30 (%)	31–40 (%)	41–50 (%)	51–60 (%)	60+ (%)
1996	1	9	30	28	26	6
1997	2	8	30	31	20	9
1998	1	8	26	30	24	11
1999	2	7	25	29	27	10

years, and this may be due to a number of reasons – for instance, the company may not directly promote its holidays to older age groups. Another observation is that the under 21 and 21–30 years age groups are not particularly well represented in the operator's profile of clients. This could be because the younger end of the market may be less able or even less inclined to participate in packaged adventure holidays due to the high cost implications of 'organized adventure' and/or the preference to put together their own 'do it yourself' trips.

When interpreting such data, it is also important to note that the independent traveller makes up a considerable proportion of the adventure market and should not be omitted from the equation. Unfortunately, there is a

---

**Box 3.1   High Places' trek grades
(source: High Places, 2001)**

Expeditions	Summer and winter mountaineering background advisable
Tough	Regular hill walking background advisable; may involve some backpacking – always stated in trip description
Steady plus	As 'Steady', but with varying extra demands – i.e. remoteness, altitude, long days, weather, lack of comforts etc.
Steady	Hill walking and camping background advisable
Fairly easy	For all recreational walkers

lack of marketing intelligence available on the independent adventure tourist market. This is because such tourists do not tend to make use of tourism organizations when organizing holidays.

The above discussion implies that age may exert some degree of influence over a person's decision-making in relation to adventure tourism. Taking this point further, it seems that an individual's age could influence whether he or she participates in adventure activities or not. One study carried out on 651 tourists to Queenstown (New Zealand) found that a person's age was significantly related to his or her participation in adventure (Berno *et al.*, 1996). The 20–34-year age group had higher rates of participation in a range of adventure activities – jet boating, bungee jumping, parapenting, white-water rafting, scenic flights, helicoptering, parasailing, skydiving, hang-gliding, river surfing, kayaking, jet skiing and climbing – compared to other age groups. Qualitative responses from individuals over the age of 45 years demonstrated a clear link between age and participation levels, as some respondents felt that they were 'too old' to engage in some of these aforementioned activities. Whilst these research findings affirm that age and participation levels are interconnected, it should be pointed out that this study only examines adventure activities of a physical nature. Tourists who enjoy other non-physical adventures whilst on holiday are more likely to span all age groups. For example, staying in a Mayan village in southern Belize and enjoying the hospitality provided by the local community may appeal to independent travellers of all age groups, as well as to students taking a 'gap' year out to work for a voluntary organization in a developing country.

As well as age being linked to participation levels – where physical adventures are concerned – it may also be associated with the type of adventure a person chooses. This can be seen in the North American adventure market, where (Loverseed, 1997: 91–92):

> Younger males, for example, gravitate towards strenuous, risky outward-bound type activities such as rock climbing or white-water canoeing. Among international travellers to Canada, those aged 45 and older like gentler outdoor activities such as bird watching.

For some tour operators that offer sport-based adventure holidays, age appears to be a less important factor when compared to a person's level of fitness. As Cater (2000) points out, some tour operators demand that their clients provide medical certificates before being allowed to take part in adventures. This requirement applies more to operators that offer physically challenging holidays that perhaps involve some degree of risk. For instance, Exodus' *Multi-Activity Brochure* (2001) advises potential clients:

> We do not have a strict upper age limit, but these are by nature adventurous activity holidays and the activities require a level of fitness and mobility. You must be certain that you are capable of fully participating in the activities involved. In certain circumstances we may require reasonable proof of medical fitness and general suitability before accepting a booking for a particular trip.

To conclude this section, it is important to note that both lifestyle and age play a role in the decision-making processes of adventure tourists. In relation to physically demanding adventure activities, people's levels of fitness and experience as well as their age seem to influence the type of activity they select, or are more suited to. It is assumed that the demand for non-physical adventure activities is not so influenced by a person's age.

The behaviour of adventure tourists

The following sections of this chapter focus on the behavioural elements of adventure tourists. Some of the main characteristics of these consumers and their position on the hard–soft adventure scale will be examined. The concept of tourist motivation will be briefly reviewed before turning to a discussion of the key motivational influences on adventure tourists. The final section presents an overview of tourists' behaviour when participating in similar (overlapping) forms of tourism to adventure tourism.

'Soft' and 'hard' adventurers

As mentioned in Chapter 1, the soft–hard continuum helps to accommodate the large diversity of adventure tourism products and consumers. The next section discusses this continuum in relation to adventure tourists.

As with any typology of tourists, the adventure tourist does not fit into a tightly defined set of personality characteristics and is considered not to have homogeneous tastes or competencies in adventurous activities. Soft adventurers usually take part in activities 'with a perceived risk but low levels of real risk requiring minimal commitment and beginning skills' (Hill, 1995: 63). These tourists are usually novices in the realm of adventure, and enjoy 'safe' activities that necessitate limited or no previous experience – for instance, bird watching on the Galapagos Islands off mainland Ecuador, whale watching off

Vancouver Island, Canada, or going on a commercially organized hiking trip to the Picos de Europa, Spain.

Soft adventurers are motivated by self-discovery, the need to escape from the routine of urban life and experience new environments (Lipscombe, 1995), the potential excitement, novelty, and the opportunity to socialize in a controlled environment (Ewert, 1989; see Lipscombe, 1995). In some senses parallels can be drawn between the soft adventurer and the mass tourist, the key difference being that the former type sporadically partakes in adventurous activities whilst the latter does not (Cloke and Perkins, 1998).

At the other end of the scale, hard adventurers thrive when exposed to 'activities with high levels of risk, requiring intense commitment and advanced skills' (Hill, 1995: 63). They are far more likely to engage in physically as well as mentally challenging outdoor activities that demand a lot of previous experience and high levels of competence. Hard adventurers procure their 'adrenaline rush' from taking risks; sometimes they can control these risks because of the level of experience they have, and other times they cannot. According to Lipscombe (1995), hard adventure tourists thrive from the elements of challenge, danger and risk that contribute towards the adventure. Activities that appeal to this type of tourist include mountaineering, sea kayaking, canyoning, bridge jumping, venturing to remote destinations (e.g. Mongolia), and going on safari in some of the untouched, less-visited wildlife areas in Africa.

The soft–hard scale illustrates not only the heterogeneous nature of adventure tourism and its associated activities, but also the broad ranging nature of participants' characteristics, motivations, skills and experience. As adventurers progress along the continuum they tend to become more adept at the activities they engage in, seek out higher levels of stimulation, and participate in riskier pursuits.

From the above discussion we can conclude that soft adventure activities would appeal to a larger proportion of people than those considered to be hard adventure. Becoming a truly hard adventurer is a challenging process, requiring the participant to have a lot of experience and nerve in the activity being pursued. In contrast, soft adventure would appeal to virtually anyone with a thirst for adventure, including novices as well as those individuals with a certain amount of experience.

These points are illustrated in Muller and Cleaver's (2000) research on the US 'baby boomer' market (see Table 3.2). Results revealed that 56 per cent of the survey's sample had taken an adventure holiday or trip in the five years

Table 3.2   Participation in 'soft' and 'hard' adventure by US residents (adapted from Muller and Cleaver, 2000)

Soft adventure activities	Demand for soft adventure (millions)	Hard adventure activities	Demand for hard adventure (millions)
Camping	64.7	White-water rafting/ kayaking	14.8
Hiking on gradually changing terrain	44.8	Snorkelling/scuba diving	12.4
Bicycle touring	27.2	Off-road biking/ mountain biking	10.8
Bird/animal watching	24.3	Backpacking across rugged terrain	8.0
Horse riding	24.1	Rock/mountain climbing	7.4
Canoeing	22.5	Spelunking/cave exploring	5.7
Total demand	207.6	Total demand	59.1

leading up to the study. Over 207 million people had taken a soft adventure holiday or trip, whereas only around 59 million individuals had participated in hard adventure. Clearly then, in relation to a rather large sample of US citizens, there is a preference for soft adventure experiences.

Evidently individuals choose to take part in soft or hard adventure for many different reasons. What one person perceives as an adventure, another may not. According to Tuson (1994; see Beard and Wilson, 2002) people have different challenge and panic zones, which place limits on the extent of adventure they can deal with. People's personalities and their prior experience of adventure influence these zones. For instance, tourists who choose to go on a gorilla-tracking holiday in Uganda would anticipate a high level of mental challenge and would undoubtedly have been on wildlife tours in the past. They would be able to control their level of panic on seeing a gorilla in close proximity. Persons inexperienced in wildlife viewing but selecting the same holiday may well find the whole experience of sighting a gorilla in its natural environment totally beyond their comfort zone, feeling panic and an overwhelming loss of control.

Some people seek a controllable adventure that does not take them out of their comfort zone – for example, hiking along a way-marked trail. Others – more than likely hard adventurers – enjoy an element of mental or physical challenge and thrive from pushing their inner strengths and relying totally on their own resources. An extreme example of the latter is climbing up Mount Everest, the most challenging endeavour in the world. Research carried out on the personalities of Everest climbers (Breivik, 1996) points to the importance of such characteristics as drive, low levels of anxiety/worry, stamina, will, and emotional stability. Individuals with this type of personality would be more likely to engage in extreme adventure activities. The fact that there are limited rescue opportunities above a certain altitude on Everest accentuates the level of danger involved in such an expedition and forces individuals to become completely reliant on their own resources.

The behavioural characteristics of soft and hard adventurers have been examined in this section. The heterogeneous nature of adventure tourists has also been explored using the soft–hard adventure continuum. For the purpose of classifying adventure tourists, this continuum has proved useful. However, as noted earlier, people's perceptions of adventure vary. Whilst the leisure and tourism industries may classify the experience of a hot air balloon ride as soft adventure, on the basis that it requires no skills or experience, a person doing this for the first time and who is of a nervous disposition would probably feel sheer panic. From this person's point of view the whole experience may feel like a hard adventure! To conclude this section, it seems apparent that people are driven to participate in different hard and soft adventures by several factors: experience, competence, skill and personality.

Tourist motivation

Tourist motivation is a complex subject that draws upon the academic discipline of psychology to explain individuals' decision-making processes and the reasons why they behave as they do both before and during their holidays. Individuals' motivations reflect their inner needs and push them to seek out holiday experiences that will bring satisfaction. People are intrinsically motivated to enjoy holidays and other forms of leisure for many divergent reasons, including relaxation, prestige, socializing, personal development, a desire for something different, excitement, adventure, experiencing different cultures/ways of life, meeting people with similar interests and intellectual enrichment. Crompton (1979; see Shaw and Williams, 1994) suggests that people take holidays to re-balance their state of disequilibrium, a 'condition' that is brought on from the routine of everyday living.

At the outset, a person feels the need to take a break from his or her usual routine. This leads to three different options for the individual:

1 To partake in leisure activities within the local area
2 To take a holiday or travel to see friends and relatives
3 To travel for business reasons.

Specific motives then shape the nature of the leisure experience, in the form of socio-psychological factors (push factors) and cultural factors (pull factors). Dann (1977; see Shaw and Williams, 1994) asserts that whilst the former set of motives determine the need for travel, the latter set affect the person's choice of destination.

Consumer motivation is important in all forms of tourism, including adventure tourism. Adventure tourists have a strong appetite for 'nerve-tingling excitement' (Krippendorf, 1987: 37). Due to their diverse profile, these tourists pursue adventure to realize many different motives. They achieve their 'holiday highs' through various activities that involve, for example, risk taking, excitement, escapism, personal development, social-izing, self-discovery and self-actualization. These are push factors, or inner needs, that urge individuals to participate in adventure. Examples of pull factors in relation to adventure tourism might include wild and rugged destination environments, suitable natural resources for adventure participa-tion (e.g. high peaks for mountaineering), or rare bird and animal species for wildlife viewing.

A number of theoretical frameworks have been devised to explain tourist motivations, but perhaps one of the most applicable to the subject of adventure tourism is the travel career ladder (Pearce, 1988). The ladder is an adaptation of Maslow's original five-fold hierarchical system of human motivation (Maslow, 1976), and is based on the premise that individuals have a career in their tourist behaviour. People seek to satisfy higher level needs or motives through their holidays as a consequence of increased tourism experience, as can be seen from Figure 3.2. The theory distinguishes (Pearce, 1996: 13):

> . . . between intrinsic and extrinsic motivation at the four lower levels of the system. The travel career ladder emphasizes all the tourists' patterns or motives, rather than a single motive for travelling. The five motivational levels described in the scheme are: a concern with biological needs (including relaxation), safety and security needs (or levels of stimulation), relationship development and extension needs, special interest and self-development needs, and fulfilment of deep involvement needs (formally defined as self actualization).

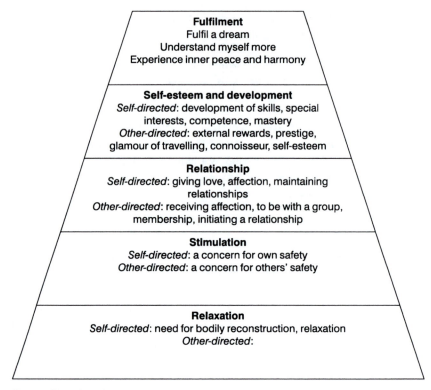

Fulfilment
Fulfil a dream
Understand myself more
Experience inner peace and harmony

Self-esteem and development
Self-directed: development of skills, special
interests, competence, mastery
Other-directed: external rewards, prestige,
glamour of travelling, connoisseur, self-esteem

Relationship
Self-directed: giving love, affection, maintaining
relationships
Other-directed: receiving affection, to be with a group,
membership, initiating a relationship

Stimulation
Self-directed: a concern for own safety
Other-directed: a concern for others' safety

Relaxation
Self-directed: need for bodily reconstruction, relaxation
Other-directed:

Source: Ryan (1998)

Figure 3.2   The travel career ladder.

In applying this framework to adventure tourists, it is evident that the majority would strive to accomplish high-level needs. As mentioned earlier in this chapter, some tourists seek out 'peak experiences' when enjoying adventures. Such experiences could well lead to dream fulfilment or inner peace and harmony – motives placed at the very top of the travel career ladder. A person may experience dream fulfilment from hiking along the Inca Trail in Peru to the famous ruins of Machu Pichu, doing a bungee jump in New Zealand, going cage diving with great white sharks in South Africa, or husky sledging in Lapland. Adventures that are non-physical can also result in the actualization of high-level needs. Examples here include going on safari in Amboseli National Park in Kenya and viewing exotic wildlife, or staying at a Buddhist retreat in the Alpujarras region of southern Spain to achieve inner peace and harmony.

Motivation plays a major role in the holiday decisions and behaviour of all tourists. However, it is important to bear in mind that other factors also influence tourists' behaviour – for example, personality, financial considerations, the amount of paid leave from work, health issues, and travelling partners. Such factors can either hinder or facilitate the realization of a person's holiday motives.

Adventure tourist motives

Due to the diverse nature of adventure tourism, it is obvious that its participants will display a wide range of motives. Some of these motives have been briefly commented upon in the section above. What follows is a more rigorous examination of some of the fundamental reasons (or motives) why people get involved in adventurous activities and holidays.

Most people take adventure holidays for a range of different reasons rather than just one. This point can be illustrated through the study on 178 exhibitors at an international adventure travel exhibition in the USA (Sung *et al.*, 1997).

Table 3.3 **Benefits of adventure travel – travellers (adapted from Sung *et al.*, 1997)**

Perceived benefits of adventure travel	Percentage of participants
Experience	
■ Discovering new experiences	27*
■ Increased sense of personal growth	25*
■ Educational opportunities	7
Activity	
■ Fun and excitement	16*
■ Integrated, better travel opportunities	16*
■ Outdoor adventure recreation activity participation	7
■ Recreational opportunity	3
Environment	
■ Improved interpretation of the environment and culture	17*
■ Return to nature	7
■ Carefree 'blown away' setting	7
■ Interaction with environment/people	5
Miscellaneous	
■ Improved awareness of physical fitness and health	3
■ Mental and/or physical stimulation	2
■ Do not know	15

* = five most important benefits of adventure travel; percentages are rounded up.

Their research found that exhibition participants associated adventure holidays with a number of experiential, activity-based and environmental benefits (see Table 3.3). 'Discovering new experiences' was the most commonly stated benefit (27 per cent), although an 'increased sense of personal growth' (25 per cent) was deemed to be virtually as important. 'Fun and excitement' (16 per cent) rated one of the highest in the activity-based benefits category, perhaps an indication of the importance of risk-seeking as an integral part of adventure travel. Other important perceived benefits of adventure travel included 'integrated, better travel opportunities' (16 per cent) and 'improved interpretation of the environment and culture' (17 per cent).

The relationship between risk and adventure

The link between adventure tourism and risk has already been highlighted, and it is fair to suggest that risk is a powerful motivator for adventurers. Indeed, 'Every adventure has its particular form and amount of risk which is a stimulatory motive to participate in the activity' (Vester, 1987; see Gilchrist et al., 1995: 12).

Definitions of adventure consistently allude to the importance of risk. Adventure comprises 'freedom of choice; intrinsic rewards; and an element of uncertainty, for instance when the experience outcome is uncertain, or its risks are unpredictable' (McArthur, 1989; see Fluker and Turner, 2000: 380). Risk therefore plays an important role in a person's enjoyment of adventure. Indeed, any absence of risk from the experience could well result in a decline in satisfaction or even a loss of the urge to participate (Sung et al., 1997).

Much of the research on risky experiences stems from the field of outdoor recreation. Such research supports the tenet that risk-seeking is an integral part of any adventure (Meier, 1978; Yerkes, 1985; Ewert, 1989). A substantial number of studies have been carried out on participants of adventurous pursuits under the guise of 'risk recreation', 'adventure recreation', 'natural challenge activities' and 'high adventure' (Ewert, 1989). Various psychological studies have also investigated the association of risk with adventure, concluding that personality is a true indicator of whether people choose to engage in risky activities or not, and of their coping mechanisms in risky situations.

Research that examines the role of risk in adventure tourism is less advanced than its application to the disciplines of recreation and psychology. Yet as the adventure travel industry continues to grow empirical research will expand accordingly, and adventure suppliers will need a comprehensive understanding of their consumers' motives, inclusive of risk. The discussion that follows should provide a justification for this.

Characteristics of risk

The concept of risk has many different connotations attached to it, and it is worth briefly examining some risk characteristics to understand more fully adventurers' motivations. People often perceive risk as the potential to lose something of value (Cheron and Ritchie, 1982; Martin and Priest, 1986) – for example, in everyday life driving a car after drinking an excess amount of alcohol could well result in the loss of one's driving licence. Working in risky professions, for instance rally car racing could result in injury or, in more extreme cases, death. In a leisure context, failing successfully to complete a deep sea diving course or turning back on a mountaineering expedition due to lack of skill or ability could well result in a blow to a person's self-esteem.

People often attach negative meaning to the word 'risk', and many regard it as a perilous component of adventure. Fortunately, risk is also associated with the pursuit of positive outcomes (Mitchell, 1983; Ewert, 1989) – otherwise why would people take part in adventures in the first place? To illustrate this point, consider the person who goes on a trekking trip through the dense Amazonian jungle, enduring an infinite number of risks *en route*, such as getting bitten by a poisonous snake or facing dehydration due to the heat and humidity of a jungle environment. At the end of the holiday, this person may feel a sense of self-fulfilment and contentment from surviving such an intensely dangerous trip.

Two distinct categories of risk exist: 'positive' risk, which a person can control and which is perceived as challenge, and 'negative' risk, which a person cannot control and which perceived as danger. These risk levels are inextricably linked to an individual's skill, experience and knowledge of the adventure activity. Johnston's investigation into mountain adventure recreation participants in New Zealand illustrates this point (Johnston, 1992; cited in Weiler and Hall, 1992). Her research found that people with experience in mountain activities perceived risk as a challenge rather than a danger. Instead of feeling threatened by the level of risk involved in mountain adventures, these people felt that risk positively contributed to their enjoyment levels. With this in mind, it stands to reason that someone who is a novice in mountain adventures may therefore experience an uncomfortable and uncontrollable level of risk. However, once this person starts to build up experience in this type of adventure, he or she will begin to view the risk component as more positive.

Often there is a disparity between a person's perceived risk and the actual or real risk involved in adventure participation. Risk can be objective, i.e. the actual number of accidents reported for a specific activity, or subjective risk, i.e. the extent of risk perceived by the participant (Rossi and Cereatti, 1993). People frequently fail to understand the objective risks involved in different physically adventurous activities, and this results in their exclusion from activities perceived as high risk. Cater's (2000) research findings back up this idea. He carried out research in Queenstown, New Zealand, and found that tourists perceived bungee jumping as a far riskier activity than white-water rafting or canyoning. In reality, though, people are far less likely to be injured by bungee jumping than during the other two activities. Such misjudgements of subjective risk result in people automatically excluding themselves from participation in adventure.

This short overview of the key features of risk illustrates that the phenomenon involves both positive and negative aspects. The way in which people view risk seems to be dependent upon the level of experience they have as well as the type of activity that they are taking part in. Also, personality will invariably be an important influence on people's perception of risk.

Risk experience and adventure

Now that we have examined what risk is, what it means to people and how it is related to adventure, it would be useful to understand how individuals actually experience risk throughout the time that they are taking part in the adventure activity. One of the most useful models to introduce on this subject is the 'risk recreation model' proposed by Robinson (1992). As its title indicates, this model focuses on recreation rather than tourism. However, as asserted in Chapter 1 and reflected in Johnston's comments that 'travel to the mountains for the specific purpose of pursuing adventurous recreation can be considered adventure tourism' (Johnston, 1992: 159; cited in Weiler and Hall, 1992), there are clear overlaps between adventure recreation and adventure tourism.

The risk recreation model identifies the different stages that individuals go through when undertaking risky leisure pursuits. The model comprises five phases that reflect an evolution from the initial allure of risk recreation to the final stage where risk taking becomes central to a person's life. It is interesting to note the importance of personality in this model. Only those individuals who have the right disposition will commit themselves to adventure/risk recreation (and adventure tourism) in the first place. A summary of this model is presented in Figure 3.3.

The five different phases are detailed as follows:

- *Phase 1.* This initial phase is concerned with whether individuals are predisposed to participating in adventure recreation. People who express a

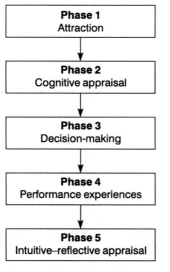

Phase 1
Attraction

Phase 2
Cognitive appraisal

Phase 3
Decision-making

Phase 4
Performance experiences

Phase 5
Intuitive–reflective appraisal

Source: adapted from Robinson (1992)

Figure 3.3   A summary of the risk recreation model.

high need for stimulation and autonomy are more likely to become involved in risky leisure activities. In a tourism context, those tourists who like to have 'active' holidays will be more inclined to experience adventure.

- *Phase 2*. Before taking part in a risky activity such as bungee jumping or white-water rafting, people will evaluate the risks involved. Cox and Stuart (1964; see Robinson, 1992) suggest that people speculate over the likelihood of failure on the activity and the consequences of potential failure. They appraise their level of competence in doing the activity, and this is weighed up against the level of perceived risk. If the perceived risk of participation exceeds the perceived competence, this could evoke feelings of threat, anxiety and fear, and the individual may not engage in the task (McGrath, 1982; see Robinson, 1992). A novice in adventure pursuits may experience such emotions if, for example, he or she is taking part in a multi-activity holiday for the first time.
- *Phase 3*. Making a decision on whether or not to take part in an adventure depends upon various factors – for example, on the extent to which individuals are motivated to succeed compared to the extent to which they want to avoid failing (Atkinson, 1974; see Robinson, 1992). Someone who is more concerned about failure avoidance will invariably engage in activities where success is virtually guaranteed. Interestingly, though, that

person could instead participate in activities that have a low probability of success. The reason for this is that failure can be blamed on the task rather than the person's lack of ability.

- *Phase 4*. This is the stage at which the actual experience occurs. Risk recreation participants enjoy optimally challenging experiences through striking a balanced relationship between the perceived risk and competencies and the demands of the risk environment (Scherl, 1989; see Robinson, 1992).
- *Phase 5*. Once the activity has been completed, participants try to understand the factors that have influenced either their success or failure in it. Immediately after the performance, individuals evaluate the experience and its associated emotions along a subjective scale ranging from unsuccessful to successful. This is known as an intuitive appraisal. The reflective appraisal then follows in which people look for the reasons why they performed in the way that they did. Where participants are positive about their appraisal, risk recreation becomes an integral part of their lifestyle.

To conclude this section, it is important to recognize that risk is a significant motive in both risk recreation and adventure tourism. Aside from risk, though, other factors come into play when people are involved in adventure. According to Robinson's model, these are competence, personality, decision-making, and the risk environment.

Sensation seeking and adventure

It seems to be widely accepted that risk taking is an important component that contributes towards a rewarding adventurous experience. There are numerous other motives that are intertwined with this element of risk, and one of these is 'sensation seeking'. This motive is judged to be highly significant in a person's pursuit of adventure. Zuckerman's (1979) pioneering research in this field has resulted in the development of the Sensation Seeking Scale (SSS; see Box 3.2), a psychological model that tests people's risk-taking behaviour in a variety of situations. The model has evolved over the past 20-plus years to take account of changing consumer behaviour, and its validity has been consistently reported through numerous studies. Zuckerman (1979: 13) defines the sensation seeking concept as:

> ... the seeking of varied, novel, complex and intense sensations and experiences and the willingness to take physical, social, legal and financial risks for the sake of such experiences.

Box 3.2   The Sensation Seeking Scale (SSS; adapted from Zuckerman, 1979)

The SSS is a 40-item questionnaire with two choices per item. It comprises an overall measure of sensation-seeking (SSV Total), plus four sub-components:

1 Thrill and adventure seeking – the preference for exciting, adventurous and risky activities (e.g. for remote tourist destinations over well-known ones)

2 Experience seeking – '. . . a desire to adopt a non-conforming lifestyle and a tendency to gravitate towards sensations through the senses and mind' (e.g. participating in skydiving to get an 'adrenaline rush')

3 Disinhibition – seeking out opportunities for social and sexual stimulation through partying and perhaps having a variety of sexual partners (e.g.: staying in backpacker hostels whilst on a round-the-world trip so as to meet fellow travellers and enjoy the 'social scene')

4 Boredom susceptibility – avoidance of tedious and unchanging situations; feelings of restlessness when things stay constant (e.g. not going on holiday with the same group of people every year to the same destination and doing the same things).

Sensation seeking is therefore not solely about risk taking, and is expressed in many areas of a person's life. Studies demonstrate that participants of risky sports, as well as people with a preference for such sports, achieve high results on the SSS. Apparently, sensation seeking is part of their personality. They thrive from doing risky and exciting activities. They need a stream of adrenaline rushes in their life, and they try to avoid routine and unchanging situations.

Research into participation in risky sports reveals that participants in parachuting (Rowland *et al.*, 1986; see Trimpop *et al.*, 1998), mountain climbing (Robinson, 1985; see Trimpop *et al.*, 1998) and downhill skiing (Bouter *et al.*, 1988; see Trimpop *et al.*, 1998) show high results on the total SSS. More recent research (Jack and Ronan, 1999) comparing people who partake in low-risk sports with those who participate in high-risk sports found divergent scores on the SSS for each group. Such research findings demonstrate the importance of sensation seeking for adventurers.

When applying the concept of sensation seeking to adventure tourists, we can assume that these people portray similar personality characteristics to participants in risky sports – certainly where physical adventure holidays are concerned. For non-physical adventures, we would expect that those people seeking out tourism experiences that are drug- or sex-based would score highly on the SSS, particularly on the 'disinhibition' and 'experience seeking' components.

Only a limited amount of research has examined the SSS in the specific context of tourism, although generally findings support the idea that sensation seeking is an integral part of adventure travel. Gilchrist (1994) applied Zuckerman's (1979) original SSS to a group of ex-overland travellers who had travelled through Africa (Kenya, Uganda, Zaire, Burundi, Rwanda, Tanzania, Malawi and Zimbabwe) with an overland adventure specialist tour operator. The SSS was also tested on a control group, similar to the travellers in age and socio-economic status. Overland travellers scored significantly higher results than their control counterparts on the total SSS, as well as on the 'thrill and adventure' and 'experience' sub-scales. Such findings imply that overland travellers are sensation seekers and:

> ... have a greater desire to engage in risky and adventurous sports and activities involving speed and danger. It also appears that they seek more experiences through mind and senses, travel and non-conforming lifestyles.

(Gilchrist, 1994: 35)

Conversely, findings revealed no significant differences between both groups on the 'boredom susceptibility'and 'disinhibition' sub-scales. In other words, overland travellers and control participants have similar desires for social (or sexual) stimulation, and express similar aversions to repetitive situations.

Achieving sensation seeking

Individuals are thought to achieve the 'feel good' sensations associated with adventure as a result of certain biological processes. These processes will be briefly highlighted in this section.

The 'adrenaline rush' that people experience when taking part in risky sports contributes considerably to the search for intense sensations. In relation to rock climbing, for instance, the pumping of adrenaline through climbers' bodies can help them to 'psyche up' and feel more focused for the climb. According to the 'catastrophe theory' the release of adrenaline helps to improve sporting ability (Fox, 2000), although this is often a short-lived effect to permit 'flight or fight' activity bursts of a physical (e.g. gaining more strength) or mental (e.g. becoming more focused and less scared) nature.

Once the adrenaline release ceases, performance can be negatively affected. The build-up of adrenaline that climbers (and other risky sports participants) feel when preparing to lead a rock climb is summed up in the quotation by Anderson (see Fox, 2000: 39) below:

> You've got to know you're going to be scared on the route. You psyche yourself up so that by the time you get there you're already full of adrenaline. Then you are really nervous when you set out on the rock, but starting to climb makes you feel better.

Adrenaline is obviously an important factor that controls people's experiences of adventure. Another primary element is the chemical balance of a person's brain. People with a strong desire for sensation seeking in their lives are thought to have different chemical balances in their brain to individuals with less of an appetite for excitement and fear-provoking situations. Certain neurotransmitters, such as adrenaline, endorphins and dopamine, are responsible for the 'feel good' factor experienced by everyone, at differing degrees of intensity. Any exciting or risky situation triggers an increased flow of these chemicals. In the case of adrenaline, this results in a 'rush of energy and alertness' (Schueller, 2000: 21). In turn, an enzyme called monoamine oxidase type B (MAO B) regulates the functioning and amount of these 'feel good' chemicals in the brain. Those people disposed to high levels of sensation seeking have less of this enzyme present than their opposites on the SSS. Therefore, individuals who are more likely to participate in bungee jumping or a conservation expedition to some far-flung destination have a higher volume of pleasure chemicals operating in the brain when they engage in risky or exciting activities.

McCobb's (1994; see Schueller, 2000: 22) STREX theory offers an alternative biological-based explanation for people's predilection for risk-taking and thrill-seeking activities. When adrenaline is released it passes through channels that are situated in adrenal cells. Some of these channels contain STREX (STress hormone regulated EXon), and are responsible for the rate at which adrenaline is released through the body:

The level of STREX will affect how quickly [the] adrenal glands dump large quantities of adrenaline. And that may have some effect on what [people] get thrills out of and the propensity to do this again.

High-sensation seekers, such as avid skydivers, would have lower levels of STREX and consequently seek out high thrill experiences to achieve an adrenaline rush.

It seems therefore that adrenaline helps people to prepare for an adventure through making them feel more active and attentive. The chemical make-up of adventurers' brains encourages them to seek out adventures so that the 'feel good' chemicals will be released and they will experience a positive outcome.

Although risk taking and sensation seeking appear to be essential elements in the enjoyment of adventure tourism or recreation, there are many other motives that stimulate people to engage in such activities. Some of these motives were noted earlier in the research findings by Sung et al. (1997). In addition, people are driven by other needs – for example, the need to enhance self-esteem, to become more competent in a certain activity, to face a challenge head on, to develop a new skill, to experience novel situations etc. It is useful to discuss the other facets underlying consumer participation in adventure in order to comprehend more fully what motivates such tourists. Before moving on, it should be noted that these facets, at the same time as being distinct, are often also linked to the motive of risk taking.

Changing consumer motives and experience

A correlation exists between the degree of experience a person has in a particular adventure activity, and changes in motivation. For instance, as people become more experienced in scuba diving, they may feel inspired to go on longer trips to more 'exciting' bodies of water. Again, the needs of independent round-the-world travellers may gradually change as they develop more travel experience. At the outset they may backpack around a well-known, 'safe' country such as Australia, but as their self-reliance and confidence grows their final month of travel may be spent in a remote part of the Amazon rainforest staying with local tribal communities, or going on walking safaris in Zambia.

The motivational changes associated with an increased level of adventure experience are demonstrated in Fluker and Turner's (2000) study. They compared the needs, motivations and expectations of both experienced and inexperienced white-water rafters. As anticipated, their research findings divulged a different set of behaviours for the experienced compared to the inexperienced rafters. Experienced rafters appeared to be more relaxed and interested in the different benefits of rafting – for instance, socializing and being in a natural environment. In contrast, novice rafters were more motivated by the novelty and excitement associated with the sport, and were also more inclined to take risks to achieve their goals.

These findings have implications for the marketing of commercial white-water rafting to meet different consumer needs. Whereas novice rafters may be inspired by banners such as 'try something new and challenging', captions such as 'bring your friends out for another enjoyable day in the wild while white-water rafting' may appeal to more experienced rafters (Fluker and Turner, 2000: 387–388). Findings from this study demonstrate that white-water rafters exhibit different behaviour according to their experience. Such findings can be broadly generalized to other areas of adventure tourism and leisure.

Experience and competence

The more experience people have in a particular adventure activity, the more likely it is that they will feel competent in that activity. Furthermore, individuals will feel competent if they have a positive adventure experience, no matter whether they are a novice or an expert in that activity. Experience and competence are important in situations where some degree of skill is required, or has to be learnt, to participate successfully in the adventure. Although adventure sports naturally fall into this category, non-physical adventures (such as going on a Buddhist retreat where the participant develops meditation skills) also involve both competence and experience.

Iso-Ahola *et al.* (1988) carried out some research on rock climbers that illustrates the above ideas. Their study detected links between people's perceived competence, self-esteem and experience. Perceived competence can be divided into two categories:

1 General perceived competence – a certain level of ability that has resulted from accumulative experience
2 Specific perceived competence – '. . .a sense of competence specific to a recent experience' (Iso-Ahola *et al.*, 1988: 34).

Rock climbers were interviewed before and after a day's climb. Those climbers that had had successful climbs on the day felt highly self-competent about their climbing ability and demonstrated a high degree of self-esteem.

Interestingly, however, self-esteem was not linked to the degree of experience a rock climber had. Furthermore, the more experience that the rock climbers had, the higher was their level of general perceived competence.

Such findings could be applied to other adventure scenarios. For instance, novice downhill skiers would not venture onto red (difficult) and black (very difficult) ski runs until they felt sufficiently competent. Someone new to paragliding would go through a series of stages to feel fully competent through initially engaging in rigorous training, moving from tandem to solo gliding, working towards gaining a pilot's licence, and ultimately achieving instructor status.

Consumer motives and continued participation in adventure

The last two sections have explored the role of individual experience within different forms of risk recreation and adventure tourism. This next section presents a model that explains the reasons (or motives) why, once people have started an adventure sport, they continue to participate in it. It shows that participants continue with a risky sport not only for the obvious reasons – for example, to gain more experience, skills and competence in it – but also for social and psychological reasons.

Shoham *et al.* (2000) devised a model, shown in Figure 3.4, which elucidates the behavioural components underlying the continuous consumption of risky sports.

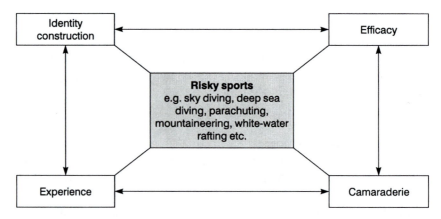

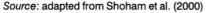
Source: adapted from Shoham et al. (2000)

Figure 3.4　The behavioural components of risky sports.

Figure 3.4 illustrates that there are four main motives that encourage a person to continue taking part in a risky sport such as sky diving or mountaineering:

1 *Identity construction.* This is '. . . a clear-cut means to organize a new, and sometimes central identity' (Celsi *et al.*, 1993; see Shoham *et al.*, 2000: 239). In other words, people participate in risky sports because they are driven by a need to undergo some sort of personal development and to acquire a new identity.
2 *Efficacy.* As individuals progress in a risky sport, their expertise generally improves and they set themselves increasingly higher standards. These elements result in people's efficacy, or ability, being maintained in the sport (Celsi *et al.*, 1993; see Shoham *et al.*, 2000).
3 *Camaraderie.* When continuously involved in an adventure sport, people experience a sense of camaraderie and feel part of a community. If they are heavily involved in the sport, they become 'members' of the group and develop certain roles and expertise. This eventually results in a clear distinction between ordinary daily life and extraordinary risky sport participation.
4 *Experience.* Risky sport participants accomplish improved levels of performance with experience, and their attention gradually moves from feeling anxious about the risks involved in the sport to feeling 'in control' of the risks. With increased experience, therefore, people enjoy the adventure sport more. Parallels can be drawn here with Fluker and Turner's (2000) research discussed earlier in this chapter.

This model has implications not only for those people who take part in risky sports, but also for those taking part in adventure tourism. For example, consider a Manchester (UK)-based mountaineering club whose members go on regular hiking day and weekend trips to the Lake District and North Wales. In winter, some members may take a few mountaineering trips in Scotland to summit a few peaks or to do some ice climbing. In summer, some members might go on mountaineering holidays to the Alps. Participation in all or even some of these activities would result in members gaining more experience and developing competence as hikers or mountaineers. They would also feel more involved in the 'club community', and perhaps assume a new identity.

The 'flow' experience

The following part of the chapter examines the concept of 'flow' and its relevance to the adventure consumer. 'Flow' is defined as (Csikszentmihalyi, 1992: 4):

... the state in which people are so involved in an activity that nothing else seems to matter; the experience itself is so enjoyable that people will do it at great cost, for the sheer sake of doing it.

Flow is an important sensation that many people desire when they take part in adventure tourism or recreation, and is a sensation that builds up throughout the duration that a person is having an adventure. The process of 'flow' ultimately leads to the 'peak experience' (highlighted earlier in this chapter). People can achieve 'flow' if they are involved in activities that demand them to actively participate, such as scuba diving, mountain biking, sea kayaking and other adventure sports. Such a state results in 'a sense of exhilaration, a deep sense of enjoyment that is long cherished and that becomes a landmark in memory for what life should be like' (Csikszentmihalyi, 1992: 3).

Flow and its associated peak experiences result in an overall feeling of happiness and an improved quality of life. Therefore, such a feeling remains with adventure participants not only whilst they are participating in the experience but also when they resume everyday living once more. However, such positive emotions only occur when an individual makes a concerted effort to achieve this state (see Box 3.3).

Much of the discussion in this chapter so far has been concerned with adventure of a physical nature and the behavioural characteristics of its participants. Different theoretical concepts have been examined and, where possible, examples applied that attempt to demonstrate the range of behaviours that adventure consumers exhibit. Many of the ideas presented have evolved from recreation- and psychology-based research. In the case of the former type of research, it is inevitable that there will be emphasis on adventure of the physical type. Unfortunately, there is less known about the behaviour of people who engage in adventures of a non-physical nature. That said, it is possible to make some assumptions about these people through examining the participants of other forms of tourism that overlap with adventure tourism. What follows is a discussion of the behaviours of ecotourists, wildlife tourists, and people who do charity challenges.

Ecotourists and adventure tourists

Before commenting on ecotourists' behaviour, it is worthwhile pointing out that the lack of a consensual view on what ecotourism truly is has contributed towards a dearth of accurate information about its consumer. Indeed,

Box 3.3 How flow and optimal experience are achieved through leading a rock climb

1 Activity requires skill and challenge. Optimal experiences emanate from goal-directed activities, such as rock climbing, that necessitate skill and psychic energy. An individual will have some rock climbing experience in order successfully to lead a climb. Bolder (hard) climbers will be interested in 'pushing their grades', i.e. setting themselves increasingly demanding route challenges. In contrast, novice climbers may feel anxious about leading a climb when they have only a basic level of skill. Climbing on indoor walls that provide a safe environment may result in an experienced climber feeling bored.

2 Total immersion in the activity. The person becomes completely absorbed in leading the climb because of the challenges that such an activity presents and the level of skill required to cope with such challenges. Subsequently, the individual becomes fully involved with the activity, as described by one rock climber: 'You are so involved in what you are doing [that] you aren't thinking of yourself as separate from the immediate activity . . . You don't see yourself as separate from what you are doing' (Csikszentmihalyi, 1992: 53).

3 Actions directed at fulfilling goal. The individual's main goal is to competently climb to the end of the route without falling off, resting or going off-route. As the person progresses up the rock face, he or she will receive constant feedback to affirm that this goal is being achieved.

4 Enhanced concentration. The individual is so immersed in leading the actual climb that he or she pushes any disagreeable parts of life to the back of the mind and concentrates on the task in hand. One climber describes such a state of mind: 'It is as if my memory input has been cut off. All I can remember is the last thirty seconds, and all I can think ahead is the next five minutes' (Csikszentmihalyi, 1992: 58).

5 Flow involves control. A climber whose skills are appropriately matched to the level of challenge will be able to exercise control throughout the climb, and be able to predict (to some extent) the differing challenges of the climb. Having this heightened sense of control will invariably result in fewer perceived risks.

6 A sense of transcendentalism. The person feels a sense of oneness with the immediate surrounding environment and a loss of the sense of self. One climber likens this sensation to 'a Zen feeling, like meditation or concentration' (Csikszentmihalyi, 1992: 62).

7 Transformation of time. Seemingly, the sense of time a person feels whilst leading a climb may be completely out of sync with the actual passage of time. The individual may think that he or she completed a 100-m multi-pitch route in a couple of hours, whereas in reality a whole afternoon may have passed by. One explanation for this loss of time is linked to the high level of concentration that the activity of climbing demands.

ecotourism is not dissimilar to adventure tourism in this respect. This lack of agreement has resulted in:

> ... an underlying assumption that because people are found in natural settings they are 'ecotourists'. For example, an individual may be visiting Tikal in Guatemala for reasons other than to view birds or learn about the outstanding Mayan ruins there (such as being able to say 'I've been there').
>
> (Palacio and McCool, 1997: 236)

These problems aside, a small number of studies have investigated the ecotourist market and come up with demographic profiles and behavioural characteristics. Some researchers conclude that ecotourists are motivated by the adventure element of ecotourism. A few of these studies will now be reviewed in a bid to understand why people pursue ecotourism experiences.

Fennell and Smale (1992) compared the travel behaviour of Canadian tourists taking holidays in Costa Rica with that of the general Canadian population. The researchers wanted to find out about the travel motives and benefits sought by each group of people. The ecotourists ranked attractions such as wilderness areas, national parks, reserves and mountains as more important to their holiday experience. In contrast, the general Canadian population regarded attractions such as indoor sports, theme parks, nightlife and entertainment as more important. Costa Rican tourists sought holiday benefits such as being physically active, experiencing new and different lifestyles and being daring and adventuresome, whilst non-ecotourists attached greater importance to more conventional motives, such as visiting friends and relatives and 'doing nothing at all'. Fennell and Smale concluded that Canadian ecotourists enjoy novel activities whilst on holiday, and crave unique or alternative holiday experiences. These research findings demonstrate that Canadian ecotourists are similar to adventure tourists in certain ways. For example, both ecotourists (in this study) and participants of physical forms of adventure tourism enjoy active holidays. Also, both groups of people seek out holidays that offer new and exciting experiences.

Another survey (Eagles, 1992), which was conducted to ascertain the motives of Canadian tourists and ecotourists, provides an insight into how adventure can often play a role in the ecotourist's holiday experience. A comprehensive set of data was analysed to establish people's preferences for particular destination environments (i.e. attraction motives) and what their general motives were for taking certain types of holiday (i.e. social motives). The 'attraction' motives that held most interest for the ecotourist group were wilderness, water, mountains, parks, rural areas and, the most highly ranked, 'wilderness and undisturbed nature'. Interestingly, the Canadian Tourism Commission (see Loverseed, 1997: 89) notes that an essential component of adventure tourism is travel to 'an unusual, exotic and remote or wilderness destination'. The most important social motives were being physically active, new lifestyles, meeting people of similar interests, adventure, and seeing the maximum in the time available.

Palacio and McCool (1997) carried out a survey on international tourists visiting Belize, a well-established ecotourism destination predominantly frequented by the North American market. From the survey results, four typologies of tourist were devised (see Figure 3.5). All four types of international tourist to Belize showed some interest in nature-based tourism. One of the more relevant findings of this discussion is that the 'ecotourist' group regarded adventure as an important anticipated benefit of their holiday. This finding supports the idea that adventure tourists and ecotourists share similar reasons for taking adventure and ecotourism holidays.

Types of international visitor to Belize

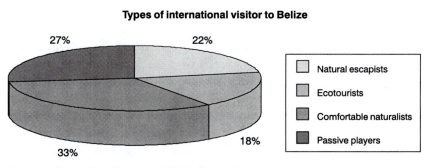

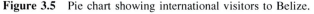

Source: adapted from Palacio and McCool (1997)

Figure 3.5 Pie chart showing international visitors to Belize.

Through briefly summarizing Diamantis' (1999) study, we can make some interesting comparisons between ecotourists and tourists who enjoy adventure of a non-physical type. United Kingdom ecotourists were divided into 'occasional ecotourists' (710 people) and 'frequent ecotourists' (1050 people). Occasional ecotourists most enjoyed the nature-based and educational components of ecotourism activities, and showed little interest in the social and outdoor elements of ecotourism. Frequent ecotourists also rated natural attractions and educational elements highly. In addition, they thought that 'the experience of traditional and natural lifestyles and local culture' (Diamantis, 1999: 101) was important to an enjoyable ecotourism experience. Tourists that engage in non-physical forms of adventure seek out the same benefits as those identified above by UK ecotourists. For example, an adventure holiday to north-west Vietnam, staying in remote tribal villages, would offer tourists an opportunity to enjoy the mountains within this region (nature element), engage in cultural exchange with local people (cultural element), and learn about the destination region, its people and its natural resources (educational element).

The four studies discussed above demonstrate a number of similarities between adventure and ecotourists. Some of the motives shared by each type of tourist include the need for novel and stimulating experiences, the need to undertake some form of physical activity, a desire to take holidays in natural and/or wilderness environments, a desire to get involved in different cultures, and a desire to learn new things.

Wildlife tourists and adventure tourists

Wildlife tourism is a niche form of ecotourism that encompasses a wide range of products, including safaris, wilderness backpacking, wildlife viewing, aquaria, circuses and zoos, many of which fit under the broad umbrella of adventure tourism. Most wildlife tourism takes place in developing countries (Shackley, 1996). Such countries are exotic destinations and are often renowned for their unique flora and fauna species. Costa Rica, Belize, Antarctica, Namibia, Kenya and Nepal are good examples of world-wide regions that have established wildlife tourism industries. Costa Rica's tourism successes, for instance, are based on its wildlife resources and a well-developed system for protecting its natural assets.

Wildlife tourists are diverse in nature, and are spread across the whole length of the soft–hard adventurer continuum. At the hard end of the scale there are tourists who are highly committed, experienced and knowledgeable about a particular area of wildlife. These tourists may go on a highly specialized botanical tour or an advanced level diving holiday, for instance. Novice wildlife tourists are at the other, soft end of the scale. They may go on safari in Kenya or go whale watching around Vancouver Island, for example.

What wildlife tourists want to experience from a wildlife holiday or activity will vary. They may want to be active participants or passive observers. They may want to view animals that are held in captivity, or encounter animals that roam freely in the wild. The main benefit for active participants is that they have 'temporary affinity with a different species or its environment' (Shackley, 1996: 60). Such an experience can be fulfilled through swimming with dolphins in their wild habitat, for instance. People who prefer to be passive observers when viewing wildlife are content simply to watch and become absorbed in the whole experience. Such satisfaction could be gained from visiting a sea-life centre in the UK or by venturing further afield to a safari destination to view large mammals in their natural habitat. Whichever of the two broad categories that people fit into, Shackley (1996: 57) asserts that wildlife tourists are searching for 'peak experiences' (a concept introduced earlier in this chapter), defined as 'those existential moments that induce a heightened sense of being alive and make the visitor happier, more confident and less stressed'.

These peak experiences are also what many adventure tourists aspire to. To illustrate this point, compare a tourist who takes a wildlife package holiday to Etosha National Park Namibia to view wild animals with a tourist who goes on an independently organized backpacking trip to the Himalayas. The wildlife tourist may achieve a peak experience on viewing wildlife at close range, whereas the adventure backpacker tourist may enjoy such a sensation on summiting a mountain.

Wildlife tourism offers a number of other benefits to its consumers. One study investigated the behaviour of international tourists visiting Penguin Place, New Zealand (Schanzel and McIntosh, 2000). Penguin Place is a conservation area that was established in 1985 to save the world's most endangered species, the yellow-eyed penguin. Visitors take a 90-minute guided tour around the colony in small groups, and have the opportunity to view the penguins close up because trenches have been dug 'so that visitors can move through the colony relatively "unnoticed" by penguins, and penguin nests are observed from within camouflaged "viewing hides"' (2000: 39). Visitors to Penguin Place commented favourably on the whole experience of being in such close proximity to the penguins. Some of the main benefits that they expressed were feelings of fascination, amazement and privilege, and a sense of exploration.

Evidently, wildlife tourists can be considered as a category of tourists in their own right or as a sub-category of adventure tourists. From the limited amount of research presented above, it is clear that both groups of tourists exhibit similar motives and gain similar benefits from their adventure or wildlife experiences. Chapter 10 provides a fuller discussion on 'wildlife adventure tourism'.

Charity challenge tourists and adventure tourists

Charity challenge 'holidays' have recently grown in popularity, and are enjoyed by individuals who feel the need to do something worthwhile and fulfilling whilst on their travels. Such holidays are often a 'once in a lifetime' experience for participants. Charity challenges form an integral part of the adventure tourism industry, and such a challenge characteristically:

> ... generally involves being part of an organized group (anything between 10 and 150) and taking part in some physical activity ranging from the relatively undemanding to the arduous. Costs to the participants are low (usually around £200) but they must raise a substantial amount of money for the charity through sponsorship (often about £2000). Supportive friends and family are encouraged to sponsor the individual, imaginative fund-raising events ensue and businesses are often willing supporters because of the team-building potential of the 'challenges'.

> (Bleasdale, 2000: 4; cited in Robinson *et al.*, 2000).

Although a limited amount of research has been conducted in this area of tourism, Bleasdale's (2000) work provides a useful insight into the motives of charity challenge participants. Bleasdale carried out a survey on people who were doing a trek in Nepal in aid of the Imperial Cancer Research Fund. A total of 31 trekkers completed the survey, either during or directly after the charity trek. The results revealed that people had divergent reasons for taking part in this charity challenge trip, and these reasons include:

1 Fundraising – the desire to do something worthwhile, help a good cause, benefit others, raise awareness
2 Physical challenge – enjoyment of walking, hill walking, preference to cycling, long-held ambition to trek in Himalayas
3 Personal challenge – sense of achievement, experience of a lifetime, rewarding experience, adventure, achieving a life long ambition, self-discovery
4 Travel motivations – experiencing other cultures, ambition to visit the area, scenery, natural beauty, remoteness
5 Social motivations – group bonding, meeting new friends, meeting like-minded people.

Respondents attributed both physical and personal challenges as the most important motives. Interestingly, 'personal challenge' motives are similar to those motives found on the top rung of Pearce's (1988) travel career ladder, verifying that some charity challenge participants are seeking to fulfil complex high-level needs.

Aside from the 'fundraising' motives identified above, the other categories of motives listed are similar to those experienced by other distinct groups of adventure tourist. For example, Fluker and Turner's (2000) research on white-water rafters (discussed earlier in this chapter) found that more experienced rafters enjoy the social element of the activity – i.e. social motivations.

Non-physical adventure tourism

We are conscious of the fact that this chapter has largely focused on physical forms of adventure tourism and leisure. Wherever possible, we have made an effort to apply research and theoretical concepts to non-physical as well as physical types of adventure. However, it is important to reiterate that it is the physical aspect of adventure tourism that has been most heavily researched in terms of people's motives and behaviour. This recognized, it is highly likely that the points made about physical adventure tourism apply, with modifications, to other forms of adventure tourism that are primarily emotional, spiritual, and intellectual. Given the broad nature of adventure tourism and the recognition that this phenomenon does not merely include physical adventures, there is a real need for more research on the motives and behaviour of those tourists who enjoy non-physical forms of adventure. Such tourists include gamblers, red light district visitors, and scholars seeking spiritual enlightenment.

Cultural differences and the adventure tourist

Much of this chapter has examined the adventure tourist generally, but we know that there are cultural and national differences in terms of the concept of adventure tourism. These differences are explored in a little detail in Chapter 4. At this stage, the authors would suggest that in terms of the basic motivators of adventure tourists they are similar – though not the same – regardless of the culture or nationality of the tourist.

Summary

In this chapter we have seen the complexity of the motivators of adventure tourists. However, we have also noted how little is known about some types of adventure tourists, particularly those engaged in non-physical adventure. We will now go on to look at how the behaviour of all these individual tourists combine in the adventure tourism market.

Discussion points and exercises

1 Critically evaluate the concept of the 'new tourist' as outlined in Figure 3.1.
2 Discuss the concept of 'hard' adventure and 'soft' adventure.
3 Discuss the factors that motivate people to take adventure tourism trips.
4 Critically evaluate the relationship between adventure and risk, in relation to adventure tourism.

4

The adventure tourism market

Introduction

In Chapter 3 we focused on the individual traveller. Here we look at the market as a whole – at the global demand for adventure tourism. However, as we have seen throughout this book, 'adventure tourism' is a complex, diverse, ill-defined field. It is therefore no surprise that we have difficulty measuring it in meaningful ways.

There are five major problems involved in endeavouring to present a global picture of the adventure tourism market:

1 There is a lack of widely recognized and agreed definitions of adventure tourism. The problem of defining the activity is highlighted by Smith and Jenner (1999):

One person's adventure may simply be commonplace to another traveller. How, then, is adventure travel to be defined? The most practical and useful method is simply to look at the marketing of a product – if a product is promoted as an 'adventure', then it can be defined as such, even if it turns out not to be particularly adventurous. In reality, some adventure holiday products are relatively tame, while some 'ordinary' holiday packages are quite demanding. Perhaps the key distinguishing feature of an adventure holiday is that it must have a quality of exploration or of an expedition about it – for the entire length of the trip, not just for one or two days.

Most data that are collected and labelled 'adventure tourism market' tend to concentrate on active trips to non-urban locations. The implicit defining of adventure tourism in this way *excludes* many of the forms of tourism the authors have identified earlier as adventure tourism, from religious pilgrimages through indoor activities to hedonism. At the same time, even within outdoor tourism in non-urban environments, there are debates over the relationship between adventure tourism and ecotourism and activity holidays, for example.

2 As the phenomenon of adventure tourism is both relatively new and very complex, comparatively little energy has yet been spent on collecting data on the market. As we will see later in this chapter, while there are data for outdoor activity-based adventure tourism there are very few data on many other forms of adventure tourism. This may also be because some of these other forms of 'adventure' are either socially frowned upon or may even be illegal – such as drug tourism and sex tourism. Yet these are still important forms of adventure tourism numerically. Likewise, data are not collected on some adventure activities because they are not easily identified and measured as 'markets' – such as 'hedonism' holidays.

3 Where data are collected, they are often not available to academics as they are not in the public domain – much data is collected by enterprises for marketing purposes and is kept confidential. Even where companies are willing to talk to researchers about their market there is the danger that operators will either exaggerate the size of their market to appear more successful than they really are, or underestimate their market because they fear the researcher will pass information to the tax authorities!

4 Government and industry awareness of, and interest in, adventure tourism is not equally developed around the world. Even in the some countries where there is a significant amount of adventure tourism, lack of recognition of the sector leads to few or no data being collected.

5 Even where data on adventure tourism are collected, there are still often problems of using these because of a lack of comparability of data between different countries. This difficulty can arise because:

■ Different countries define adventure tourism in different ways
■ Data are collected using different methodologies
■ Data relate to different time periods.

For all these reasons, measuring the adventure tourism market is extremely difficult if not impossible. Notwithstanding this fact, we will now endeavour to look at several aspects of the adventure tourism market (or markets). We will look at the geography of demand and the demand for different types of adventure travel, as well as considering the segmentation of the market and market trends.

The international adventure tourism market

According to Millington (2001), the international adventure tourism market amounted to between 4 and 5 million trips in 2000. This represents about 7 per cent of all international trips taken during that year.

However, it is important to recognize that this is based on a definition of adventure tourism that focuses on sport and nature tourism and (to a lesser extent) cultural tourism, in the wilderness, or at least in remote non-urban locations. It therefore excludes much of the non-physical adventure tourism considered in this book. Nevertheless, very importantly, it has been estimated that the potential international market for even this limited view of adventure tourism is around 60 million or 14 per cent of all international tourism trips (Millington, 2001).

According to the World Tourism Organization (WTO) and Millington, this potential international adventure tourism market is made up as follows:

Market	Number of tourists (millions)
Current market	4–5
50% of skiers	18
50% of scuba divers	3
50% of surfers	2.5
50% of nature-based tourists	15
25% of cultural tourists	15–18
Total	58–61

These figures show the rather crude way in which such forecasts are developed, as well as giving a clear view of how the WTO and others view adventure tourism.

The geography of demand

Before we look at the geography of adventure tourism market in detail, we need to recognize that there are generally three aspects of demand:

1 Outbound
2 Inbound
3 Domestic.

It is impossible to produce a comprehensive review of all three types of demand, world-wide, because of a lack of data. All we can do, therefore, is provide some selective data to try to give the reader a flavour of the global picture of demand for adventure tourism.

Outbound adventure tourism

On a regional basis, the geographical distribution of outbound adventure tourism world-wide is:

Europe	1 000 000
North America	2 000 000–3 000 000
Rest of the world	1 000 000
Total	4 000 000–5 000 000

(Source: Travel Industry Association of America, 2001.)

These data clearly show the domination of North Americans in the outbound adventure tourism market. However, it is important to recognize that around 80 per cent of all adventure trips taken by North Americans are domestic trips.

Much of the outbound adventure tourism world-wide takes place as part of organized packages, offered by tour operators. According to Millington (2001), the European market for organized packaged adventure holidays in 2001 was around 950 000 trips. The leading national outbound markets were:

Market	Customers (thousands)
Germany	225
UK	173
France	138
Italy	138
Scandinavia	86
Netherlands	86
Spain	52
Switzerland	26
Belgium	17
Austria	17
Total	958

(Source: Millington, 2001.)

This is clearly an underestimate, as several countries are not included in this list – notably Ireland, Portugal and Greece. It also excludes Eastern Europe, and is based on outbound and not domestic adventure tourism.

In recent years growth rates in this market have been consistently higher than those for other forms of tourism, and it was estimated that the volume of such trips in Europe would roughly double between 1998 and 2003, from 550 000 to just over 1 million (Smith and Jenner, 1999). The figures quoted above for 2001 seem to indicate this will prove to be correct.

The data show that per head consumption of such packaged adventure tourism product is higher in the UK than in Germany, which in turn has a higher participation rate than France. However, in Germany, UK, France and the Netherlands, adventure tourism in the late 1990s accounted for less than 1 per cent of all tourist spending, although this figure is rising (World Tourism Organization and Travel and Tourism Intelligence).

On the other hand, there are interesting characteristics of the market in different European countries. Clearly, in Germany tourists are willing to pay a relatively high price for such an experience, with average prices up to DM 4500 (Euros 2300) in 1998/1999. The German market is perhaps the most fragmented in Europe, with a large number of small operators, some serving as few as 300 clients per annum.

The UK market is less fragmented, with several major operators dominating the market. The age profile is clearly varied, with some packages aimed at young travellers while others focus on the older customer. Most holidays are booked generally with the operator rather than in a travel agent's.

The French market tends to be a little lower in its spending than its German counterpart, and it also has a focus on North Africa as a destination, reflecting French colonial history.

The Dutch market has the highest consumption of adventure tourism per head in the whole of Europe.

One major operator dominates the Belgian market, with an average spend of 2300 Euros per vacation. Interestingly, this company sells mainly to Flemish-speaking Belgians but not to their Walloon-speaking countrymen. The client in Belgium is relatively young, with an average age of around 30 years.

The Italian market is split between two major companies, whose clients pay average prices of 1500 Euros and 2200 Euros respectively.

Overall, the European market is forecast to grow in the future, with a trend towards shorter trips than the two- or three-week vacations that appear to be the norm today.

Most of this section has been focused on organized tourism packages, and it excludes the 'grey' sector of independent travel. It also does not include the activities of 'backpackers', who travel independently on journeys that are a personal adventure. The phenomenon of backpacking is featured in a case study later in the book.

Inbound adventure tourism in selected destinations

We have constantly seen in this book that adventure tourism is a complex and diverse field. This is also true of the pattern of adventure tourism seen across the world. In this chapter the authors will endeavour briefly to highlight some of these differences by looking at inbound international adventure tourism in several countries. Any such exercise is fraught with problems due to the lack of comparable data between countries, and the lack of data on certain types of adventure tourism such as hedonism and urban adventure. Nevertheless, some interesting differences can be observed.

Botswana

The main 'adventure' attraction in Botswana is wildlife, focused on the extensive national park and reserves. In 1997 these parks and reserves received 140 693 paying visitors (Travel and Tourism Intelligence, 2000), and these were divided between people on self-drive safaris, those using mobile tents, and those using permanent camp sites or lodges. Some 72 per cent of visitors stayed overnight, although the length of stay was generally only one night.

In 1997 the breakdown of visitors was as follows:

Area	Percentage of visitors
Europe	42
South Africa	18
USA and Canada	10
Australasia	7
Asia	3
South America	2
Others	18

The number of visitors to the reserves and parks is still relatively low but it is growing rapidly, with annual rates of growth in generally in double figures every year. Wildlife tourism is now worth in excess of US$2 million to the government in parks and reserve admission fees alone.

Brazil

Brazil has two totally different major adventure tourism markets; the Rio Carnival, and the Amazon region. The Rio Carnival attracts in excess of 40 000 international visitors to the city of Rio de Janeiro during the carnival season, and their hotel bills alone contribute an estimated US$75 million to the city economy (Travel and Tourism Intelligence, 2000). Furthermore, the carnival is now the symbol of Brazil to many foreigners. Attending the carnival is truly an adventure, with visitors being encouraged to let their hair down and indulge in hedonistic pleasures while coping with the ever-present threat of street crime!

The Amazon region is another globally recognized symbol of Brazil, but it is the least developed tourism asset in Brazil. This is partly because to Brazilians it represents a wilderness to be developed or avoided, and not an attractive tourist destination. The region of Brazil with perhaps the most potential tourism is outside the Amazon basin, the Pantinol region, a wetland environment.

Chile

Chile is a huge country with a variety of landscapes, wildlife and even climatic zones. Adventure tourism is not well established in the country, although there are a few exceptions, notably:

Table 4.1 Activities undertaken in Namibia by country of residence, 1997 (%, multiple responses; source: Ministry of Environment and Tourism, 1997; Travel and Tourism Intelligence, 2000

Activities	South Africa	Other regions	Germany	UK	France	Italy	Other European regions	Others	Total
Game viewing	35	29	87	92	71	60	81	64	73
Bird watching	30	15	77	60	81	63	67	47	62
Nature tours	25	13	70	56	72	63	59	42	56
Hunting	3	–	7	2	2	–	6	8	6
Horse riding	3	3	7	2	2	3	4	6	5
Sport fishing	15	–	4	14	–	–	7	2	6
Ballooning	1	–	2	3	2	–	4	3	4
Trekking	12	19	31	28	37	26	20	22	21
Shopping	56	67	55	65	68	81	57	59	57
Others	1	1	–	–	–	–	1	1	1
No. of respondents	1345	238	3929	320	292	139	628	660	7551

- Skiing between June and September, which attracts a limited number of North American and European serious skiers who want to be able to ski all year round, even when the snow has disappeared in their own countries. It is also popular with affluent skiers from neighbouring Brazil.
- Patagonia and Tierra del Fuego, which attract 'die-hard' wilderness and wildlife tourists from Germany, Austria, Spain, Brazil and North America. Tour operators are also now trying to exploit this destination and broaden the market.

Namibia

In recent years, Namibia has emerged as a major adventure tourism destination, with a strong emphasis on wildlife. The activities of different nationals in Namibia are shown in Table 4.1.

Wildlife watching is clearly the main activity, with all other activities trailing well behind shopping! In general, research shows that international visitors to Namibia rated the sightseeing tours quite highly. (Travel and Tourism Intelligence 2000).

New Zealand

New Zealand is seen as a pioneer of adventure tourism, first for its domestic market and then increasingly for foreign visitors. The country is marketed and perceived as an outdoor adventure destination. However, Table 4.2 illustrates the fact that its appeal to international tourists is much wider than this.

Around 154 000 international visitors took part in jet boating during their visit in 1998–1999. This is still less than those who visited a museum/gallery. However, New Zealand has been very successful in attracting people from the Northern hemisphere who want to continue to ski and snowboard during their own winter.

Many foreigners do not appreciate that gambling is also quite a highly developed form of adventure tourism in New Zealand. In 1998–1999, 136 000 international tourists visited a casino – which is nearly as many as those taking part in jet boating (Travel and Tourism Intelligence, 2000).

South Africa

South Africa is the major player in Southern African tourism, and again a large part of its tourism is based on wildlife watching. However, unlike some other countries in the region it has also succeeded in developing other forms of tourism such as beach tourism, wine tourism and cultural tourism. For those

Table 4.2   Main activities participated in by international visitors in New Zealand (year ending 31 March 1999; source: IVS, Travel and Tourism Intelligence, 2000)

Activity	No. of visitors (thousands)
Eating out/restaurants	738
Shopping	639
General sightseeing	605
Walking in city	466
Friends/family/people	399
Sightseeing tour	340
Geothermal	326
Museum/gallery	326
Beaches	280
Botanical/gardens	230
Business/conference	205
Maori performance	203
Scenic cruise	184
Scenic drive	171
Bar/nightclub	168
Gondola	165
Jet boating	154
Casino	136
Sky tower	127
Glacier walk/helicopter	125
Farm show	124
Other natural attractions	123

seeking 'fantasy' it also offers the resort complex of Sun City. Under apartheid this was a place where white South Africans met for 'adventures' that were not legal in their own country! 'Adventure' also exists in some cities, such as Johannesburg, where crime levels are high!

Sri Lanka

Sri Lanka has been marketed abroad largely as an inexpensive beach destination. For tourists on such vacations the only element of 'adventure' is the threat of tension due to the civil war that has raged on the island for years! In spite of these problems, tourist expenditure grew by 350 per cent between 1990 and 1998. (Travel and Tourism, 2000).

As yet adventure tourism is relatively under-developed in Sri Lanka, but tour operators are now offering packages including trekking, paragliding and wildlife-watching. However, Sri Lanka is also developing traditional health treatments based on Hindu philosophies and practice. This may prove very attractive to Western tourists looking for both better health and spiritual enlightenment. The government hopes that once the war is over it will be able to develop adventure tourism further, and include diving on the coral reefs.

Zambia

Scenery and wildlife are at the heart of Zambia's appeal to foreign adventure tourists. Tour operators are reaping annual growth rates for adventure tourism spending of over 18 per cent per annum (Travel and Tourism Intelligence, 2000). The market in Zambia is mainly 20–44-year-olds, and focuses on activities such as bungee jumping and microlight flying.

However, the government is also keen to develop other forms of tourism, including watersports on Lake Tanganyika, visits to traditional villages, and bird watching.

Other countries

The diversity of adventure tourism is shown by the fact that if we had looked at another selection of countries the picture would have been different. For example, we could have considered:

- Indonesia, where diving, visiting traditional villages and wildlife-watching are major attractions
- Russia, where hunting and wilderness trips in Siberia are high on the list of attractions
- Morocco, with its 'unofficial' drug tourism and its desert activities
- Iceland, with its whale-watching, four-wheel drives across the interior 'desert', glacier walking, and white-water rafting
- Nepal, with its mountain trekking and 'drug tourism'
- India and Thailand, playgrounds for the backpacker and places where tourists go for spiritual enlightenment 'adventures'
- Australia, where the appeal is divided between activities such as diving on the Great Barrier Reef and exploring the outback.

Domestic adventure tourism

We should not forget that in many of the countries domestic tourists are the core of the adventure tourism market. They often discover the adventure tourism potential of the country first, and are followed later by foreigners. This is certainly the case with New Zealand, for example.

Even in a relatively poor country like Botswana, its citizens and residents represented 15 per cent of all visitors to parks and reserves in 1997 (Travel and Tourism Intelligence, 2000). Chileans are the majority market at many of the country's nature attractions.

As might be expected, the USA has a massive domestic adventure tourism market. In 1999, half of US adults claimed to have taken an adventure trip in the last 5 years. Average expenditure on these vacations was high, at US\$ 1300 per head (Travel and Tourism Intelligence, 2000).

In the US market, a distinction is made between hard and soft adventure, based on definitions used by the US Travel Industry Association.

Table 4.3 shows us the most popular adventure activities within the domestic US market.

Table 4.3   Cross-participation in adventure activities in the USA by US travellers (source: Travel Industry Association of America, 1997)

Other activities also undertaken during previous five years	Four most popular activities			
	Camping	*Hiking*	*Cycling*	*Bird/animal watching*
Soft activities				
Camping	100	76	82	85
Hiking	53	100	72	70
Cycling	35	44	100	38
Bird/animal watching	28	38	34	100
Horse riding	27	35	36	33
Canoeing	29	32	39	29
Water skiing	26	26	35	21
Snow skiing	23	29	38	24
Wilderness tour in off-road vehicles	19	25	27	30
Sailing	15	20	24	19
Photo safari	6	10	7	16
Dude ranch	8	10	9	11
Hard activities				
Rafting/kayaking	16	18	19	17
Snorkelling/scuba diving	13	14	20	16
Mountain biking	12	13	25	11
Backpacking across rugged terrain	10	14	17	14
Climbing	8	13	13	13
Caving	8	8	10	8

The segmentation of the adventure tourism market

There are many potential ways in which we can segment the adventure tourism market. We have already, in this chapter, segmented the market geographically by looking at where the tourists live. The market is clearly dominated by North Americans and Europeans at present, although it is growing in other regions of the world. Of course it is also possible to segment the market demographically, in terms of age, sex, stage in the family life cycle, income, and ethnic origins.

Traditionally, adventure tourism has been perceived to be a younger person's activity. However, in recent years we have seen a growth of adventure travel by 'empty nesters' – older people keen to enjoy new experiences once their children have left home. What appear to vary are the motivators of adventure tourists at different ages. According to the work of the US travel industry, 'travellers in their 20s tend to take an adventure trip for the thrill, those in their 30s pursue an interest in the environment, and those in their 40s or 50s to get away from job stress' (Millington, 2001).

Women in the USA are as likely as men to take adventure trips, although there is still a bias towards men in the market for some types of adventure tourism.

In the past, adventure tourism has usually been seen as an activity for adults, done in couples or in groups. However, we are seeing an increase in family adventure travel. A survey in 1997 in the USA showed that many parents now take their children with them on adventure trips. The percentage who were accompanied by their children was as follows (Travel Industry Association of America, 1997):

Campers	45
Water skiers	41
Cyclists	40
Snow skiers	40
Hikers	38
Horse riders	38
Canoeists	34
Bird/animal watchers	33

Adventure travel is often an activity for those in the higher income groups. A major US on-line adventure travel company estimated that the average income of its customers in 2000 was $75 000 (Millington, 2001). However, there has been a growth in participation amongst those households on more modest incomes.

Ethnic minorities are still under-represented in the adventure tourism market, just as they are in the tourism market in general.

Psychographic segmentation is very important in adventure tourism, as can be seen from Chapter 3 where we talked about the motivators and determinants of individual adventure tourists. However, it has not yet developed greatly in terms of empirical research in the adventure tourism market.

There are numerous other ways of segmenting the adventure tourism market, including:

- According to the activity
- Whether it is hard and soft adventure
- By the level of interest in adventure tourism
- Into independent travellers and those who take organized packages.

Activity

The market can be segmented according to the activity. There are two tiers to such segmentation:

1 Generic types of activity, e.g. air sports or watersports
2 Sub-types of these generic activities, such as paragliding, microlight flying and so on in relation to air sports.

Some of these sub-types of activities are sizeable in their own right – for example, it is estimated that there are 6 million scuba divers world-wide, and this is forecast to rise to 10 million by 2005. However, we have to recognize that many adventure tourists are interested in more than one activity.

Hard or soft adventure

Adventure tourists can be divided into those participating in hard or soft adventure, which Millington (2001) has defined as follows:

> Hard adventure travel requires an element of experience in the activity being undertaken, and because it encompasses an element of risk, participants must be physically and mentally fit. It includes an intimate experience with the environment and culture of the destination.

Participants should be prepared for all weather conditions, sleeping arrangements and dietary restrictions. Examples include: climbing expeditions, arduous treks, hang gliding, rock climbing, white-water kayaking and wilderness survival.

Soft adventure requires less physical risk, little or no experience, and offers more convenience in terms of sleeping arrangements and cuisine. Many activities are similar to those in the hard adventure category, yet they occur at a less physically demanding level. Soft adventure offers a wider range of activities and adventure experiences for the traveller. Examples include horseback riding, rafting, sea kayaking, snorkelling, bicycle touring, camping, canoeing, cross-country skiing, dog sledding, surfing, walking tours, wildlife watching and windsurfing.

However, many tourists will of course take part in both types of activity, possibly even during the same vacation.

Level of interest

The market can also be segmented into three main segments on the basis of the tourists' level of interest in adventure tourism:

1 Those who only take adventure vacations
2 Those who take adventure vacations as well as other types of vacations
3 Those who take non-adventure vacations, but take part in adventure activities once or twice during their vacation.

There are also, of course, many people who have absolutely no desire to take part in adventure travel at all.

Independent travellers or those on organized trips

A division may be made between independent travellers and those who take organized packages. However, some people may indulge in both forms of travel at different times.

Furthermore, those who take organized packages are not a single homogeneous group. Millington (2001) reports that for a leading UK specialist tour operator, their market consists of three main segments:

1 Older, often retired people who finally have the time and money to fulfil their dreams

2 Ex-backpackers who used to travel to exotic locations independently, and still want an element of adventure in the limited holiday time they have available

3 A new group of consumers accustomed to beach package holidays, who see adventure tours as something more exciting.

The adventure day trip market

This chapter has so far been concerned with the staying vacation market. However, adventure is also playing a leading role in the day trip market. People now have the opportunity to escape for a day from their normal routine and environment, for example to:

- Have a go at driving a Formula One racing car
- Make a parachute jump
- Learn to scuba dive
- Go whale-watching.

Some companies specialize in arranging such 'day trips' – such as 'Red Letter Days' in the UK, about which there is a case study later in the book.

The hidden adventure tourism market

As well as the problems arising from how we define adventure tourism, the data on adventure tourism are incomplete because some demand is 'hidden' from view because it is either illegal or seen as socially unacceptable. For example, in many countries hunting tourism is either not recorded or is under-counted because of its controversial nature. The same is true of 'walk on the wild side urban tourism' and sex tourism. In many countries these markets are of great significance, such as Russia in relation to the former and Manila and Bangkok in terms of the latter.

Non-physical adventure tourism markets

Most of this chapter has focused on physical adventure in wild, remote regions. However, it is now time to say a few words about the market for non-physical adventure.

There are many forms of non-physical adventure tourism, and we will consider four of them here.

Gambling

For a number of tourist destinations gambling is their main attraction, including most notably Las Vegas. Many casinos also serve as day trip leisure attractions for people from their host region. The scale of the gambling market can be gauged from the following data, which are taken from *Travel and Tourism Analyst* (1999):

- Commercial casinos in the State of Nevada, USA, employed 180000 people in 1997
- State gaming taxes in Clark County, Las Vegas, were worth $457 million in 1998
- Tunica County in Tennessee opened a casino to attract visitors in 1992, and now attracts around 15 million visitors per year
- Foxwoods Casino, in New England, attracts up to 40000 people a day on busy weekends.

The same report on the US gaming business also noted that in 1997, 89 per cent of visitors to Las Vegas had gambled. Each day these visitors passed around 4 hours gambling, and they spent a total of about $515 on gambling during their stay in the resort.

It is interesting to look at who the gamblers are, although the profile of casino users varies from place to place. A study of Northern Cyprus by Scott and Asikoglu (2001) looked at Turkish visitors and divided them into three groups:

1 General holidaymakers who were not attracted to Northern Cyprus for the gambling (A)
2 Those whose main motive for visiting was gambling (B)
3 Those who wished to combine a general holiday with gambling (C).

Table 4.4 shows how the behaviour of these groups differed from each other.

Interestingly, the same research showed that 32 per cent of those in Group A, with no apparent interesting in gaming, gambled during their visit to Northern Cyprus.

Table 4.5 also shows the characteristics of casino gamblers in Black Hawk, Colorado – a former mining town.

Table 4.6 illustrates the motives for gambling at Black Hawk.

Table 4.4 Age, status and income profile of groups in North Cyprus (A = main purpose holiday, B = main purpose gambling, and C = gambling + holiday; source: Scott and Asikoglu, 2001)

	A (%; n = 206)	B (%; n = 230)	C (%; n = 136)
Age (years)			
18–25	7	2	4
26–35	24	17	20
36–45	38	41	41
46–60	23	38	32
60+	8	2	3
Total	100	100	100
Status			
Married	80	86	81
Single	19	12	13
Divorced	1	2	6
Total	100	100	100
Children?			
Yes	74	74	77
No	26	26	23
Total	100	100	100
Income (in million Turkish Lira per month)			
100–199	2	1	0
200–299	11	1	1
300–399	16	12	10
400–499	26	44	43
500+	45	42	46
Total	100	100	100

While many of the respondents of this survey were not tourists in the strictest sense of the word, it is likely that their motivators are similar to those of tourists.

A recent Travel and Tourism Intelligence report on the Japanese outbound market showed how the propensity of Japanese tourists to indulge in gambling differed depending on their destination. For example, 20 per cent of Japanese visitors to the USA indulged in gambling, 11 per cent of visitors to Oceania,

Table 4.5   Characteristics of casino gamblers in Black Hawk, Colorado (source: Park *et al.*, 2002)

Variables	Frequency	Per cent
Age (years)		
< 20	3	0.6
21–30	25	4.9
31–40	42	8.3
41–50	96	18.9
51–60	114	22.4
61+	228	44.9
Sex		
Male	205	39.6
Female	313	60.4
Education		
Grade school	20	3.8
High school	224	43.0
College	217	41.7
Graduate school	60	11.5
Marital status		
Single	72	13.9
Married	333	64.3
Divorced/separated	66	12.7
Widowed	47	9.1
Residence		
Colorado	442	84.5
Other states	79	15.1
Foreign country	2	0.4
Income ($)		
< 19 999	91	19.8
20 000–39 99	152	33.1
40 000–59 000	113	24.6
60 000–79 000	65	14.2
80 000–99 000	18	3.9
100 000+	20	4.4

but only 7 per cent of visitors to East Asia and 7 per cent of visitors to Europe. Japanese visitors to the USA and Oceania were more likely to gamble than to indulge in any other 'adventure'.

According to Cai *et al.* (2000) Chinese travellers to the USA also show a high propensity to gamble during their stay, with nearly 14 per cent of Chinese tourists visiting a casino in the USA.

Table 4.6   Motives for casino gambling, Black Hawk, Colorado (after Park *et al.*, 2002)

Involvement items

Self-expression

Gambling says a lot about who I am

Gambling helps me maintain the type of life I strive for

I find that much of my life is organized around gambling

Gambling is important to me

When I gamble, others see me the way I want them to see me

You can tell a lot about a person when you see them gambling

Enjoyment

Gambling offers me relaxation and fun when pressures build up

Gambling is one of the most enjoyable things I do

When I am gambling I can really be myself

I have little or no interest in gambling

I get bored when other people talk to me about gambling

Centrality

Most of my friends are in some way connected with gambling

When I am with friends, we often talk about gambling

Eigenvalues

Percentage variance (%)

Cumulative percentage variance (%)

Most data on gambling tourism focuses rigidly on casino gambling, but other forms of gambling can be important in certain locations – such as on-course betting on horse races.

Finally, we have to recognize that gambling tourism is often controversial. In Australasia, for example, there has been a vigorous debate over the building of new casinos designed to put a place on the tourist map as a destination. Often the casino is not frequented by wealthy tourists but by less affluent local people spending money they cannot afford, which clearly causes social problems.

Religious tourism

Travelling for religious reasons has been with us for centuries, and still represents a personal spiritual adventure for those taking part in it.

Traditional pilgrimage tourism is still a massive phenomenon in tourism terms. A report in *Travel and Tourism Analyst* No. 5 in 1999 offered data that are now rather dated but still make the point about the significant scale of

Table 4.7 Major places of pilgrimage, by religion and country (source: Meyer et al., 1991)

Religion	Country of pilgrimage destination	Place or shrine
Baha'i	Israel	Bahji (Akko)
		Haifa (Shrine of the Bab)
Buddhism	Myanmar	Shwe Dagon
	China	O'mei Shan
	India	Bodh Gaya, Isipatana Kusinagara, Rajagrham, Sravasti, Sanchi
	Japan	Kamakura, Nara, Hongan-Ji
	Thailand	Wat Phra Doi Suthep, Temple of the Emerald Buddha
Christianity	Austria	Mariazell
	Belgium	Banneaux
	Canada	St Anne de Beaupre
	Egypt	Mount Sanai, Cairo
	France	Ars, Lisieux, Lourdes, Tours
	Germany	Altötting
	India	Goa
	Ireland	Downpatrick, Knock
	Israel	Bethlehem, Jerusalem, Galilee
	Poland	Gzestochowa
	Portugal	Fátima, Lisbon
	Spain	Santiago de Compostela
	Turkey	Ephesus
Hinduism	India	Ayodhya, Badrinatha, Benares, Dvaraka, Haridwar, Kusi, Mathura, Puri, Ramaswaram, Ujjain
		Rivers: Ganges, Godavari, Indus, Cauvery, Narmada, Servaswait
Islam	Iran	Meshed
	Iraq	Karbala, Baghdad
	Israel	Jerusalem
	Saudi Arabia	Mecca, Medina
Jainism	India	Belgola, Dilwara, Kesariaji, Rajgir, Ranakpur, Samata Sikhara, Satrunjaya, Sravana
Judaism	Israel	Jerusalem, Meron, Mod'in, Hebron, Mount Carmel, Safed, Tiberias
Shinto	Japan	Shikoku, Ise
Sikh	India	Amritsar, Anandpur, Panta
	Pakistan	Nankana

religious tourism to many destinations. The main pilgrimage sites for different religions are listed in Table 4.7.

Table 4.8 shows the number of tourists from different European countries who visited a religious site in 1996.

Table 4.8 Estimated number of tourists to religious sites by selected European country of origin, 1996 (source: ETM, Borsa Internazionale de Turismo, World Tourism Organization, and national tourism authorities or respective countries)

Country	Religious tourists
Italy	19 050
Germany	19 050
Spain	10 160
France	4 440
Ireland	3 810
Austria	3 170
Belgium	2 540
Netherlands	1 270
Total of eight countries	63 490

For some destinations, pilgrimage tourism is the main motivator of their visitors. For example, *Travel and Tourism Analyst* No. 5 (1999) reported that 1 080 000 foreign pilgrims visited Saudi Arabia in 1995–1996. In 1998, the same report estimated that around 135 000 American pilgrims alone visited Israel.

However, as well as the traditional pilgrimage tourism we are also seeing the rise of 'religious spiritual adventure tourism' where people go in search of religious inspiration from other religions. This phenomenon largely concerns 'westerners' seeking spiritual enlightenment from 'the East'.

In 1999, *Travel and Tourism Analyst* No. 5 noted that:

There has been a small but growing enchantment in the western world with the religions of the Orient and Far East, perhaps as a counter to an ever more materialist and spiritual-less culture. Western interest in Buddhism and its related activities of yoga and meditation is certainly on the rise and it is conceivable that this could lead to more exploration of Asian countries where Buddhism is the dominant religion.

An example of this is the International Buddhist Meditation Centre in Bangkok, which draws people from all over the world for meditative retreats. Another, more remote destination is a 120-acre forest temple in the Surat Thani province of Thailand, 580 kilometres south of the Thai capital. Called Suan Mokkh, meaning 'The Garden of Liberation', the temple is in fact a teaching monastery of Buddhists, offering ten-day meditation courses, set amid a coconut grove.

India is another Asian country which is seeking to attract more foreign tourists through the charms of its spiritual heritage. Indian tourism authorities have announced a target of 5 million international arrivals by 2004.

This trend looks set to continue in the future.

Gay tourism

Gay tourism is a form of adventure tourism in itself because the participants are people whose sexual orientation can attract discrimination and even persecution in places. This fact was well detailed in a report in *Travel and Tourism Analyst* No. 2 (2001) as follows:

> There are distinct regions of the world where homosexuality remains a social taboo and government-sanctioned homophobia prevails. These can be broadly defined as the Caribbean, some Latin countries, most of Africa and parts of the Middle East. Recent examples include the Jamaican government's refusal to grant basic human rights protection for gay and lesbian citizens and visitors. Meanwhile, the UK's five Overseas Territories of Anguilla, the British Virgin Islands, the Cayman Islands, Montserrat and the Turks and Caicos islands have so far refused the request from London to repeal their anti-gay legislation in line with European human rights legislation.
>
> Experience shows however, that a prevailing homophobic culture does not necessarily put a country out of bounds to gay travellers. What tends to happen is that gay holidaymakers stay in all-inclusive, self-contained resorts where interaction with local people is voluntary rather than unavoidable.
>
> Discrimination exists at the micro level, of course – that is, prejudice encountered by lesbians and gay men from hotel staff, travel agents and other travel industry staff.

Yet the gay holiday market is substantial and growing. In 2000 it was estimated that 2.8 million gay people would take holidays in 2002, of whom only 118 000 would take vacations designed specifically for gay people (Mintel, 2000a).

At the same time, a growing number of gay people are taking activity/soft adventure holidays. A selection of those offered by US tour operators is shown in Table 4.9.

City breaks seem to be very popular with gay travellers. Mintel estimated that gay travellers were more than twice as likely to take city breaks as non-gay travellers. Gay pride events have also become a major focus of travel by gay people, and some of the leading such events worldwide are listed in Table 4.10.

Table 4.9   A calendar of selected activity/soft adventure holidays for gay travellers, 2001 (source: gaytravelnews.com)

Date	Holiday/event	Tour operator	Price per person (US$)
1–8 April	Rafting on the Rio Grande	Spirit Journeys	1250
21–27 April	Moab Red Rocks Explorer	OutWest Global Adventures	1150
3–18 May	Amazon and Machu Picchu	Mariah Wilderness Adventures	na
3–15 May	Sailing on Turkish coast	Coda International	3795
15–26 June	Kenya Safari	na	3799
1–8 July	White-water rafting through Grand Canyon	OutWest Global Adventures	1450
1–8 August	White-water rafting through Grand Canyon	Toto Tours	2000
24–31 August	Sailing Ibiza and Minorca	Toto Tours	na
1–8 September	Diving in Fiji	Undersea Expeditions	2395
31 October–12 November	Galapagos Islands and Ecuador	Mariah Wilderness Adventures	4600
17–25 November	Thanksgiving in Costa Rica	Toto Tours	1595

Table 4.10   Leading Pride/Mardi Gras events, 2001 (source: Travel and Tourism Intelligence, 2001, no. 2)

Event name	Date	Expected attendance (thousands)	Major travel sponsors
Sydney Mardi Gras	9 February–3 March	600	Qanta
San Francisco Pride Parade and Celebration	23–24 June	300–400	United Airlines Hyatt Hotels National Car Rental
New York City Gay Pride	31 July–28 August	450	No travel sponsors
Brazil Pride, Sao Paulo	14–16 June	20	No travel sponsors
Christopher Street Day, Berlin	23 June	400–500	Swissair Sabena
Lesbian and Gay Pride, Paris	24 June	300	No travel sponsors announced
London Mardi Gras	30 June	90	Virgin Atlantic Eurostar
Europride, Vienna	28–30 June	250	Cosmos Travel

An interesting final point is that only a small proportion of the vacations offered specifically for gay people are for women; this may well change in the future.

Female romance and sex tourists

That men travel in search of sex is a well-known and heavily studied phenomenon. However, relatively little attention has been paid to women who take vacations with similar motives. Yet this is a phenomenon seen in a number of developing countries and in some Mediterranean destinations.

In 1994, Eugenia Wickens published a paper on hedonistic tourism in Greece. One of the segments she identified, in her study in the Halkidiki area, were women she termed the 'Shirley Valentines' – after the title of a contemporary film about such women. Wickens (1994) described the 'Shirley Valentines' as follows:

The 'Shirley Valentines' are women on a mono-gender holiday who hope for romance and sexual adventure with a 'Greek God'. This particular 'expectation of pleasure' is based on the Greek male stereotype, which has been perpetuated by newspapers and the film *Shirley Valentine*. These 'seekers of sexual adventure' often date with Greek waiters or other local men. Escape 'from domesticity', 'from family life', plus a 'break in the sun' were identified by this type of tourist as contributory factors in their selection of this holiday resort. This type of tourist has also been observed in other Greek holiday regions, including Rhodes and Crete (see Kousis, 1989).

For these women, their vacation is a personal, escapist adventure. Usually no money changes hands in these situations, although gifts may be given to the male lover. Wickens (1994) reported the views of one of her research respondents, about why she enjoyed this type of vacation:

> You are here to please yourself ... As far as I can, I leave my everyday life behind. When I'm in England, I'm fitting into an appointed role of somebody's wife, somebody's secretary. Here, you can relax, and rub off some of the sharp corners. You are not restricted. Greeks are very tolerant of us ... If you give yourself a chance, you can find out things about yourself that you did not know about before ... I like sex but not with my husband ... I come to Greece for a bit of fun.

In 2001, Herold, Garcia and Demoya explored the long-recognized phenomenon of women who travel to the Caribbean – in this case the Dominican Republic – and develop sexual relationships with local beach boys. Often the opportunity for such relationships is a motivator for these women to take such vacations. Herold *et al.* (2001) suggest that this phenomenon could be seen as either romantic adventure tourism or sex tourism. The beach boys, who are usually between 16 and 20 years old, tend to take the initiative with the women, who are usually significantly older – and are the willing recipients of the attention. As well as receiving money for their services, the boys often hope that their foreign female lovers will help them emigrate to a better life abroad. This clearly gives the women great power within the relationship, and leads to suggestions that they exploit their power to their own advantage. In general, this looks like a form of sex tourism rather than a romantic adventure.

The future of the market

In the final chapter of this book, we look forward and predict how adventure tourism may develop in the future. However, at this stage it is important that we say something about the probable future direction of the overall adventure tourism market.

It seems likely that much of the current latent demand will turn into real international adventure tourism trips in the future, including:

- Those with an interest in particular activities who have not yet taken an adventure tourism vacation
- Growing outbound tourism from countries that have not previously been thought of as generators of international tourist trips, such as Russia, India, and China

We will also see other changes in the adventure tourism market in response to social, economic and technological change, notably:

- A growth in family adventure tourism
- More short-break adventure packages
- An increase in independent adventure travel.

On the other hand we must recognize that the future of the adventure tourism market is uncertain, and there are factors – from climate change to political instability – that could threaten its continued growth.

Nevertheless, it seems likely that adventure tourism of all types will grow steadily in the foreseeable future.

Summary

In this chapter we have seen how the global adventure tourism market is a complex phenomenon, and that data are often difficult to find and interpret. We have noted a number of ways in which the market can be segmented. It has also been shown that, by and large, the non-physical adventure sector suffers greatly from a lack of research and data, which is a real problem for tourism planners. Finally, we have suggested that the adventure tourism market will grow significantly and steadily in the future.

Discussion points and exercises

1 Discuss the reasons why the global adventure tourism market appears to be dominated by North America.

2 Critically evaluate the application of 'traditional' segmentation techniques to the adventure tourism market.

3 Compare and contrast the motivators for gambling tourism and religious tourism.

4 Select a country. For your chosen country you should try to produce a report covering domestic, inbound and outbound adventure tourism in the country. You should note the problems you experience in carrying out this project, together with any elements of the task you were unable to complete.

Part
C

The supply side

5

Destinations and venues

Introduction

In this chapter, we will look at the places where adventure tourism actually takes place – namely the destinations and venues. Let us begin by discussing the role of destinations.

Adventure tourism destinations

The role of destinations in adventure tourism

In many well established forms of tourism, such as Mediterranean 'sun, sand, and sea' vacations, one could often be forgiven for thinking that the actual destination is of secondary importance to many tourists. Providing the sun shines and the sea is blue, most such tourists do not really mind if they are in Albufeira or Rhodes, Palma Nova or Agadir, providing the price is right!

However, in other types of tourism the destination is of prime importance for the tourist. Adventure tourism is an excellent example of this latter form of tourism.

In almost all varieties of adventure tourism the destination is the core of the experience, giving a unique flavour to the experience. These destinations provide the key attraction that motivates the tourist to take a trip in the first place. For example:

- Pilgrimages focus on destinations with major religious buildings and shrines, such as Mecca, Jerusalem, and Rome
- Mountaineering trips tend to concentrate on the desire to conquer particular peaks or explore certain mountain ranges, hence the popularity of Chamonix (for the Mont Blanc massif) for example.

However, destinations do not usually provide just the attractions desired by the adventure tourist. Unless the trip is truly a wilderness experience, destinations also provide the services the tourist requires – such as accommodation, equipment, food and transport – since destinations often serve as gateways for regions that may have only limited or non-existent tourist services.

A gateway destination like this may serve a region of tens of thousands of square kilometres, as in Alaska and Siberia. Often such settlements have an airport or rail station, which is the only way in which tourists can arrive in the region as a whole.

The geographical hierarchy of adventure tourism destinations

As with all types of tourism, there is a geographical hierarchy of adventure tourism destinations (see Figure 5.1).

Different regions of the world are associated with particular types of adventure tourism. In 2001 Millington put some of these associations into words (see Table 5.1).

An individual country can include a wide variety of different types of adventure tourism destinations. For example:

- Thailand offers sex tourism in Bangkok, jungle adventure tourism destinations, and religious retreat destinations
- The USA offers destinations that specialize in gambling tourism, rock-climbing, white-water rafting, and wilderness adventures

Table 5.1   Regions of the world associated with particular types of adventure tourism (source: Millington, 2001)

Central and South America and the Caribbean	Central and South America have become almost synonymous with adventure travel and ecotourism. Costa Rica has the Cloud Forests, then there are the deep rainforests of the Amazon basin, the Andes Mountains in Peru, and the Atlantic coast in Brazil. Ecuador offers the biodiversity of the Galapagos Islands, Argentina houses the 6960-m (22 834-ft) Mount Aconacagua, and Chile the Class V Rio Futaleufu for hard-core white-water rafters. For ancient civilizations there are the Mayan ruins in the jungles of Guatemala, and Machu Picchu in Peru. Most adventure activities in the Caribbean revolve around the water, with scuba diving, sailing and surfing being the most popular activities.
Europe	Despite being heavily populated and having a well-developed infrastructure, Europe still provides some of the best adventure travel opportunities available world-wide. Ireland, Scotland, England, Belgium and France offer some of the world's best hiking and biking, with tours that traverse lush rolling countryside. Germany, Switzerland, eastern France and northern Italy are popular for skiing, hiking and climbing in the Alps. Scandinavia is home to mountains and fjords for a range of land- and water-based activities, whilst Russia provides adventure travellers with the Caucasus Mountains and the Kola Peninsula.
Middle East	Being at the centre of the Old World, in three continents, the Middle East offers a rich cultural as well as natural destination. Trekking by foot or by camel is popular in the deserts of Iran and Turkmenistan, whilst hiking and skiing are more popular in Kazakhstan, Uzbekistan and Tajikistan. At the southernmost point in Jordan, as well as in Yemen and Oman, there is some of the world's best diving in the Red Sea and Indian Ocean. Desert trekking opportunities are also abundant in the region, especially in Oman, the United Arab Emirates and Saudi Arabia.

Table 5.1 Continued

Asia	Asia offers some of the most unexplored masses of land in the world. Mongolia has excellent trekking opportunities through the Gobi Desert, and China offers rivers and mountains with excellent climbing opportunities on Mount Songnisan and Mount Soraksan. The smaller islands of Japan's mainland are well known for scuba diving and surfing. Wildlife safaris in India provide scope for considerable game viewing of, among others, tigers, elephants, monkeys and pythons. Nepal not only has the world's highest peak, Mount Everest, but also some of the best climbing and trekking in the world on its lower slopes. Thailand, Malaysia and Indonesia all offer a combined product of wildlife watching and excellent seas for diving and other water-based activities.
North America	North America covers a massive area, and as a result offers just about every option for the adventure tourist. The USA has Alaska's Mount McKinley, the tropical waters of the Florida Keys National Marine Sanctuary, opportunities for kayaking on Main's Island Trail, and biking in Arizona's Sonoran Desert. Canada's variety ranges from the temperate rainforests of Vancouver Island to the snowy dogsled trials of the Yukon to the padding options offered by the diversity of Algonquin Provincial Park.
Antarctic	The Antarctic is the last vast wilderness and the most isolated continent on the planet, and in the last decade it has been tourism rather than oil drilling that has been the continent's growth industry. There are several options for travelling to the Antarctic – all by ship – with most being from South America, although there are options from Australia. Great care is being taken not to spoil the environment, and only a limited number of people are allowed on to the shore at a time. For those wanting to see the South Pole in greater luxury, a Melbourne-based company is operating twelve-hour flights from Australia over the South Pole on a Qantas-chartered Boeing 747.

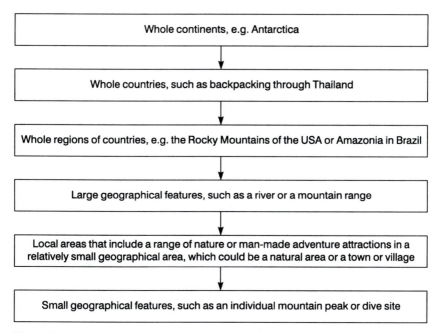

Figure 5.1   The geographical hierarchy of adventure tourism destinations.

Table 5.2   A selection of Venezuela's National Parks (source: www.think-venezuela.net, Travel and Tourism Intelligence, Country Reports, November 4, 2001)

Name of park	Size (hectares)	Attractions
Archipelogo Las Roques	221 120	Coral reefs, keys, beaches, swamps
Canaima	3 000 000	Savannas, forests, tepuis, waterfalls
Cerro Saroche	32 294	Arid lands
Ciénagas del Catatumbo	226 130	Swamps, flooded forests
Curva de Quebrada del Toro	4885	Caverns with underground rivers
Chorro El Indio	16 000	Humid rainforests
Guaramacal	21 491	Cloud forests, moors
Henri Pittier	107 800	Cloud forests, dry forests, beaches
Laguna de Tacarigua	39 100	Swamps, lagoon, beaches
Mochima	94 935	Beaches, reefs, islands
Parima-Tapirapec	3 900 000	Source of Orinoco, Amazon rainforest
Serrania La Neblina	1 360 000	Amazon forest
Sierra Nevada	276 446	Glaciers, moors, forests, lagoons
Turuépano	70 000	Swamps, channels, aquatic fauna

- Australia has places for diving, outback adventures and skiing
- Libya offers desert adventure destinations, mountain trekking adventures and remote archaeological site destinations.

Even in terms of a single type of adventure tourism, such as nature watching in the wild, a country can offer a number of different types of destination. For instance, Venezuela has a number of national parks that offer different types of wildlife adventure (see Table 5.2).

Typologies of adventure tourism destinations

It is possible to clarify adventure tourism destinations in a number of ways:

1 Traditional, long-established destinations vs modern destinations – the latter are often the result of the development of a new adventure activity or government tourism development policy
2 The geographical location of the destination (see Figure 5.2)
3 Destinations associated with particular types of activity (see Figure 5.3)
4 The seasonality of adventure tourism destinations (see in Figure 5.4)
5 Destinations that are wholly or solely based on adventure tourism vs those destinations where other types of tourism are also important
6 Adventure tourism destinations with a predominantly domestic market vs those destinations with a largely international market
7 Destinations where visiting them is an adventure in itself, due to climate, political tension or the lack of infrastructure, vs destinations that are comfortable to visit but offer facilities for adventure activities

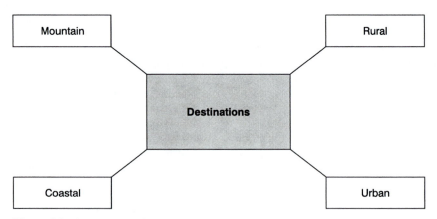

Figure 5.2 The geographical location of destinations.

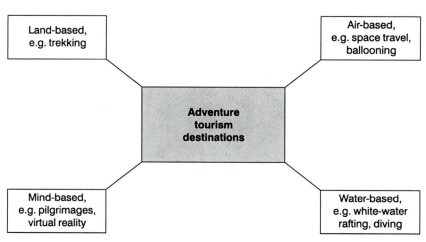

Figure 5.3   Types of activities.

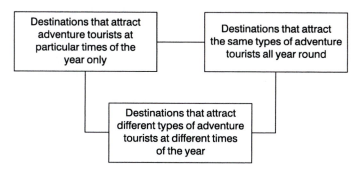

Figure 5.4   Seasonality of adventure tourism destinations.

8 Destinations that actively encourage adventure tourism vs those destinations that do not encourage adventure tourism but attract adventure tourists anyway

9 Destinations where the whole area offers adventure tourism opportunities vs those destinations where the adventure activities are restricted to individual, single unit venues.

Adventure tourism venues

Venues are the individual sites or units, within destinations, that offer facilities and/or services for adventure tourism. Adventure tourism venues can be classified in several ways (see Figure 5.5).

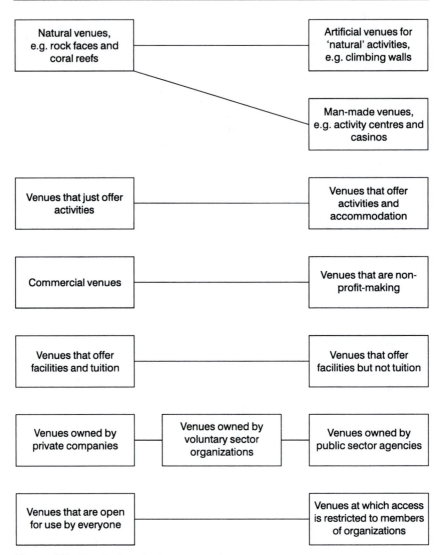

Figure 5.5 Typologies of adventure tourism venues.

The diversity of venues

The diversity of adventure tourism is reflected in the variety of venues around the world that provide facilities and services for adventure tourists. As well as natural sites there are a plethora of different types of man-made venues for different forms of adventure tourism, as can be seen from the following examples based on the promotional material issued by the venues in question.

Adventure sports, Carnkie, Redruth, Cornwall, UK

Adventure Sports is a UK-based activity centre

Adventure holidays, active holidays, outdoor holidays,
adventure sports holidays

It provides the following outdoor pursuits

Surfing, Paragliding, Windsurfing, Sailing
Power boating, Waterskiing, Jetskiing, Wakeboarding
Climbing, Abseiling, Mountain Biking
Coastal Safaris, Snorkelling and Orienteering

In the following ways

5- and 7-day multi-activity residential holidays
Weekend and short activity breaks
Stag and Hen Adventure weekends
Corporate Weekends
Specialist Paragliding Training
Specialist Powerboat & Jetski Training

for the following

Singles, couples, groups
Families with older children
Stags, Hens and Corporate groups
No previous experience

Adventure Sports provides the ultimate in multi-activity holidays for adults, set in beautiful Cornwall amongst Europe's most spectacular beaches. Our holidays are fun, challenging and safe with an opportunity to meet like-minded adventurous people. No previous experience is necessary and singles or groups are welcome. We offer an unrivalled range of quality activities which include water-skiing, surfing, paragliding, windsurfing, sailing, climbing, abseiling, jetskiing, power boating, wakeboarding, coastal safaris, snorkelling, mountain biking, coasteering and orienteering plus a range of optional extras such as horse riding and quadbiking. Established in 1982 the centre is run by qualified and extremely experienced outdoor pursuits instructors, not businessmen or hoteliers. Our staff are talented athletes with a level of expertise that ensures you are in good hands. Accommodation is basic but comfortable

129

in a small rural complex with a choice of self-catering farmhouse rooms, chalet bunkrooms or camping, sharing bathroom, showers and toilets. Laundry and drying facilities are available along with TV/briefing room and recreation area. All rooms are equipped for cooking light meals but eating out at inexpensive pubs and restaurants is allowed for in our low price, and is part of our lively evening social programme which includes watching live rock and jazz bands, night clubs, ten-pin bowling, indoor go-karting and barbecues. All evening activities are optional but great fun with the group. A variety of good food is available locally, including lunch at the resorts. Accommodation, tuition and equipment including wetsuits are all part of the package, with free transport daily to resorts and from train or bus terminals. No hidden extras.

(Source: Company Website)

Planula, 'Diver's Retreat', New South Wales, Australia

We specialize in diving/accommodation packages with a difference, offering more than your average divers' bunk bed lodge. Check out our *rates* for package deals. Planula Divers Retreat is equipped with everything a diver needs and more:

- gear washing and drying areas
- safe equipment storage
- extensive reference library with identification books and literature on marine biology, diving locations and more
- underwater photo cameras for hire
- gear hire available
- Tim can go out diving with you and *video* your dive, giving you an everlasting memory of Byron Bay.

(Source: Company Website)

The Arctic Icebreaker *Sampo*, Finland

An Arctic Ice Adventure

The *Sampo*, the world's only tourist icebreaker, operates on the northern Gulf of Bothnia out of Kemi in Finnish Lapland. After serving for thirty years as an icebreaker in Arctic waters, the vessel has been given a new, more fascinating task – to act as a base for ice adventurers.

The *Sampo* sails from the middle of December to the end of April. The trips last four hours. For scheduled sailings, it's worthwhile making a reservation well in advance. We recommend these cruises both for individual travellers and for groups.

The ship can also be booked entirely for private use. All charter trips are conducted to a programme selected by the customer, and prepared package tours are also offered.

The *Sampo* operates as a restaurant during the summer and can also be booked for conferences.

Designed for extreme conditions, the ruggedly simple vessel conceals quite a surprise within it. Ornamented with hardwood and brass, the cosy salons and cabins sweep you into an authentic maritime atmosphere even as you sit in the harbour.

Technical information

- length 75 m, width 17.4 m
- height of bridge above sea level 14 m
- weight 3540 tonnes, draught 7 m
- engine power 8800 hp
- speed in open water, 16 knots
- speed in 50-cm solid ice, 8 knots
- icebreaking capability, 70–120 cm solid ice
- passenger capacity, 150 people
- crew, 16 people
- built in 1961.

Service facilities

- Captain's Saloon, seats 20
- Icebreaker Bar, seats 80
- Arctic Restaurant, seats 80
- Lapponia Shop, souvenirs.

(Source: Company Website)

Foxwoods Resort Casino, New England, USA

In 2000, Foxwoods Resort Casino complex consisted of five casinos with over 300 000 square feet of gaming space, 5842 slot machines, 370 gaming tables, a 3000-seat high stakes bingo parlor with $1 million jackpots, a 200-seat Sportsbook, a keno lounge and the popular pull-tabs. Table games included Baccarat, min-Baccarat, Big Six wheels,

131

Blackjack, Caribbean Stud Poker, Craps, Pai Gow, Pai Gow Tiles, Red Dog, Roulette and a number of novelty games. One of the casinos is non-smoking.

Run by the Mashantucket Pequot Tribe, the Pequot made an agreement with the state to only allow one other casino operation in the state, the Mohegan Sun in Uncasville. Both casinos pay the State of Connecticut twenty percent of their slot machine profits, which totaled over three-hundred eighteen million dollars the previous fiscal year.

The Foxwood complex had four hotels in 2000, the Grand Pequot Tower with 800 guest rooms and suites; Great Cedar Hotel with 312 rooms and suites, a health spa and heated pool; Two Trees Inn with 280 rooms and suites, a pool and fitness room; the Mystic Hilton. Randall's Ordinary is an 18th century-style Inn in North Stonington, CT for weddings.

In total there were, in 2000, 23 shopping areas, 24 food and beverage outlets, a Cinedrome 360 theatre, 85 000 square-foot Mashantucket Pequot museum, a Fox Grand Theatre with Las Vegas style entertainment, a Turbo Ride, Fox video Arcade, gift shops, with over 1400 rooms, suites and villas ranging in price from $140 000 to $525 000.

Food prices are high at the Foxwoods. Expect a simple snack in the food court for two to run between $12 and $15. A full meal without extras $30 to $70 per couple. You won't find the bargains Las Vegas or Atlantic City offers guests.

(Source: Company Website)

Hedonism II, Jamaica

Hedonism II is an all-inclusive resort catering to both singles and couples over age 18. Included: accommodation, all meals and snacks, wine with lunch and dinner, unlimited premium brand bar drinks at any of 6 bars (bar service available 19 hours per day), all land and watersports, and nightly entertainment.

There are 280 bedrooms, all air-conditioned with private bath and shower. Rooms have either 2 twin beds or 1 king-sized bed. Rooms can be booked on a shared basis. This means that a guest travelling alone automatically shares with someone of the same sex. A guaranteed single rate is available.

Activities (includes the use of all sports equipment and facilities with instruction)

- Watersports: sunfish sailing, water-skiing, snorkeling, glass-bottom boat rides, windsurfing school, kayaks, scuba diving. For scuba diving one has to be certified; if not, a resort scuba course is available.
- Landsports: badminton, shuffleboard, basketball, volleyball, table tennis, bicycles, squash (2 air-conditioned courts), clinics daily, tournaments on Wednesdays.
- Tennis: 6 tennis courts, lit for night play, with resident pros. Clinics twice daily. Tournaments on Tuesday and Thursdays.
- Beach/pools/jacuzzis: private beach which is divided into two sections, of which one is for nude bathing with a nude Jacuzzi and pool. In addition, a large freshwater swimming pool with spacious sundeck and Jacuzzi is situated close to the main entertainment area.
- Fitness centre: stationary bicycles, stair climbing machine and a rower, along with 11 piece Nautilus equipment and complete weight room with instructor. Aerobic classes 5 times per week.
- Circus workshop: our exciting circus workshop features flying and swinging trapeze, trampoline clinics, juggling, tightrope walking, unicycle, and bicycle balancing acts. Available Sunday to Friday.

Special activities

Reggae dance classes 3 times per week. Lunchtime Spin each day (except Tuesday), Olympic Day (Tuesday), and Island Picnic (Wednesdays), Pyjama Party (Tuesday nights), Toga Party (Thursdays), Disco Welcome Party (Sundays), Jamaica Day (Friday). Toga tying and sumo wrestling (Thursday), Karaoke (Monday and Tuesday).

Entertainment

Monday	Reggae Dance Demo and Competition
Tuesday	Class of the Titans, Pyjama Party
Wednesday	Reggae Beach Party, Vegas Night
Thursday	Toga Party: Guest/Staff Talent Show
Friday	Beach Party with Live Band, Fun and Games, Circus Show
Saturday	Cabaret Show
Sunday	Oldies Night, Retro Cabaret Dance

Weddings

The hotel offers complimentary weddings, which include wedding cake, champagne, marriage license, non-denominational marriage officer and flowers. Witnesses are provided on request. All the necessary paperwork is handled by the resort. One working week's notice is required to complete the formalities. You are required to be in Jamaica 48 hours before the ceremony can be performed.

(Source: Company and Customer Websites)

Franciscan Renewal Center, Scottsdale, USA

The Franciscan Renewal Center is located only minutes from Sky Harbor International Airport. We offer 23 acres of a lush desert oasis set at the base of Camelback Mountain in the heart of the Scottsdale/Paradise Valley resort district. As a retreat house for sponsored and private retreats, we offer 56 sleeping rooms, each with a private bath. For non-profit conferences, we offer 14 meeting rooms and A/V services.

For the spiritual reflection of our guests, the chapel and Meditation Chapel are open daily with scheduled masses. For the physical relaxation of our guests, we offer a therapy pool, swimming pool, and many walking paths. We have a very active and inspiring campus. If you would like to join us for one of our many weekend retreats, a private retreat, our classes and workshops or for a conference, please contact us for further information and reservations.

(Source: Company and Specialist Websites)

Summary

In this chapter we have looked at the characteristics and scope of adventure tourism destinations and venues, noting their diversity. There are clearly links between destinations and venues, as the latter exist within the former. However, if a venue grows and develops ancillary services it may develop into a mini destination in its own right.

Destinations and venues are crucial because they are the places or sites where adventure tourism takes place. However, it is now time for us to look at the organizations that make up the adventure tourism industry.

Discussion points and exercises

1 Discuss the role that destinations play in adventure tourism.
2 Critically evaluate the typologies of adventure tourism destinations offered in Figures 5.2, 5.3 5.4.
3 Using examples, compare and contrast the role of venues and destinations in adventure tourism.
4 Select an adventure tourism venue and analyse its products and markets.

6

The adventure tourism industry

Introduction

Adventure tourism is a complex industry with a wide variety of elements and suppliers. Some of these suppliers are also part of the mainstream tourism industry, such as accommodation operators, while others are specific to adventure tourism, like equipment manufacturers. The structure of the adventure tourism industry is illustrated in Figure 6.1.

It is also possible, as we will now see, to look at the structure of the industry in several other ways.

The structure of the industry

A wide range of suppliers meets the demand for adventure tourism, and these can be looked at in different ways as in Figure 6.2.

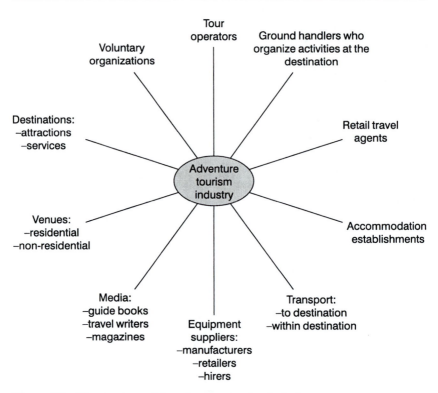

Figure 6.1 The structure of the adventure tourism industry.

Clearly this is a gross over-simplification. For example:

1 Some types of suppliers, such as equipment supplies and tour operators, can be found in both the generation zone and the destination zone.
2 Some types of suppliers can be sub-divided into many different categories. For example, accommodation for adventure tourists could encompass:

- Sleeping in the open in the wilderness where no permission is required, no equipment is needed, and no fee is paid for the accommodation
- Camping in the wilderness, which is free, and camping on owned land where a fee is payable
- Building a shelter in the wilderness or on owned land where a 'rental price' for the land may or may not be payable
- Making use of existing buildings or shelters that are either derelict or are usually used for a different purpose
- Using accommodation that has been tailor-made for adventure tourists, such as mountain refuge huts

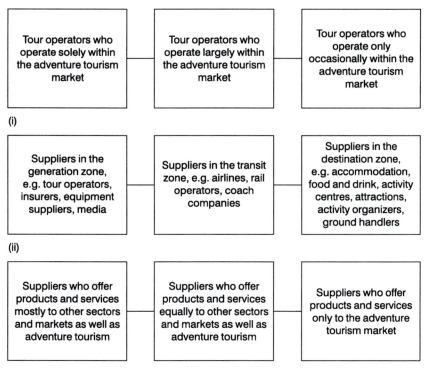

(i)

(ii)

(iii)

Figure 6.2 Three dimensions of the supply side of adventure tourism.

- Combined transport and accommodation, such as long-distance sailing races where competitors sleep on board their boat
- Novel indigenous forms of accommodation, such as rorbus, yurts, and ice caves
- Shared use of destination accommodation that is also used by other leisure and/or business tourists
- The use of both serviced and self-catering accommodation
- The use of luxury accommodation so that the adventure is a daytime activity only, while the nights mean pampering, warmth, and safety.

3 Figure 6.2 has clearly not distinguished between suppliers who are in the private, public and voluntary sectors. As we will see in the chapter on marketing, this distinction has a great influence on the nature of products, pricing levels, and promotional messages. Public and voluntary bodies often offer basic level products with social objectives such as education or conservation, while private sector suppliers tend to focus on generating profits and satisfying the tastes of their clients with a higher-level product.

Let us now look at each of the elements of the industry identified in Figure 6.1 in a little more detail.

Adventure tour operators

The growth of adventure tourism has been fuelled by the activities of specialist tour operators who focus on adventure tourism. Generally these tour operators are small-scale and specialize in particular types of activity or region of the world. Where larger corporations have 'dipped their toes' in the adventure tourism sector, they have often been unsuccessful and have withdrawn.

Millington (2001) provided data on a number of the world's major adventure tourism tour operators:

- Explore Worldwide (UK) was owned by its founders until it was bought by the mainstream tour operator, the Holidaybreak Group, in 2000. In 2001 the operator sold around 22 000 packages, and made £1.3 million profit between September 2000 and March 2001. Explore offers a wide range of activities in many different regions of the world.
- Exodus (UK) is a close competitor of Explore Worldwide, and carries around 12 000 passengers a year. The company started in 1974 with tours to Afghanistan, a destination that was very trendy with young travellers in the 1970s.
- Dragoman (UK) has been in business for a quarter of a century, and has a strong reputation for working with local communities.
- Abercrombie and Kent (UK) was founded in 1962, and is renowned for offering packages at the luxury end of the adventure travel market. Therefore many of its packages are not true 'adventure experiences', and only a proportion of its 180 000 clients per year can be truly seen as adventure tourists. A new offshot, A & K Active, focuses more on activity holidays than the traditional Abercrombie and Kent vacation, which tends to be more about sightseeing.
- Trek America (USA), which is now 30 years old, focuses on selling adventure packages in the USA, Canada and Mexico to Americans and foreigners. Its on-line brochure site enjoys around 4 million hits per annum.
- Lindblad Travel (USA) has been around since 1958, and concentrates on taking Americans for adventures on other continents. Now it even owns its own ships for adventure cruising.
- Mountain Travel Sobek (USA) is a result of a merger in 1991 between Mountain Travel (mountain expedition specialists) and Sobek (a river-rafting company). Since this merger, the company has sought to boost its market appeal.

- Geographic Expeditions (USA), set up in 1983, concentrates on small-scale special interest vacations to adventurous destinations, and has around 4500 clients every year.
- Canadian Mountain Holidays (Canada) concentrates on vacations to very remote, little visited places, but with an emphasis on luxury. The company was founded in 1979 and carries about 4000 passengers each year. It claims to have invented heli-skiing, and now has a range of products aimed at families.
- Wikinger Reisen (Germany) is more than 30 years old, and now services some 16 000 clients per annum and employs 200 staff.
- DAV Summit Club (Germany) focuses on walking and climbing holidays all over the world.
- Terres d'Adventure (France) carries around 17 000 passengers per annum, and focuses on solo adventure and family adventure.
- Explorator (France) focuses on four-wheel drive vehicle tours and services around 4000 (generally high income) clients each year.

This survey illustrates the diversity of tour operators in adventure tourism, but they all share the characteristic that they are small, niche-market operators. They are therefore quite weak in relation to larger operators, and hence it is not surprising that many small operators are forming strategic alliances to give them more power in the marketplace. For example, Exodus in the UK has teamed up with Peregrine Adventures and Geckos to form 'This Amazing Planet', which focuses on environmentally responsible tourism. Each company has different target markets, but they are involved in joint marketing activities.

Most adventure trips are not 'hard' vacations but are relatively 'soft', in small groups. Two examples are given here from the UK-based company Sundowners' 2001 brochure.

KARAKORAM & KASHGAR
21 Days, £1960 Twin Share

Pakistan and China

From the North West Frontier Province to the great mountain regions of northern Pakistan, the Hindu Kush, Karakoram and Pamir ranges collide to produce some of the world's most breathtaking scenery.

Hidden valleys and high passes lead the way through Chirtal, Chilgit and Hunza to the Khunjerab pass and China's Xinjian province. This was the way of the silk caravans on their journey from Xian to Kashmir and in more recent history the lands where the rivalries for territory between Britain and Russia became known as the 'Great Game'. To travel this region independently is to follow in the footsteps of Silk Road merchants, spies, geographers and eccentrics who were the pioneers of travel to this incredible land. A truly remarkable travel experience.

Itinerary Guideline

Day 1 Islamabad
Pakistan's capital is a modern planned city

Day 2 Taxila to Peshawar
Visit the ruined city of Taxila en route to the frontier town of Peshawar

Day 3 Peshawar
The bazaar reflects Peshawar's location as gateway to the Khyber Pass; opium and hashish, arms and ammunitions vie for space alongside carpets and spices, food and clothing

Days 4–6 North West Frontier Province
North to the Swat valley, over the Lowari pass (3118 m) to Chitral and visit the Kafir people of the Kalash valleys

Days 7–9 to Gillgit
Through the spectacular Hindu Raj mountains and over the Shandur Pass (3734 m) to Gilgit

Days 10–12 To Hunza
Walk in the Hunza valley with magnificent views of Rakaposhi (7788 m) and the surrounding peaks and glaciers before continuing to Sust

Days 13 & 14 Khunjerab Pass to Kashgar
Over the Khunjerab pass (4730 m) to China and the old fortress town of Tashkurgan and on to the legendary Silk Road market town of Kashgar

Days 15 & 16 Kashgar
The Sunday market is not to be missed as Uighar, Tadjik and Kyrgyz gather to buy, sell and exchange in an age-old tradition

Days 17 & 18 Across the Karakoram
Return to Pakistan and the Hunza valley

Days 19–21 Karakoram highway
Down the Karakoram highway via Chilas and Besham to Islamabad

Details

Commences – Daily from Islamabad [Saturday recommended]

Travel by	– Four-wheel drive jeep, local and chartered vehicle
Stay in	– Hotels and guesthouses 18 nights, camping 2 nights
Meals	– Included when camping from lunch day 7 to lunch day 9
Grade	– ***Adventurous***
Notes	– Some hard travelling and high passes ––expect an outstanding adventure. Travelling season May to October. Supplements for single travellers £1440
Dossier	– Available on request

IN THE FOOTSTEPS OF ALEXANDER
26 Days, £1990

Conquer Asia on this truly epic journey. Follow in the footsteps of Alexander the Great and Marco Polo from the fertile Indus Valley, cradle of civilization, across the vast and inhospitable deserts of Central Asia, through ancient Persia to the Bosphorous – gateway to Europe. Between lies a world of lost civilizations, amazing architecture and mysterious and fascinating people.

History unfolds as you follow this ancient route of trade and conquest, revealing the rise and fall of monumental empires and the legendary heroes, ancient and modern, who ventured into this land of fable suspended between East and West.

Your Itinerary

Days 1 & 2 – Arrive Lahore. Enjoy a full day sightseeing, including Badshahi mosque. Lahore fort, Shalimar gardens and the old city. *3* Drive to Multan, known as the 'city of saints', via one of the Indus valley's most important ancient cities, Harappa. Explore the fascinating ruins dating from 3500 BC. *4* A morning tour of Multan includes the Shah Tukne-Alam tomb and Agahi bazaar, one of the most colourful in Pakistan and full of pottery and handicrafts. Then to Uchh, famous for the beautiful tombs of the Sufi saints. Then to

Bahawalpur. *5* Drive to Sukkur on the banks of the Indus river. *6 & 7* Morning boat ride on the Indus before departing for the ruins of Mohenjodaro, one of the Indus valley's earliest civilizations. Then through the spectacular Bolan pass to Quetta. *8 & 9* Across the remote Baluchiastan desert to Iran. *10* To Bam, where we explore the beautifully preserved citadel. *11* To Kerman, carpet capital of the world. *12 & 13* To the cultural centre of ancient Persia, Shiraz. We visit the massive stone ruins of Darius the Great's Persepolis. *14 & 15* To the majestic city of Isfahan, with the greatest concentration of Islamic monuments in the country. *16 & 17* To the capital Tehran and on to Tabriz. *18 & 19* To Turkey, passing Mt Ararat, fabled resting place of Noah's Ark. Visit the spectacular Isak Pasa Sarayi fortress before heading across eastern Anatolia to Erzurum. *20–23* North to the Black Sea with time to explore the quaint coastal towns and beaches before driving to the capital Ankara. *24–26* To Istanbul, Turkey's most exciting and interesting city. Visit the infamous Blue Mosque and old town before our epic journey concludes at this meeting point of East and West.

Details

Escorted – Maximum Group size: 15

Travel by – Chartered and local vehicles, some sightseeing by foot and boat

Stay in – Budget hotels/guesthouses

Meals – Not included

You will experience – An epic journey that links Asia with Europe, revealing the rich cultures and history of Pakistan, Iran and Turkey little seen by the western traveller

Grade – Adventurous

Notes – Although this journey is scheduled in the most favourable season, temperatures can still be high during the day and it can be cold overnight, particularly in the desert regions. The distance covered should not be underestimated – there are some long travelling days. Combines with 'Oases of the Silk Road' Dossier – Available on request.

Adventure ground handlers

Tour operators are the companies in the country from which the tourist travels, which organize the whole package. Within destinations, there are ground handlers. These are the companies that organize activities within the destination, either on behalf of the tour operators or for independent travellers. These ground handlers usually specialize in particular activities. They are important because they determine the quality of the adventure experience, as they are the actual people who offer the activities to the tourists on a face-to-face basis. Some idea of the nature and scope of ground handlers is illustrated in the following examples:

- Salty's in Bundaberg (Queensland), a company that runs diving trips on the Great Barrier Reef
- Gecko Canoe Tours, which offers three- to six-day canal trips from Kalterine in the Nitmiluh National Park
- Impacto Turismo, which runs eco-tours in the Pantanal wetlands region of Brazil
- Amazon's Indian Turismo, which is run by Amazonian Indians and offers basic jungle-trekking and wildlife trips in Brazilian Amazonia
- Svalbard Polar Travel of Norway, which offers a five-day adventure cruise around Svalbard involving landings in isolated locations
- Idide Ride Sled Dog Tours, which offers short day sled tours in the Kenai Peninsular of Alaska
- Tien Shan Travel in Bishbek, which offers heli-skiing trips, as well as trekking, in the mountains of Kyrgyzstan
- Small plane sightseeing tours of glaciers on Alaska, at $90–$140 dollars per person, offered by several local ground handlers.

The ground handlers play a vital role in adventure travel in that, as the organizers of the adventure activities, they are primarily responsible for the safety of travellers.

Travel agents

Most adventure tourism tour operators sell their products directly to clients without the need for intermediaries. However, several travel agencies specialize in selling adventure packages or making travel arrangements for individual adventure travellers and backpackers.

Trailfinders (UK), for example, was founded in 1970 and now makes travel arrangements for around 800 000 people per annum. It accounts for 20 per cent of all British leisure travellers to Australia. The company also works with specialist tour operators such as Exodus, Trek America, Journey Latin America, Guerba, Dragoman Encounter, Contiki, and the Imaginative Traveller (Millington, 2001).

Equipment suppliers

Much adventure tourism is based on activities that require specialist equipment. This in turn creates a need for equipment manufacturers, retailers and hire companies. Some of this equipment (such as micro-light aircraft) costs thousands of pounds, while other items cost just a few pounds. Equipment includes the hardware people need to undertake an activity as well as the specialist clothing required to take part in the activity. Major considerations in relation to the purchase of equipment include safety and fashionability.

Manufacturers and retailers of equipment and clothing advertise heavily in the adventure travel magazines. The range of equipment suppliers involved in adventure tourism is illustrated by the contents of a randomly selected issue of *Adventure Travel Outdoors* magazine from 2001. This magazine contained the following:

- Fifteen advertisements for equipment manufacturers
- Twenty-four advertisements for equipment retailers
- Seven advertisements for specialist clothing
- Thirteen reviews of new pieces of equipment
- Eight advertisements for services offered to adventure tourists.

The scope of equipment in adventure tourism is shown by the following selection of types of equipment, clothing or service advertised in the same issue of *Adventure Travel Outdoors*:

- Blister cream
- Duvets
- Expedition packs
- Guidebooks
- Food
- Gaiters
- Insect repellent
- Insurance
- Knives
- Rucksacks
- Torches
- Watches
- Waterproof clothing
- Maps
- Tents

Equipment manufacturing and retailing tends to take place in the tourists' home country. However, many adventure travellers rely on hiring equipment and clothing in their destinations. This is particularly the case where:

- Tourists decide to take part in activities that they did not envisage participating in when they planned their vacation
- Tourists participate in a new activity while on vacation
- The cost of transporting the tourists' own gear and clothing is prohibitive
- Local conditions demand specialist equipment that is designed specifically for the locality.

Some idea of rental charges is given in the following examples taken from the USA in 2000 (prices are in US dollars):

- Bike hire in Alaska – $20 per day
- Kayak rental in Alaska – $50 per day for a single
- Cross-country skis – $20 per day
- Wetsuits and surfboards – $30 per day
- Bear-resistant food containers, in national parks – free from the park authorities.

Accommodation

Adventure tourists require sleeping accommodation, but often it is very different from that used by mainstream tourists. The most popular forms of accommodation for adventure tourists are:

- Sleeping rough, in the open
- Camping
- Youth and other hostels
- Mountain huts and refuges.

Much of this accommodation is either free or is offered at very low cost by non-profit-making organizations.

Some adventure tourists like to stay with local people, in everything from longhouses in Borneo to bed-and-breakfast in Alaska. Here the price paid is a 'commercial' rate, but it is paid to private individual or families and not to commercial operations.

Often the form of accommodation is part of the actual adventure experience, but sometimes the accommodation is the core of the adventure. This category may include ice-hotels or igloos in the Arctic North of Scandinavia and North America, or the 'tree hotels' in several jungle regions of the world.

At the higher end of the adventure market there are those who want to sleep in luxurious or at least comfortable accommodation, and then be transported to the adventure each day.

Transport

The transport needs of adventure tourists are of two kinds; first to the destination, and then within the destination. Because of the remoteness of many adventure tourism destinations, travel to them is often a complex process involving several flights, bus journeys or slow train journeys.

Furthermore, the riskiness of the journey to the destination can be part of the adventure itself, providing stories for the traveller to recount in the years to come. These risks can involve old aircraft, bad weather, dangerous terrain, or the threat of terrorist action.

Once at the destination a wide variety of modes of transport are utilized including:

- Walking
- Cross-country skiing
- Aircraft and helicopters
- Cycling
- Horse, camel and donkey riding
- Hire cars
- Commercial lorries
- Buses and coaches
- Trains
- Canoes, boats and ferries.

One particular way of travelling is hitching – a way of moving around that is an adventure in itself. There are risks of being attacked or of simply not getting a lift. Hitching is viewed as a particularly adventurous or risky activity for lone women travellers.

Finally, sometimes the act of travelling is in itself the adventure. This is true of great rail journeys such as the Trans-Siberian Express or the Orient Express, together with seaplane flights and trips on ice-breaking ships.

Media

The adventure tourism media consist of four major elements:

1 *Guide books*. Adventure tourists have had an increasingly large choice of guide books in recent years to help them plan their activities. Some focus on particular types of activity, such as skiing or wildlife watching, but the most popular and influential guide books are those produced for whole countries – such as those published by Lonely Planet, Let's Go, and Rough Guide. These books particularly influence the growing market of independent adventure travellers and backpackers. Their influence is reinforced by

the websites they offer. These books and websites are often the only major source of information about a country for a traveller, so they have a great responsibility in terms of where tourists go and how they will behave.

2 *Travel writing.* Travel writing, particularly in relation to adventure tourism, has boomed in recent years and now takes up many shelves in large bookshops around the world. Traditionally such writing focused on expeditions to remote and dangerous places. Today, however, adventure travel writing covers a wider variety of tourism experiences, notably:

- The explorations of solo female travellers like Dervla Murphy
- Visits to war zones and areas where there is a major terrorist threat
- The travels of disabled people
- Personal spiritual or emotional travel experiences
- Sexual and romantic adventures while on vacation.

   Later in the book the reader will find a short case study which focuses specifically on adventure travel writing.

3 *Specialist magazines.* Specialist adventure travel magazines have grown in number dramatically in recent years, particularly in the so-called developed world. Some focus on particular adventures, such as gliding or mountaineering, while others focus on destinations. Such magazines are a key influence on the positive decisions of adventure travellers in terms of both destinations and equipment. A case study of two UK-based adventure travel magazines is to be found later in this book.

4 *Television adventure travel programmes.* Television – terrestrial and satellite – has taken to adventure travel and has realized that it makes attractive television. If an adventure activity or destination is featured in a television programme, it will stimulate demand. Television has also started to play a role in organizing some experiments in adventure travel – for example, in 2000 a production company produced a top-rating show based on putting a selection of ordinary people on an isolated Scottish island as 'castaways'. Likewise, many programmes are now being made about ordinary people being sent into the wilderness with the aim of adapting to their surroundings and 'surviving'.

All of the media outlined here share responsibility for the results of their activities, which may cause problems in terms of achieving sustainable adventure tourism by:

- Raising the profile of, and stimulating people's desire to visit, fragile, remote environments
- Encouraging behaviour that is not sensitive to the environment or host community, e.g. scuba diving

- Photography, and four-wheel driving
- Failing to give travellers information to allow them to be sensitive tourists.

Voluntary organizations

Most of the adventure tourism industry is commercial and is profit-oriented. However, the voluntary sector plays a significant role in the industry in several ways; for example:

- There are activity centres and mountain holidays and refuges that are run by voluntary, non profit-making bodies
- Professional bodies that are wholly or largely voluntary sector, such as the British Mountaineering Council, often regulate adventure activities and/or develop codes of conduct for participants
- It provides voluntary labour such as instructors and group leaders.

Venues

While most adventure tourism is outdoors based, some of it is based in or on venues. This subject is dealt with in further detail in Chapter 5, but venues include:

- Outdoor activity centres
- Facilities such as gliding and flying clubs and diving centres
- Artificial climbing walls.

New venues can help put places on the map as adventure tourism destinations.

Destinations

Destinations for adventure tourism are discussed in detail in Chapter 5. Suffice it to say at this stage that destinations are crucial to adventure tourism. Sometimes the destination is the core of the experience because of its landscape or climate, while at other times it is an incidental background to the activities. In any event, it is the place where tourists enjoy their adventure tourism experience.

It is now an appropriate time for us to look at the nature of entrepreneurship in adventure tourism – a sector where the small business dominates.

Entrepreneurship in adventure tourism

Adventure tourism, as we have seen, is an 'industry' dominated by small and medium-sized enterprises and the entrepreneurial flair of individuals.

Any study of businesses in the sector reveals the existence of a certain type of enterprise, as shown in Figure 6.3.

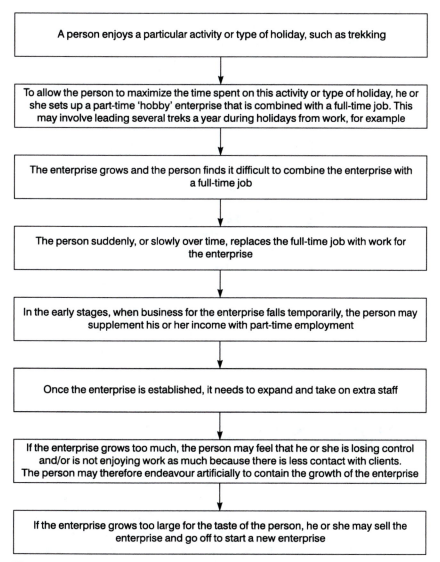

Figure 6.3   The evolution of small enterprises in adventure tourism.

Of course many enterprises do not follow this pattern, for they never become established and fail. However, enterprises like those described in Figure 6.3 can be seen throughout adventure tourism.

These enterprises also give lie to the capitalist theory that entrepreneurs will always seek to maximize profits. Many entrepreneurs in this sector clearly do not try to make as much money as possible, but instead endeavour to achieve a high quality, balanced lifestyle that provides enough money to allow them and their families to live comfortably while giving them enough free time to enjoy leisure activities or time with their family. This approach to entrepreneurship seems to be growing in popularity in today's world, and adventure tourism offers some excellent real world examples.

Clearly this phenomenon is not unique to adventure tourism; it is also being seen elsewhere, such as in the small hotel sector and in other industries such as information technology.

An interesting final point is that the very act of setting up a new enterprise, of becoming an entrepreneur, is in itself an adventure – a step into the unknown!

The non-physical adventure sector

Understandably we have focused on physical adventure, which is the heart of the adventure tourism industry. However, spiritual, intellectual and emotional adventure tourism have their own infrastructure or suppliers – for example:

- Spiritual adventures – monasteries and religious retreat communities
- Gambling – casinos
- Hedonism – night clubs.

At the same time they also make use of transport and have their own specialist media.

Human resources in adventure tourism

Adventure tourism is a service industry where the human resources that staff the industry are of great importance. The safety and enjoyment of adventure tourists is often dependent on the quality of people such as tour leaders, guides and instructors. There are many technical qualifications and professional bodies that regulate the quality of such staff, but there is still a lack of formal education and training for those involved in the management of adventure tourism.

Volunteers also play a significant role in staffing the adventure tourism industry. It is, of course, more difficult to manage and control the activities of volunteers, but they are an indispensable resource for many adventure tourism organizations.

Summary

In this chapter we have seen that the adventure tourism industry is complex and multi-faceted. It has been noted that adventure tourism uses elements of the mainstream tourism industry as well as having its own specialist suppliers. We have also recognized that the bulk of the industry is dominated by small enterprises. It is now time for us to move on to look at how adventure tourism is marketed.

Discussion points and exercises

1 Compare and contrast the structure of the adventure tourism industry with that of the mass market package tourism and business tourism sectors.
2 Choose several adventure tourism tour operators and see if they conform to the model offered in Figure 6.3.
3 Discuss the implications of the growing influence of the media on the adventure tourism market.
4 Discuss the role of voluntary sector organizations in adventure tourism.

Part
D

The management of adventure tourism

7

Marketing

Introduction

The complexity of adventure tourism as a phenomenon, which we have noted throughout the book, is reflected in the nature of marketing within the sector. Some of the intricacies of adventure tourism marketing are identified in Figure 7.1, and we will look at each of these in a little detail.

Complexities of marketing

1 *The producers and suppliers of adventure tourism products and experiences have a variety of different objectives.* These affect their approach to marketing. For many companies, adventure tourism is a business from which they want to make a healthy profit. At the other extreme there are voluntary or non-profit-making organizations offering adventure tourism experiences, where the aim is

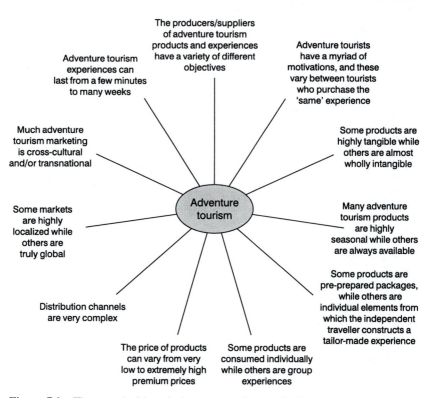

The producers/suppliers
of adventure tourism
products and experiences
have a variety of different
objectives

Adventure tourism
experiences can
last from a few minutes
to many weeks

Adventure tourists
have a myriad of
motivations, and these
vary between tourists
who purchase the
'same' experience

Much adventure
tourism marketing
is cross-cultural
and/or transnational

Some products are
highly tangible while
others are almost
wholly intangible

Adventure
tourism

Some markets
are highly
localized while
others are
truly global

Many adventure
tourism products
are highly
seasonal while others
are always available

Some products are
pre-prepared packages,
while others are
individual elements from
which the independent
traveller constructs a
tailor-made experience

Distribution channels
are very complex

The price of products
can vary from very
low to extremely high
premium prices

Some products are
consumed individually
while others are group
experiences

Figure 7.1   The complexities of adventure tourism marketing.

largely social. This could include those who run 'charity challenges', or 'character building', 'horizon-widening' holidays for disadvantaged children. In between there are those adventure tourism enthusiasts who set up enterprises that allow them to pursue their former 'hobby' as a full-time profession. They often do not see profit maximization as their aim, but rather seek to balance an enjoyable lifestyle with earning enough income to enjoy a reasonable standard of living. These differences in objectives will be reflected in the approach taken to promotion in terms of how much is done and the nature of the messages transmitted about the product.

2 *Adventure tourists have a myriad of motivations, and these motivations vary between tourists purchasing the 'same' experience.* If you think about all the types of adventure tourism mentioned in this book and then try to 'brainstorm' motivations people could have for taking part in them, you will need a very large piece of paper or white board. Motivations could include everything from gaining status to the desire for sensual

pleasure, escaping from the conventions of everyday life to meeting people, testing oneself to improving one's health. If we looked at any single group of people on a specific adventure tourism trip, then it is likely there would be significant differences between the motivations of each participant.

3 *Some products are highly tangible while others are almost wholly intangible.* Physical adventure trips tend to rely heavily on tangible features such as rivers and mountains. These physical natural resources are the core of the experience for white-water rafters and mountaineers respectively, for example. On the other hand, the adventure tourist who is looking for spiritual enlightenment is concerned with gaining an intangible benefit from experiences that are largely based on intangibles – such as the atmosphere in pilgrimage destinations, and religious practices. Marketing such intangible experiences is difficult, because you cannot easily communicate the nature of the product and its benefits to potential customers.

4 *Many adventure tourism products are highly seasonal while others are always available.* The seasonality of adventure tourism has two main aspects; attractions and accessibility. Some adventure tourism attractions are highly seasonal, such as white water, snow, and special events, for example. However, in some places it is not the attraction that is seasonal but rather the accessibility of the attraction – at certain times of the year the attraction may be less accessible because of bad weather or reduced transport services, for instance. On the other hand, there are products where the attraction is both permanently available and accessible. Seasonality, as elsewhere in tourism, affects both pricing and the potential volume of demand.

5 *Some products are pre-prepared packages while others are individual elements from which the independent traveller constructs a tailor-made experience.* A single adventure tourism attraction can be part of a pre-prepared package or can be selected by an independent traveller to be part of a personally tailor-made experience. This is true of everything from ski slopes to hunting reserves, visits to religious retreats to trips to desert regions. The same is of course also true of accommodation and transport services that are aimed at the adventure tourist.

6 *Some products are consumed individually while others are group experiences.* Many adventure tourism experiences are intensely personal, solo activities. Often, not only do these 'independent' tourists not want to take their vacation as part of a group but they would also prefer it if there were no other tourists around at all in their destination environment. Conversely, a number of adventure experiences tend to be group activities

with the enjoyment coming partly from the interaction between participants. This is clearly an important issue to bear in mind when promotional messages are being designed.

7 *The price of products can vary from very low to high premium pricing.* Some adventure tourism can be free, at least in terms of the use of natural attractions, for example. However, even in these areas most adventure tourism involves paying a price to use certain attractions, accommodation, transport and so on. Some products are aimed specifically at disadvantaged sections of the community for social reasons, and these are low priced or may even be free to the consumer, thanks to public sector or voluntary sector subsidies. On the other hand, some adventure vacations are priced very highly as high status products. Interestingly, people on low-priced and high-priced trips may find themselves sharing the same core product, such as a mountain or a river, at the same time in the same weather.

8 *Distribution channels are often very complex.* The distribution of adventure tourism products often involves the use of numerous distribution channels. For example, magine a small specialist adventure activity organizer in an established tourist destination. It could distribute its product as follows:

- Within the destination, directly, to individual customers who visit its office
- Within the destination, directly, to groups of customers who visit its office
- As 'tailor-made packages' for local hotels and travel agencies
- As 'tailor-made packages' for externally based tour operators
- Directly with individuals/groups via the Internet.

  This range of different distribution channels has implications for the pricing of the product by the organizer, as well as for its promotional campaigns.

9 *Some markets are highly localized while others are truly global.* In some destinations, the majority of the adventure tourism market is local. This tends to be the case in countries or regions with a sizeable population and a developed economy, and which are a considerable distance from major tourism markets. Until recently this was the case with New Zealand, for instance. However, destinations are attracting an increasing number of people from other countries and even continents. There is now also a segment of tourists who are keen to take adventure holidays all over the world. Many destinations now have markets that are truly global. The geographical catchment area of a destination market clearly has great implications for its pricing, promotion and destination.

10 *Much adventure tourism marketing is cross-cultural and/or trans-national.* The phenomenon of adventure tourism that crosses cultural and/ or national boundaries is increasing due to the falling real cost of long-haul travel and the growing interest in adventure tourism in emerging outbound tourism markets. Where such cross-cultural tourism occurs it poses challenges for marketers, with a need to reconcile cultural differences between the destination and markets in terms of everything from concepts of what constitutes adventure to ethical standards, attitudes towards risk to dietary needs, food preferences, languages, and legal contracts concerning how products can be advertised.

11 *Adventure tourism experiences can last from a few minutes to many weeks.* Adventure experiences can last for a very short period, such as a few minutes in the case of bungee jumping or a flight in a Russian MiG fighter. This puts great pressure on the product to deliver instant satisfaction to the tourist. Conversely, trekking or overland expeditions can last for several weeks. Here the emphasis is on providing highlights throughout the trip to sustain satisfaction, as well as ensuring that the total cost is affordable for the target market.

Furthermore, we can identify a number of characteristics that distinguish marketing in adventure tourism from that in other sectors. These include the following:

- An emphasis on psychographic segmentation because so many of the motivators and determinants of the behaviour of adventure tourists relates to their personalities and lifestyles. It is clear that this fact is well understood by the adventure tourism industry just by looking at the brochures produced by specialist tourist operators in the field.
- Recognizing the importance of bestowing status on purchasers of adventure tourism products is vital in the marketing in this sector. However, the concept of status clearly varies between different kinds of products and experiences. It may mean exclusivity on the basis of the rarity value and uniqueness of the experience and/or high price. Alternatively, an adventure tourist may gain status from being away from other tourists or visiting exotic destinations at low cost as a budget traveller. Here, the lower the price paid the greater the status enjoyed by the tourist. This is particularly the case in the student backpacking market.
- Most adventure tourism marketing is carried out by small and medium-sized enterprises, whether tour operators, travel agencies or even destination marketing agencies. This is in contrast with many other sectors of tourism, where marketing is now dominated by large-scale, often trans-national companies.

- Specialist media play a significant role in promoting adventure tourism products and destinations. These specialist media include general adventure tourism magazines (such as *Wanderlust* in the UK) as well as periodicals that focus on one activity like mountaineering or sailing. The modern types of destination guides, such as Lonely Planet and Rough Guides, also often promote adventure tourism opportunities within destinations.
- The Internet probably plays a greater role in adventure tourism marketing than it does in other sectors for several reasons. First, it is a form of promotion and distribution that suits small and medium enterprises that do not have the budget to produce glossy brochures and do not sell enough holidays to be attractive to travel agents. Second, in a rapidly changing business it allows producers regularly to update their selling messages, reflecting daily changes in snow conditions for example. Third, in a market that is truly global the Internet means that products and destinations can take bookings from clients anywhere in the world, day and night. Finally, the Internet is a relatively inexpensive form of promotion and it is very effective in targeting niche markets, like adventure tourism, effectively.
- With most adventure tourism products there is a great emphasis on brand loyalty and repeat business, as this is much less expensive than having constantly to find new customers in a numerically small specialist market.

We will now look at some other issues relating to the marketing of adventure tourism, beginning with market segmentation.

Segmentation and marketing

Segmentation is at the heart of modern marketing. No longer do we see markets as monolithic, homogeneous mass markets. Instead we divide the potential market into segments, or groups, who share similar characteristics. These characteristics can be geographical (i.e. where the tourists come from), demographic (age, sex, race and so on) and psychographic (lifestyle and personality).

The first two methods have traditionally been used in tourism, and for adventure tourism marketers there are interesting trends in relation to both:

- More and more people from countries that previously generated few adventure tourism trips, including Taiwan, South Korea, China, India and Russia, are now taking adventure vacations

- The growing number of empty nesters and senior citizens who are enjoying the benefits of improved health care, and are keen to try new adventure experiences, and are healthy enough to take part in them
- The increasing participation of women in adventurous travel, particularly some sports and backpacking
- The trend towards couples with children taking part in family adventure vacations.

At the same time psychographic segmentation is at the core of adventure tourism marketing, because personality type is a key determinant to whether or not people will take adventure trips. Adventurous risk-takers are more likely to take such vacations than cautious people. However, when designing products and promotional messages the industry needs to recognize that cautious, non-risk-takers may find themselves taking such trips to please their more adventurous partners and friends. These people may refuse to go on some trips unless they can be reassured that the vacation is safe.

Personality also plays a part in determining if people will travel individually or in groups, and whether they will take independent trips or buy organized packages.

The lifestyle of tourists also affects the type of adventure trip they will take. Often they will take a vacation that allows them to pursue an interest or hobby they enjoy at home, such as rock-climbing or partying. Alternatively, the adventure trip can be a total contrast with the everyday life of the tourist.

Adventure tourism organizations also have to recognize that there are 'shades' of adventure tourist, from the occasional participant in a particular type of activity to those who seek adventure in every moment of every holiday they take.

As we are about to talk about the Internet, it is worth saying that many believe that the opportunities for customized, targeted communication that the Internet offers mean that in future we will be able to treat every individual as a separate, unique market segment.

The role of the Internet

The Internet is revolutionizing the marketing of adventure tourism in several ways:

1 It allows small-scale tour operators to promote their products at a minimal cost. This is important, given that such tour operators have not traditionally

been able to sell via travel agents because of their low sales volume. Previously they have had to rely heavily on relatively expensive press advertisements and glossy brochures.

2 It provides an opportunity for entrepreneurs to regularly update their promotional message and prices in response to changes in market conditions.

3 It has changed the traditional 4 'Ps', or marketing mix, by combining promotion and place or distribution. Websites both provide information and allow the customer to make a reservation in a single transaction at the same time. This facilitates the spontaneous 'impulse purchase' decision.

4 Given that small operators are unable to staff reservation offices 24 hours a day, seven days a week, the Internet provides them with a low-cost way of taking bookings at all hours of the day and night. This is particularly important when selling on a global scale, where clients may live in countries in different time zones.

5 It is an effective tool for both relationship marketing and the targeting of small niche markets.

6 Guide book publishers, such as Lonely Planet, have set up their own websites that, while independent, recommend particular adventure tourism destinations and suppliers.

7 Many travellers are now creating their own websites or contributing to those set up by others, and on these sites their experiences are shared. This can help, indirectly, to promote particular adventure tourism destinations and operators; however, it can also have the opposite affect if the experiences were negative.

There seems little doubt that the Internet will play an increasing role in the marketing of adventure tourism because, as Millington (2001) notes:

> For the adventure travel operator, the Internet is proving to be the perfect mechanism for selling holidays. The profile of the average Internet user clearly matches that of a consumer who is likely to participate in adventure travel.

However, to be effective sites must be well designed and simple and quick to use, which is not always the case currently.

Promotional strategies

The promotional strategies used in the adventure tourism industry reflects the fact that most players within the sector are small and medium-sized enterprises. In other words, the emphasis is on finely targeted activities that maximize cost-effectiveness.

For the typical adventure travel tour operator, the promotional mix could include:

- The production of a relatively small number of glossy, high-quality brochures, which are not distributed widely but are instead only sent out in response to a specific enquiry. We will look at the brochures in a little more detail later.
- Websites featuring colourful images, factual information, and prices, together with a booking facility. There may also be a section containing testimonials from previous customers.
- Exhibiting at specialist adventure travel trade shows. Several UK cities now have at least one such show each year, where potential customers visit to look at what is on offer for the following year. One special exhibition in the UK, The Adventure Travel and Sports Show, attracted 2000 exhibitors and 28 000 visitors in 2000 (Millington, 2001).
- Direct mail marketing, particularly to past customers, to encourage brand loyalty and repeat purchase. Incentives may also be offered to existing customers who recommend new potential clients to the organization.
- Trying to obtain favourable mentions of the company's products in the travel media, including newspapers, magazines and television programmes.
- Placing small advertisements in specialist magazines or in the travel supplements of newspapers.
- Doing talks or film shows for potential clients.

However, the brochure still remains the mainstay of most adventure travel marketing, although this may change with the growth of the Internet.

Looking at these brochures, certain similar themes seem to emerge regardless of which company it is or which destination. Some of the main messages that are used in adventure travel brochures are illustrated in Table 7.1, through real extracts taken from five current brochures.

In adventure travel brochures, in general the companies are keen to reassure potential clients that they:

- Are experienced and have trained, highly skilled tour leaders
- Offer value for money
- Give the traveller extraordinary experiences

Table 7.1   Key messages in five selected adventure travel brochures

Message	*Brochure*
Experience more on small group exploratory holidays	Explore World-wide 2002–2003
The Ultimate Adventure	Kumuka Expeditions 2001–2002
Discovery and Adventure	Exodus 2001–2002
Join us on one of the best holidays you will ever have – your world will never be the same again	Explore World-Wide 2002–2003
Small group adventures – how much fun can you handle?	AmeriCon Adventures 2001–2002
Our holidays are great fun, good value, professionally run, educational, and responsible	Discover the World 2001–2002
By joining a Kumuka tour you can enjoy freedom as an individual traveller, whilst having the back-up and support of our experience	Kumuka Expeditions 2001–2002
Get away from it all with American Adventures and Roadrunner!!	AmeriCon Adventures 2000–2002
Since 1974 we have been running trips for people who want to experience the world as well as see it	Exodus 2001–2002
There are prices to suit all pockets, from £420 to more than £6000	Discover the World 2001–2002
Warning! Adventure Travel can be habit-forming	Explore World-wide 2002–2003
Adventures for the young and young at heart	AmeriCon Adventures 2000–2002
We travel in small groups causing as little environmental impact and cultural disturbance as possible. We use local resources and services wherever possible making our tour itineraries individual enough to be a positive and sustainable alternative to mass tourism	Explore World-Wide 2002–2003

Table 7.1 Continued

Message	Brochure
Experience Central and South America by travelling with local people and enjoying insights into the Latin lifestyle	Kumuka Expeditions 2001–2002
At Kumuka we know that your crew are the most important part of the tour. That is why we select our crew for their organizational skills, energy, and friendly personality. They undergo an extensive training programme, and as fellow travellers themselves, have a genuine enthusiasm for travel	Kumuka Expeditions 2001–2002
Our groups are small and, unlike many other operators, wherever possible we charter boats exclusively to provide maximum space for observation and photography	Discover the World 2001–2002
We try at all times to ensure that all our trips are socially, economically, and ecologically sound, because these are the three essential issues of any responsible tour policy	Exodus 2001–2002
Our business thrives on word of mouth. The majority of our clients have either travelled with us before or have been recommended by friends and relatives	Discover the World 2001–2002
Our Leaders will not only look after the practitioners, they will also ensure that you enjoy your trip whatever happens	Exodus 2001–2002
Our tours have been thoroughly planned for our clients to enjoy value for money and to ensure that you take home life-long memories	Kumuka Expeditions 2001–2002
We are pleased to announce that in the inaugural Wanderlust Readers Travel Awards, Exodus was voted top tour operator	Exodus 2001–2002

- Do not arrange travel in large groups
- Are responsible organizations that are sensitive to the needs of the environment and host communities.

The brochures tend to differ from those of mass market tour operators in a number of ways:

- They focus less attention on prices and discounts and more on value for money and exclusivity
- They provide much more detail on the itineraries and destinations
- They offer guidance on which kind of people each tour will suit rather than suggesting that they will appeal to everyone.

The marketing of adventure tourism destinations

Having focused on how individual companies market their adventure travel products, it is now time to consider the marketing of adventure tourism destinations.

The first thing to say is that there is much more adventure tourism going on than there was a few years ago. New destinations are being launched all the time as countries and regions seek to attract the economic benefits that such tourism can bring. However, like all destination marketing, the 'selling' of adventure tourism destinations is a complex matter for the following reasons:

1 Most marketing is undertaken by public sector destination marketing agencies who do not own or control much of the product and its pricing or distribution. Agencies therefore have to focus on the one element of the marketing mix they can control, or at least influence – namely promotion.
2 Some forms of adventure tourism are lucrative and controversial at the same time, notably wilderness hunting. Destination marketing agencies that publicly promote such products may alienate other types of tourists and make them go elsewhere.
3 Tourists' perceptions of the identity of a particular destination may conflict with the boundaries adopted by the public sector bodies charged with marketing these destinations. For example, tourists may think of the Austrian Tyrol as a single entity, but it may be marketed by different individual municipalities with different (and perhaps conflicting) objectives and marketing strategies.

4 The perceptions about the destination held by potential visitors are largely influenced by external sources over which the destination has little or no control, such as foreign tour operators and the media.

5 Destination marketing in most countries is organized in a hierarchical fashion. National governments promote whole countries usually through a few key images of what are perceived to be the leading attractions of the country. Regional authorities often promote regions within countries, again highlighting their own selection of the leading attractions. The individual municipalities or local government authorities seek to market their own corner of the region. There is often tension between the different geographical levels of marketing, and mixed, confusing messages are often given to the markets as a result.

6 Often the nature of adventure tourism in a particular destination changes from one season to the next. In a mountain area, winter means skiing, spring may be the peak season for white-water rafting, summer the time for hang-gliding, and autumn the prime season for trekking. This means marketers have to modify the marketing mix several times during a single year to meet the needs of different market segments.

7 Adventure tourism is a very competitive business today, and therefore most adventure tourism destinations face considerable competition from:
- Neighbouring regions in the same country with similar attractions
- Regions elsewhere in the world that offer similar attractions
- Regions elsewhere in the world that offer different attractions but similar benefits for tourists
- Adventure sports and activities that 'tourists' can undertake in their home area.

It is not surprising, therefore, that destinations make great use of a range of promotional techniques such as advertising, brochures, press and public relations, and attendance trade fairs to try to sell the unique aspects of their destination.

Summary

In this chapter we have explored a number of issues relating to the marketing of adventure tourism. First, we have seen that it is a complex activity that is complicated by the characteristics of both the product and the market. Second, we have noted that brochures will play a crucial role in promoting adventure tourism products. Third, we have seen that the Internet is playing a growing role in adventure tourism marketing. Finally, we have seen that destination marketing adds a new level of complexity to adventure tourism marketing.

Discussion points and exercises

1 Discuss the suggestion that adventure tourism marketing is more complex than marketing in other sectors of tourism.
2 Discuss the advantages and disadvantages of the Internet as a marketing tool in adventure tourism.
3 Critically evaluate the view that psychographic segmentation is more important than other segmentation techniques in adventure tourism.
4 Select an adventure tourism organization and critically evaluate its use of the marketing mix.

8

Risk management

Introduction

With a series of widely publicized incidents in recent years, risk management has become a major issue for organizations involved in all areas of adventure tourism – including adventure sports centres, specialist tour operators and trekking companies. At the same time, these organizations cannot eliminate the risk and also need to recognize that the risk itself is part of the motivation for most adventure tourists.

However, for adventure tourism organizations the failure to manage risk effectively can have four related, negative consequences, as we can see from Figure 8.1.

In this chapter we will consider three aspects of the issue of risk management:

1 Risk management in a particular sector of physical adventure tourism, namely, mountain

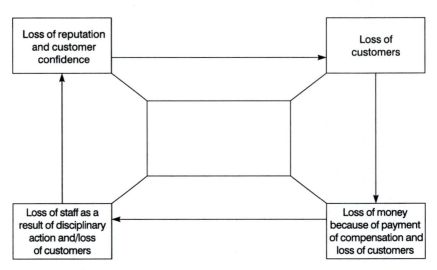

Figure 8.1   The negative consequences of inadequate risk management.

tourism. This section focuses on the duties of operators involved in this sector, and concludes with general comments on the nature of risk that are also relevant to the rest of the chapter

2 Risk management and independent physical adventure tourism

3 The concept of risk management in non-physical adventure tourism.

The final section of the chapter covers the issue of crisis management.

Risk management and mountain adventure tourism

It is generally recognized that risk is a key feature of most adventure tourism activities. Some people, who would undoubtedly be classified into the hard adventure category, thrive from this element of risk and its associated 'highs' caused by adrenaline rushing through their bodies and minds. Others enjoy a certain level of risk in their adventures, although some degree of perceived control is essential to their overall enjoyment of the experience. It is important to recognize, however, that participants in adventure recreation or tourism accept these risks, to a lesser or greater extent, as an integral part of the destination's environment because they have a strong desire to be in this type of environment. Suppliers of adventure tourism need to ensure that a fine balance is maintained between exposing their clients to risk and managing this risk so that the latter do not become victims as a consequence of their participation.

Simply by noting some of the fatal accidents that have occurred over the past few years we can see the need for risk management in adventure tourism. Take, for example, the deaths on two commercial expeditions to Everest on 10 May 1996 (Krakauer, 1997); the death of a porter in Nepal in 1996 (Duff, 1998); the 21 deaths in the Swiss canyoning accident on 27 July 1999 (Dodd, 1999); and the death of a teenage girl on Mount Kinabalu in 2001. Indeed the necessity for risk management throughout the entire tourism industry is important, as 'the increased volume of global tourism activity has combined with the attractiveness of high risk exotic destinations to expose tourists to greater levels of risk' (Faulkner, 2001).

On the general theme of why accidents happen, some academics adopt a human psychology approach to causation – such as Reason's (1990) study of human error and his development of the generic modelling system. In contrast, others take an organizational approach. For instance, Turner (1979, 1994) accepts that accidents are often sparked by a technical failure, but believes that they are amplified by the institutional, administrative and organizational context within which they occur. Whilst theorists have sought to understand why accidents happen, the real task of risk management is to develop strategies to prevent or minimize these for individual organizations.

Although a body of literature exists on the generic theme of risk management, research into the use of this management technique within the tourism industry and more specifically within the adventure travel sector is sparser. However, there are several useful studies that have contributed knowledge to risk management in tourism. For instance, Hollman and Forrest (1991) developed a model to explain risk management in service companies (tourism is a service industry *par excellence*) on the basis that 'risk management involves the protection of a firm's assets and profits'. The model is a five-stage process involving the discovery of loss exposure, the evaluation of loss exposure, operational techniques, implementation of strategy, and monitoring. Risk-management strategies are divided into two broad categories: 'operational techniques' are measures that reduce loss exposure, for example fire-fighting equipment; and 'financing techniques' aim to minimize the effects of loss on a business, for instance transferring the financial consequences of loss to an insurer.

Though Faulkner (2001) acknowledges the vulnerability of tourism to natural disasters and terrorism, he argues that 'few tourism organizations at the enterprise or destination level have properly developed disaster strategies as an integral part of their business plans'. He proposes a 'tourism disaster management framework that involves formulating disaster contingency plans based on risk assessment of both potential disasters and the probability of their occurrence'.

In an attempt to determine appropriate risk management strategies for tourist scuba-diving operations, Wilks and Davis (2000) developed a risk evaluation matrix (see Figure 8.2). The matrix entails four components: risk retention is the assumption or acceptance of loss by the operator; risk transfer is the use of insurance to cover infrequent but potentially costly accidents; risk reduction is the adoption of 'best practice' to keep the likelihood of accidents to a minimum; and risk avoidance is achieved by eliminating those activities that are too risky from the operators' product portfolio.

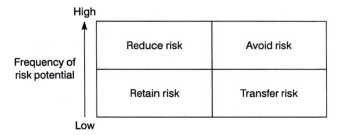

Figure 8.2 Risk evaluation matrix (Wilks and Davis, 2000: 595).

The conclusion that Morgan (2000) draws from an investigation into white-water rafting in New Zealand is that operators target an optimal safety level through an assessment of the desired level of risk. The assessment involves numerous criteria, including the technical abilities of employees, the standard and type of equipment used, the physical location of the activity, and legal obligations. Operators have to 'estimate the level of actual control that participants will require to meet the actual risks from the physical hazards to be encountered'. Furthermore, operators have some influence over the client's perception of risk; guides can talk the risks up to make the experience seem more exciting or talk them down to avoid over-arousal and subsequent loss of control by the clients. Clients can enjoy an optimal adventure experience so long as the operator understands clients' expectations and their perceived levels of risk in the activity.

Priest and Gass (1997) examined risk management in outdoor education – a sector that is closely linked to adventure tourism. They view risk management as the:

... policies, practices and procedures used ... to appropriately address potential personal injury and financial losses, protecting [the] adventure organization from the economic cost of being sued and reducing [the] organization's financial obligation if a suit is successful.

They argue that accidents are a result of the interaction between environmental dangers, objective hazards that arise from the local environment, and human dangers – subjective perils within human control. To illustrate this, consider an alpine ascent where objective dangers exist in the form of crevasses. High temperatures cause these ice formations to be less stable, resulting in a greater accident potential. This can be reduced by crossing the danger zone at night when temperatures are lowest. The authors propose a ten-step plan for assessing dangers in outdoor education environments (see Table 8.1), although these procedures are not always adhered to due to a

Table 8.1 Procedure for analysing dangers (Priest and Gass, 1997)

Step	Explanation
1 Plan ahead	Recognize that accidents will happen; pre-plan
2 Identify dangers	Be continuously aware of dangerous situations and conditions
3 Point out potential dangers	Ensure that all group members are aware of the existence of potential dangers once identified
4 When appropriate, remove elements that contribute to dangerous situations	If warning does not adequately deal with the danger, remove it as long as it does not increase risk
5 Avoid dangerous situations	Change pre-planned activity or route to safer alternative if possible
6 Identify and classify dangerous situations	What are the perils and hazards? How can hazards be minimized?
7 Assess risk and re-classify danger	Are the dangers environmental or human?
8 Estimate potential losses	What are the number and strength of dangers?
9 Minimize losses	Adopt course of action that keeps the accident outcome as acceptable and recoverable as possible
10 Make appropriate adjustments	Adopt pre-planned accident countermeasures

number of inhibiting factors. These include: the unfamiliarity of new or unexpected situations, 'smelling the barn' (i.e. the rush to get home when the activity is nearly complete), and a relaxation of concentration caused by fatigue, carelessness or over-familiarity.

The four risk management strategies identified in the risk evaluation matrix by Wilks and Davis (2000; Figure 8.2) are similarly employed by Priest and Gass. They view litigation as a key consideration for outdoor education providers, in which liability is defined as 'the degree of legal responsibility or obligation that people or programmes have for repairing damages (often by paying money) for injuries to participants' (Priest and Gass, 1997: 124). In the context of mountain adventure tourism, the tort of negligence is the most applicable – i.e. 'unintentional breach of legal duty causing damage reasonably foreseeable without which breach the damage would not have occurred' (Van der Smissen, 1990; quoted in Priest and Gass, 1997). However, providers can avoid lawsuits through adopting various measures. One measure is to aim to prevent the accident in the first place by having proper safety procedures. This would act as a good defence should a case arise, illustrating to courts that the operation was conducted professionally. Another defence is to inform clients fully of the potential risks and likelihood of accidents involved in the adventure activity. Priest and Gass conclude that a post-accident strategy is paramount to effective risk management. This should include such measures as first aid, evacuation procedures and keeping accurate records of incidents.

Brown (1999) also approaches risk management from an outdoor education perspective. His Adventure REACT model (see Figure 8.3) involves 'the recognition, evaluation, adjustment, choice and tracking phases of risk management', and the associated risk-management strategies are again based on retention, reduction, avoidance and transferral of risk. Brown stresses the need for an effective 'critical incident management plan' that should address staff responsibilities and tasks, communication protocols, first aid and rescue procedures, evacuation policies, and procedures for fatality management. However, he accepts that 'safety cannot necessarily be guaranteed by a set of rigid standards' due to the fact that objective dangers exist that are difficult to control. In essence, no matter how good the risk management plan is it is impossible to avoid every single risk.

In the same vein, Cloutier (2000) affirms that risk is an innate component of all adventure activities and hence risk management 'is about managing or optimizing risk' rather than abolishing it completely. There-fore, for the activity to remain adventurous the risk management process

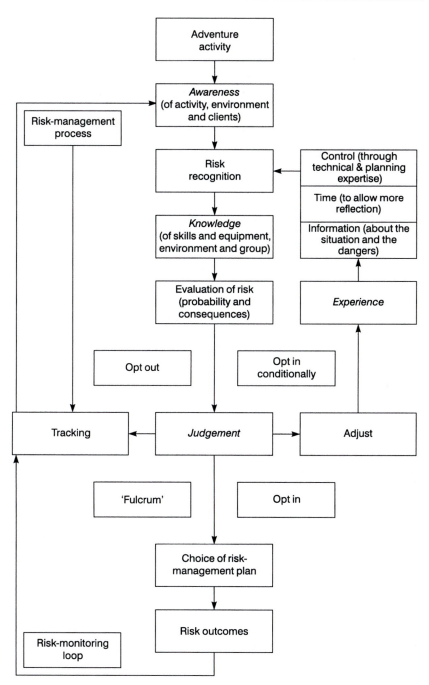

Source: Brown 1999

Figure 8.3 Adventure-REACT model of managing risk.

needs to determine acceptable exposure levels for clients and operators alike, identify risks, select suitable risk-management strategies, implement these, and make the appropriate responses to incidents. Cloutier (1998, 2000) divides risk management strategies into two broad approaches. Risk control concerns the decision not to undertake a trip or activity due to the high risk involved. It also refers to risk-reduction measures such as client briefings and increasing instructional ratios for activities considered of greater risk. Risk financing follows on from risk control, and involves both risk retention and risk transfer. He recommends the preparation of an 'emergency response plan' (Cloutier, 1998: 1–2) for each trip, comprising risk management objectives, identification of hazards, evaluation of hazards, risk-management strategies, incident response strategies, action plan and controls. A number of techniques can be used to ascertain hazards – for example, site inspections and hazard checklists. In evaluating hazards, providers should examine the frequency and severity of their occurrence and consequently 'assign a high, medium, low priority to each, and create strategies to mitigate their effects' (Cloutier, 1998: 7). The incident response strategy should clearly set out the roles and responsibilities within the organization in the case of an incident, considering such factors as identifying the staff member who would mobilize and activate the incident response strategy.

A model of risk management

Whilst the aforementioned studies provide clear guidelines on what adventure operators should do in terms of their risk management strategies, only a limited amount of actual primary research has been conducted in this field. Cloutier's (1998) work, for instance, is written from the perspective of advising his students as to which methods they should adopt. In a bid to ascertain how the risk management process operates in practice, Hibbert (2001) conducted an investigation into the mountain adventure tourism sector. He undertook a series of in-depth interviews with tour operators who offered mountain adventure products, and in addition sought the views of the governing body of British mountaineering, the British Mountaineering Council (BMC). A model of 'risk management practice in mountain adventure tourism' emerged from these primary findings (see Figure 8.4). The model incorporates contemporary viewpoints drawn from risk management literature, and details specific risk management strategies that mountain adventure tourism operators employ in practice. A broad overview of the interview results and recommendations is presented here.

A model of risk management

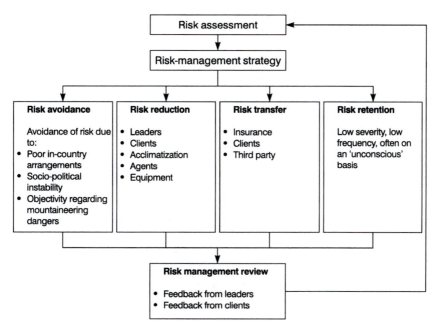

Figure 8.4 Model of risk management practice in mountain adventure tourism (after British Mountaineering Council).

Risk assessment

All operators considered the elements of risk involved in their adventure products at the trip planning stage. At the same time, it was recognized that unforeseen risks could occur on a day-to-day basis throughout the trips. Hibbert (2001) concluded that most mountain adventure risk management is conducted during the actual trips rather than in the company's office beforehand. Some operators assessed risk through reconnaissance trips to the destination. As one operator explained, 'it's the first-hand experience that proves how much of a risk the trip is likely to be'. Hibbert advocates the implementation of formal written risk management planning, based on Cloutier's (2000) argument that it 'forces the business manager to think through individual and corporate philosophies, acceptable procedures and legal-liability ramifications'.

The model incorporates the four risk management strategies identified in previous research:

1 *Risk avoidance.* Operators employ this strategy when there are poor in-country arrangements, socio-political instability at the destination, or

objective mountaineering dangers. The latter hazards are specific to mountain environments and are usually beyond a person's control. An example of this can be seen in one of the operator's trips to Naya Kanga, where the higher than normal temperatures and lack of snow cover led to an increased objective danger of stone fall to a level that was deemed unacceptable. Risk avoidance can also be achieved through offering a trip in an alternative format. For example, one operator offers a trip to the Karakorum region of Pakistan, visiting the site of the K2 base camp and crossing the high pass of the Gondor La, while most companies offer this trek by ascending the Baltoro Glacier and then crossing the pass and dropping into the Huche Valley. The first operator goes the other way round due to the risk of stone fall in the pass. Ascending from the Huche Valley increases the chances of getting over the pass early in the morning whilst the rocks on the surrounding slopes are still frozen in place, thus reducing the objective danger.

2 *Risk reduction.* Operators utilize a number of risk reduction strategies. They look for trek leaders who have appropriate qualifications, as qualifications serve as an indication that leaders have a minimum level of experience and have undertaken some formal training in practical mountaineering skills and party management. Leaders also need to be mentally robust enough to make unpopular decisions to ensure the safety of their clients. In Hibbert's research, operators stressed the importance of clients choosing the right trip in accordance with their experience, skills etc. This was achieved through requesting clients to provide an outline of their experience before booking the trip. Some operators also assessed their clients' capabilities during the early part of a trip before committing to the main objective. In addition, operators assigned grades to their trips, to assist clients in making the correct choice. However, Hibbert notes that no uniform system of grading is available, and hence clients may face problems when comparing the holiday products of one company against another. As many mountain adventure tourism activities involve clients being at high altitude, an acclimatization programme is necessary to reduce the risk of altitude sickness. Operators stressed that trips should be of an adequate length to ensure clients' acclimatization. Local agents were seen as key to risk reduction, and whilst some operators had established good working relationships with these companies over several years they also noted difficulties in finding agents in whom they had complete confidence when breaking into new destinations.

3 *Risk transfer.* The transfer of risk from the operator to others is a key method used in managing risk (Hollman and Forest, 1991; Priest and Gass, 1997; Wilks and Davis, 2000). In Hibbert's study, operators identified three ways

in which risks were transferred out: to the operators' own insurers, to the clients, and to third parties. Transferring risk to insurance companies is the main method used, and operators must hold public liability insurance as a legal requirement. All operators encouraged clients to recognize the risks involved in any particular trip. For instance, in the booking conditions one operator states: 'Please understand that there are certain hazards involved in climbing expeditions, which you must accept at your own risk. The company will not be liable for any illness, injury or death sustained during an expedition, nor will it be liable for any uninsured losses of your property'. On the issue of transferring risk to third parties, operators used different measures. For instance, one company did not transfer any risks to third parties whilst another transferred some risk to its local agents indirectly through imposing financial penalties if a trip had serious problems.

4 *Risk retention.* Risk retention occurs where risk is not transferred to others and is accepted deliberately, either unconsciously or owing to the inability to transfer it to others (Cloutier, 1998). It usually covers those risks that are low in both severity and frequency (Wilks and Davis, 2000). Risk retention did not seem to form a major part of the risk management strategies of operators. Hibbert notes that operators may take risks on unconsciously, for example one operator commented that some risk in loss of equipment was 'part and parcel' of the operation. This would explain the lack of risk retention strategies.

Hibbert also investigated how operators deal with the issues of litigation and emergency planning. The importance of having a strategy to avoid litigation was recognized by operators. As one operator commented, 'you can't get into this game without accepting at some point someone may possibly sue you or there may be a problem that may require a call on your professional indemnity insurance'. Three methods of dealing with litigation emerged: the avoidance of accidents through risk management strategies, a willingness to settle small claims out of court if it was felt the client had a case, and financial protection from the consequences of litigation through insurance. Emergency plans differed according to the destinations, but were greatly affected by local conditions. The contrast between Nepal (where helicopter rescue was fairly advanced) and Bolivia and Mongolia (where such facilities were minimal or non-existent) was made by operators. This meant that local agents who could advise on the necessary arrangements were particularly important.

Risk management review
The risk management review forms the final component of the model. Within any management system, a feedback loop that allows operations to be

reviewed and procedures and policies to be modified in the light of experience is vital. Some operators stated that it was a formal requirement for their leaders to submit a written report at the end of each trip as part of their contracts, whilst others used a verbal reporting format. Client questionnaires were also completed post-trip by a number of operators and, whilst no specific safety comments were requested, all operators felt that any concerns would be brought up.

Risk management and independent physical adventure tourism

The previous section focuses on mountain tourism that is largely group-based and involves commercial and not-for-profit operators offering services to mountain adventure tourists. However, a major component of physical adventure tourism is independent travel rather than being organized by specialist operators. Individuals or groups make their own arrangements and are therefore also responsible for their own risk management.

If we imagine a group of friends who want to take a trip heli-skiing in the Caucasus Mountains, the potential risks they face are many and varied, including:

■ Financial risks if, for example, they book their travel before they obtain a visa, then discover they will not get visas and cannot claim a reimbursement of their travel costs
■ Health risks in terms of disease (such as diphtheria), illness (such as food poisoning) or injury
■ Safety risks, such as travelling in inadequately maintained helicopters in difficult terrain, or kidnapping by terrorist groups.

They will endeavour to manage this risk as best they can by:

■ Reducing the risks where possible – for instance, they may consult guidebooks, government embassies and websites to gain information that will help them be better prepared for their trip
■ Putting plans in place to ensure that if the worst does happen, the damage is minimal – this may, for example, involve purchasing specialist medical insurance that guarantees evacuation by air in the event of an accident on the slopes.

As in any risk management situation, our group of intrepid skiers will need to balance the benefits of taking such actions with the financial and time costs involved. This means they will need to carry out an evaluation of the chance that a particular risk will become a reality against the severity of the consequences if it does happen.

To reduce the risk while maintaining the predominantly independent quality of the tourism experience, they may hire a local guide for part of their time in the Caucasus. On the other hand, they may relish the idea of the riskiness of endeavouring to take a trip where they are wholly reliant on their own abilities.

Whatever approach they take, they will also need to develop their own formal (or more likely informal) guidelines covering the responsibilities of each group member towards fellow travellers in terms of the management of risk. Will they make a group decision, for instance, to avoid particularly dangerous slopes, or will each individual member make an individual choice? If the latter, will the individual concerned expect the others to attempt a rescue if anything goes wrong?

It is easy to try to answer such questions while sitting at home planning such a trip, but it is very different when tourists are on the slopes, with the adrenaline pulsing through their veins!

The concept of risk management in non-physical adventure tourism

Most analysis of risk in adventure tourism focuses on physical adventure tourism. However, not all adventure tourism is physical in nature, and nor are the risks of adventure tourism always physical. Table 8.2 endeavours to illustrate this point by looking at different types of non-physical adventure tourism, the risks involved, and how tourists can seek to manage these risks.

The risks identified in Table 8.2 are, of course, in addition to the normal risks involved in all travel.

It must also be recognized that in any situations there will be those who perceive no risks and accordingly practise no approach to risk management at all. At the same time, we must note that the division between physical and non-physical adventure tourism and risks is largely artificial. In most cases adventure tourism has both physical and non-physical elements, and the risks associated with it are of both types too. For example, a young female backpacker travelling through South-East Asia faces both physical risks (attack or illness) and non-physical risks (verbal sexual harassment and the constant attention of beggars).

Table 8.2 The risks involved in non-physical adventure tourism

Type of adventure tourism	Nature of risk	Approaches to risk management
1 Hedonistic tourism	■ Sexually transmitted diseases ■ Alcohol poisoning ■ Getting involved in fighting ■ Arrest by the police for bad behaviour	■ Don't care; will take no precautions and will deal with problems only if and when they arise ■ Go with friends for mutual support ■ Take precautions such as using contraception in the event of indulging in casual sex
2 Travelling to another country to study	■ Could fail due to lack of knowledge of other country's language and learning culture, with resulting loss of face ■ Possible inability to integrate into host community/potential rejection by fellow students	■ Careful choice of country and educational institution, which may mean choosing a country with the same language ■ Prepare for the study abroad by improving language skills ■ Make a concentrated effort to fit into the host culture
3 Gambling tourism	■ Losing more money than one can afford ■ Becoming the victim of criminals	■ Only take a certain amount of money ■ Only go with friends who can offer support or control your behaviour ■ Avoid particularly risky casinos or neighbourhoods
4 Travelling in search of spiritual enlightenment	■ The experience could, in extreme cases, lead to psychological problems and a sense of isolation from your own family, community and background ■ The chance of perhaps losing money to 'charlatans'	■ You may not see any potential risk ■ Choose to travel with others for mutual support ■ Only visit places with established reputations
5 Travelling to learn a new skill, such as cookery or craft-making	■ You may dislike the activity and therefore gain little benefit from the expenditure of time and money	■ Choose a skill you already have some interest in ■ Only choose a vacation package that is recommended by acquaintances, guidebooks or professional bodies

Having looked at the nature of risk, it is now time to move on to the associated subject of crisis management.

Crisis management

Crisis management is about what happens when the risk becomes reality. It is always better to develop crisis management plans in advance of the crisis, rather than managing it in an *ad hoc* manner in the 'heat of the moment'.

Organizations such as specialist tour operators need crisis management plans for all foreseeable emergencies. These should be written down and communicated to all staff so that when a crisis occurs everyone knows exactly what to do. The plan should, for example, say what will happen in the event of the drowning of a client on a white-water rafting trip, including:

- Who will inform the relatives and how
- Whether the press will be informed and, if so, what will be said and who will say it
- How the authorities will be informed of the event and by whom
- Whether the trip should continue or be terminated immediately for all participants
- What communication should take place with other clients on the same trip, and what counselling should be made available to them.

All the relevant information (key telephone numbers, etc.) should be in an easily accessible crisis management file.

Crisis management is a specialist field in its own right, but some general rules can perhaps be elucidated, such as:

- Staff who have been directly involved in the tragedy should *not* talk to the media, as they are too emotionally involved
- Only one trained, experienced spokesperson should speak on behalf of the company
- No speculation should be entered into about possible causes of the tragedy before a full enquiry has taken place
- No suggestion of liability should be even hinted at before the completion of the aforementioned enquiry.

Even individual and independent adventure travellers need informal crisis management plans – ideas of what they will do if things go wrong. For many travellers, this may simply be calling their insurance company, friends or parents!

For many adventure tourists, dealing with a crisis or potential crisis enhances their enjoyment of a trip. On the other hand, failing to deal with it can ultimately ruin the trip or have even more tragic consequences.

Summary

In this chapter we have looked at a number of aspects of the issue of risks in adventure tourism, where the desire to experience risk is often a motivator for trips. A range of different approaches to risk have been discussed, including risk avoidance and risk reduction, as well as the question of risk assessment and risk evaluation. Finally, it has been noted that when risk becomes reality then crisis management comes to the fore.

In recent years, the question of risk has become a major ethical debate in adventure tourism. It is therefore appropriate that we should now move on to focus on the ethical challenges faced in the field of adventure tourism.

Discussion points and exercises

1 Discuss the value of the Risk Evaluation Matrix, illustrated in Figure 8.2, for adventure tourists and the adventure tourism industry.
2 Develop a crisis management plan for a tour operator engaged in organizing treks to remote mountain regions.
3 Carry out a survey of a small number of people who engage in adventure tourism to see how they perceive risk, and whether they follow the model shown in Table 8.1.
4 Discuss the contention that a high level of risk is an essential prerequisite for all adventure experiences.

9

Ethical issues in adventure tourism

Introduction

Well-publicized tragedies such as the deaths of
Nepalese porters on Himalayan expeditions, and
the controversy over whether people should risk
their lives to rescue adventure tourists who get
into difficulties, illustrate one dimension of the
ethical issues involved in the field. However, the
range of ethical concerns in adventure tourism is
bewildering.

The scope and nature of ethical issues

The scope and nature of these ethical issues is
clearly demonstrated by Figure 9.1, which presents a number of typologies of ethical issues in
adventure tourism.

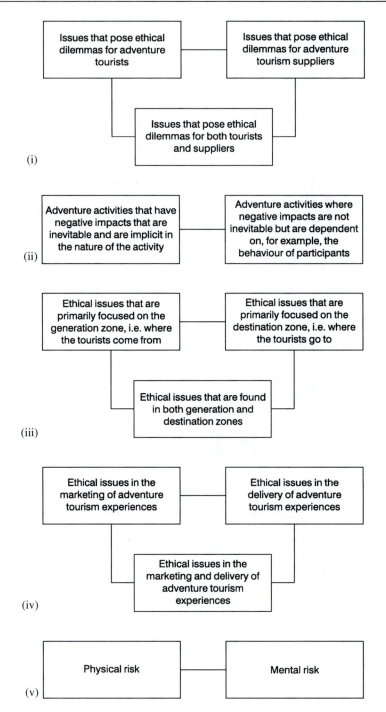

Figure 9.1   Typologies of ethical issues in adventure tourism.

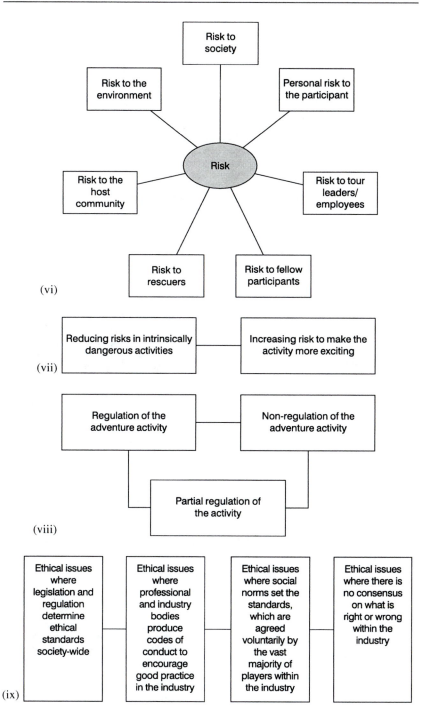

Figure 9.1 Continued.

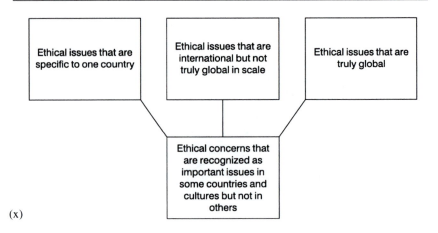

(x)

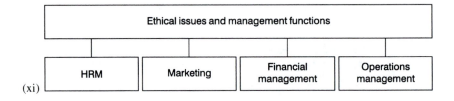

(xi)

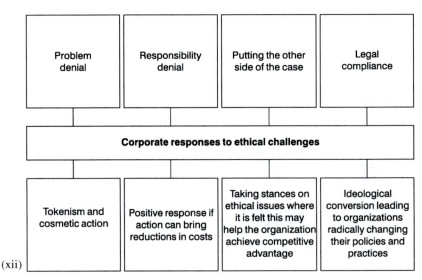

(xii)

Figure 9.1 Continued.

It is clear from this set of typologies that ethical issues in adventure tourism can be divided into sub-types based on various criteria, including:

- Who is affected by the issue – in other words tourists, including (for example) organizations or host communities in destinations
- The geographical area where the issue exists, whether it be the destination or the tourist's own area
- Issues that are highly localized against those that are national or international
- Ethical concerns that relate to management facilities, such as marketing
- A number of issues based on the theme of risk and risk management
- The degree and nature of state regulation of markets and activities.

These typologies clearly illustrate what we suspect is already clear to any reader – that ethics is a complex, broad subject. This fact is also clear from the following diverse examples of ethical issues in adventure tourism:

- The morality of affluent tourists from developed countries visiting developing countries as adventure playgrounds
- The apparent way in which many people with disabilities are discriminated against in many aspects of adventure tourism
- The debate over ecotourism and whether or not it is harmful or beneficial for the destination
- The level and type of expectation raised by the marketing of adventure tourism products
- The management of risk in waterparks
- The problems caused by backpackers travelling in remote areas whose cultures they do not really understand
- The level of wages paid to adventure tourism industry employees, and discrimination on the grounds of age, sex or race, for example.

There are three other important points to be made about the question of ethics in adventure tourism. First, ethics are in the 'eye of the beholder' in that each individual has an opinion on which constitutes an ethical dilemma, as well as personal views on the dilemmas. These opinions and views are a result of a person's unique personal circumstances in terms of personality, life experience, education, parental influences and cultural background. Second, the views of every individual on ethical issues are continuously being affected by external influences, including:

1 The media, which highlights particular issues – often in a sensationalized manner

2 Pressure groups, which may often present issues in a biased way (consciously or unconsciously) to further their particular interests

3 Professional bodies, which often play down ethical concerns to reduce the risk of government intervention, or take action on particular issues to improve the image of the industry as a whole

4 Governments, which may choose to tackle issues that they think will be of most interest to voters.

The third point to be made follows on from this. All four of the external influences noted are highly subjective and political in their approach to any ethical issue in adventure tourism – rarely does a newspaper article or a pressure group publication attempt to give a balanced, even-handed account of any issue. This can lead to issues being seen, crudely and unrealistically, as being polarized between good and bad, right or wrong. Yet in many countries some things that are criticized by pressure groups and the Western media are traditional, deep-seated elements in the culture of the indigenous people. For example, in many Western countries all hunting trips are seen as wrong, but for some poor residents in inhospitable environments hunting is part of their everyday life, and hunting tourism may be their only viable means of employment.

However, there are sections of 'adventure tourism' where virtually everyone is agreed that the type of tourism is intrinsically unethical and immoral. Perhaps the most important example of this phenomenon is sex tourism involving children. Men travelling to Asia and other regions for such sex will even risk criminal prosecution to indulge in this perverted form of adventure tourism.

Corporate responses to ethical challenges

Much criticism of adventure tourism (as with all tourism) in terms of ethical issues tends to focus on the activities of commercial enterprises within the sector. They may be accused of everything from risking the lives of their employees and customers to paying their staff badly, causing environmental problems through their products and so on.

When faced with criticism of their actions on ethical grounds, companies in the field may adapt one of a number of approaches. Some of these are shown in part (xii) of Figure 9.1.

We can illustrate these potential responses with a hypothetical case study. Let us imagine a small tour operator who offers ecotourism adventures in a

Table 9.1   Corporate responses to ethical challenge

Response	Example
Problem denial	'Our tours cause no problems, they are small scale and our clients are sensitive and careful not to cause any damage'
Responsibility denial	'Yes we know there are some problems with such tours, but they are caused by the lack of government action on conservation and visitor development, together with the lack of a proper infrastructure'
Putting the other side of the case	'We know such tours can cause environmental damage, but on the other hand we employ local guides who otherwise would have no job or income'
Legal compliance	'In running these tours we are doing nothing wrong, they are perfectly legal'
Tokenism and cosmetic action	'We do our bit for the local community by donating £1 for every client to a nature conservation voluntary group in the rainforest'
Cost reduction	'We are going to make more use of the Internet rather than brochures in our marketing to save paper' (and money!)
Competitive advantage	'We will no longer take clients to village X because it is overcrowded with tourists taken there by our competitors, who are not behaving as responsibly as us'
Ideological conversion	'Wow – we had never thought about it like that before. We'll stop offering these tours from today'

South American rainforest destination. People criticize the operator's activities because of the effects tourism will have on the rainforest. The operator could respond as in Table 9.1 – although, perhaps not surprisingly, the final response is very rare!

The responsibilities of the adventure tourist

As well as industry taking its fair share of responsibility for the ethical issues in adventure tourism, it is important that the consumers or tourists should also do so. After all, it is tourists' desires that lead to the development of different adventure tourism products, and it is the tourists who have the power to make or break enterprises. Furthermore, sometimes it is the behaviour of the tourists themselves that can cause problems. Tourists can, for example, exploit staff through their demands, while ignorance of local custom can lead to offence being caused in the host community.

Every year the activity of irresponsible adventure tourists cause the deaths of fellow tourists through accidents.

Figure 9.2 puts forward an ideal model for ensuring that tourists behave responsibly and ethically.

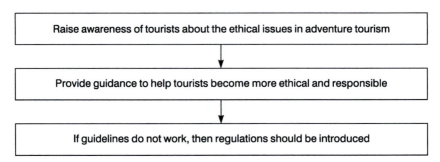

Figure 9.2 A process for ensuring adventure tourists behave more ethically.

The problem is that behaving more responsibly or ethically is not a high priority for many adventure tourists because:

■ Some forms of adventure tourism, such as hedonistic tourism, have irresponsibility as a major motivator – the opportunity to behave outrageously
■ For many tourists, holidays are the one time of the year when people feel they do not have to behave responsibly or worry about ethical issues.

It seems, therefore, that regulation may be the only answer where tourists are required to behave responsibly. Clearly the case of child sex tourism shows us that sometimes regulation is the only way to tackle unethical tourist behaviour, and even then it can be an uphill task!

Evidence from many areas of life leads us to believe that public sector campaigns to change the behaviour of the public have only limited success. People who feel they are being lectured do tend to rebel. That is why this idea of writing brochures to 'educate' adventure tourists to be more ethical is probably naive. Instead, perhaps, behaviour will only change if and when the media, which is now massively influential in the tourism market, begins to take this issue seriously.

The impacts of adventure tourism

Like all forms of tourism, adventure tourism has three main impacts – economic, environmental, and social. Most research has focused on the impact tourism has on the destination and the host community. However, the economic and social impacts are also seen, to a lesser extent, in the country of origin of the tourist through the jobs created in the tour operations and equipment suppliers, as well as in the impact it has on the tourists themselves. This section focuses mainly on the destination.

Economic impacts

The economic impacts of adventure tourism are illustrated in Figure 9.3.

Some figures from *Travel and Tourism Intelligence Reports* published in 2000 illustrate the economic value of adventure tourism:

- The US domestic adventure travel market is an estimated US$25 billion, based on figures of participation rates and average spending per trip
- Hotels earned around US$16 million from the carnival in Rio in 1998
- Tourism in Brazil, much of which is based on different kinds of adventure, earned US$3.7 billion in foreign earnings for the country in 1998

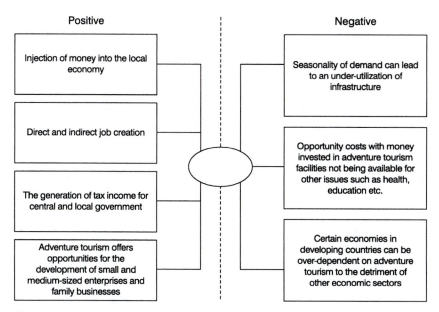

Figure 9.3 The economic impacts of adventure tourism.

- The skiing industry in New Zealand is worth approximately NZ$43 million per annum
- Zambia, whose tourism industry is largely based on adventure travel, aims to be earning some US$171 million from tourism by 2004 – double the figure achieved in 1998.

Overall it appears that the economic impact is positive in most destinations, although there is always the potential problem of 'leakages', particularly in developing countries, where the industry is dominated by 'foreign' enterprises.

However, the economic impact of adventure tourism is not limited to the destinations. The equipment suppliers, who are not usually based in the destination, represent a valuable economic sector in their own right. Individual items of gear or clothing often cost hundreds (and sometimes thousands) of pounds. Globally, those who supply the adventure tourism industry must generate hundreds of millions of pounds for their national economies.

Environmental impacts

Adventure tourism often involves direct contact with the physical environment – indeed, this environment is often the main attraction for the adventure tourist. It can be argued that adventure tourism has had a positive impact on environmental conservation, because it has given the environment a monetary value and destinations a financial incentive for conservation. However, adventure tourism has had many negative impacts on the environment around the world, in a number of ways:

- The development of facilities for activities can cause problems – for example, the construction of ski slopes causes deforestation and can increase the danger of avalanches
- The leaving of waste that is not biodegradable is a phenomenon that is now even seen on Mount Everest!
- Some activities involve causing damage to the environment, such as climbing with artificial aids (where metal pegs are hammered into the rock)
- High-volume safari tourism can disrupt both the feeding and breeding patterns of the animals
- Diving can irretrievably damage coral reefs
- Visiting places where man does not normally live, such as Antarctica, introduces alien influences that disturb the fragile balance of the ecosystem.

It is difficult to argue that the environmental impact of adventure tourism outside cities is not overwhelmingly negative. A prime motivator in adventure tourism is often the desire to get 'off the beaten track' and away from other tourists, and this means that this form of tourism spreads its negative impacts over a relatively wide geographical area. On the other hand, in purely environmental terms urban-based adventure tourism is relatively low impact as the urban environment is much more resilient and less fragile.

Social impacts

Many adventure tourists from so-called developed countries visit places where populations are from much less privileged backgrounds and very different cultures. This can cause all sorts of problems and negative impacts. For example:

- Tourists can behave in ways which local people find offensive. For example, in Indonesia backpackers tend to dress skimpily and often expose their 'belly buttons'; this is very fashionable in Europe and Australasia, but is highly offensive to local people as this part of the body has great spiritual significance in their religion.
- Tourists can introduce 'bad habits' to the local population, such as drug taking.
- Tourists can become role models for local young people because they are perceived to come from 'advanced' countries. The copying of the habits of the tourists by the young people can cause tension within families.
- Sex tourism causes, or at least perpetuates, health problems and individual suffering within destinations.
- Adventure tourists, with their apparent greater wealth than the locals, may unwittingly stimulate an increase in crime
- Tourists giving local people gifts and money may also encourage a culture of begging, which will harm the ability of the community to develop economically.

However, adventure tourism can have a positive social impact on the destination. Some tourists in developing countries take volunteer holidays, where they work free of charge on conservation or aid projects. The growth of tourism can sometimes also lead to recognition of the need to improve education for local people. At the same time tourism can provide job opportunities, particularly for women and young people. It also provides a relatively low-cost way to develop small, locally owned businesses, such as guiding.

It is clear that the social impacts of adventure tourism are both positive and negative, and that they affect both urban areas and non-urban areas.

Social impacts of adventure tourism on the tourist

For many adventure tourists their trip is just like any other holiday; it allows them to have fun and recharge their batteries so they can carry on with their daily lives. However, in some cases their trip can have a profound impact on the tourists. For example:

- For some, such as backpackers to India and other Asian countries, it can result in them questioning everything about their life and maybe changing their lifestyle or religion or both
- It can be the beginning of a new hobby or even obsession that will last for the rest of their lives; such as snowboarding, micro-light flying or scuba-diving
- Seeing wildlife in its natural habitat can make them become actively involved in conservation when they return home
- Seeing new and exciting places may mean that tourists take these new influences back into their homes, from food to clothes to styles of decoration and furniture.

Clearly, the impact on the tourist will depend on the type of adventure tourism experience undertaken. However, while these impacts are generally positive they can be a problem, with the tourist feeling out of place or dissatisfied on returning home.

The future

The adventure tourism sector clearly provides examples of a wide range of ethical issues, and in relation to tourism generally these issues can be viewed in terms of three types:

1 Issues seen in adventure tourism but not generally in other forms of tourism, such as unsafe behaviour on ski slopes or rock faces
2 Issues that are similar to those seen in tourism in general, for instance economic impacts
3 Issues that are much less important in adventure tourism than in other forms of tourism, such as traffic congestion.

Looking to the future, new ethical issues may emerge as adventure tourism develops in different ways, including:

- The growth of adventure tourism in new 'destinations' and 'venues', such as space, the Antarctic and underwater 'resorts'
- The development of outbound adventure tourism from different countries and cultures, notably China, India and Latin America
- The rise of new forms of adventure tourism that cannot yet be predicted.

What we can predict with confidence is that adventure tourism will continue to provide examples of a wide range of complex ethical challenges.

Summary

We have seen that adventure tourism has both positive and negative impacts on destinations. It seems that in general, the economic impacts are positive and the environmental impacts are negative while the social impacts are a mixture of good and bad. It has also been noted that the impacts are usually more marked in rural areas and wilderness zones than they are in urban areas. At the same time, it seems clear that the impacts are more significant when the destination is a developing, rather than a so-called developed, country.

Some tourism commentators have agreed that adventure tourism is a relatively low (negative) impact form of tourism because it is often smaller scale than mass-market beach tourism, for instance. However, this view is open to criticism because:

- Adventure tourism often involves people travelling off the beaten track into fragile environments and/or communities that are socially vulnerable
- Small-scale adventure tourism destinations today tend to become mass-market destinations tomorrow, as the message about them spreads – this has been seen everywhere, but notably with the safari destinations in Kenya.

We need a better understanding of the impacts of adventure tourism if we are to manage its development more effectively.

Discussion points and exercises

1 Critically evaluate the typologies of ethical issues illustrated in Figure 9.1.
2 Discuss the circumstances in which organizations may utilize the different strategies outlined in Figure 9.1, part xii.
3 Discuss the relative responsibilities of tourists, the industry and governments for making adventure tourism more ethical.
4 Select an adventure tourism destination and analyse the economic, social and environmental impacts of adventure tourism on this destination.

Part

E

Key sectors of adventure tourism

10

Wildlife tourism

Introduction

This chapter explores some of the prominent features that constitute adventure in the interaction of people with wildlife. We will look at the idiosyncratic form that adventure takes, and show how wildlife adventure is indeed as diverse as the people that take part in it. The chapter also offers an insight into some rather unusual wildlife adventures – physical, physiological and psychological – and we will explore some of the more exotic drives that fuel the thirst for wildlife excitement.

First we will look at the some of the existing literature and explore how terms are problematic as they are defined, re-defined and become interchangeable. We will then examine the multiple use of nature within the tourism industry, and illustrate how, for example, character, rarity, exclusivity, danger and many other phenomena play a key role in the reshaping and re-branding of wildlife through image makeovers to create suitable tourism products.

The 'nature' of wildlife adventure

Three key texts that examine the use of nature in tourism are those by Shackley (1996), Fennell (1999), and Wearing and Neal (1999). All three offer an extensive array of case studies of wildlife tourism from around the world. Shackley's work includes a brief examination of the way that tourists interact with wildlife, focusing very much on the resultant management issues. She considers traditional wildlife tourism in some detail, setting it very much in a broad tourism and ecotourism context. The work focuses strongly on the management of wildlife and visitors and their impact, and the involvement of local communities. Fennell, on the other hand offers a critical examination of many social, environmental and political issues associated with the industry, and concentrates on ecotourism policy, economics, marketing, management and product development. Fennell also explores the relationship of ecotourism to adventure tourism and, interestingly, notes that many writers subsume ecotourism within adventure travel. Wearing and Neal also offer a strong focus on philosophy, policy and planning, as well as examining community issues and the many problems associated with defining and practising sustainability. To some extent the main differentiating factor between ecotourism destinations and adventure tourism destinations is the focus on the need for environmentally 'compatible' and sustainable recreational opportunities required, supposedly, by the former. In recent years we have seen a rapid growth in so-called 'ecotourism' at the interface between wildlife and tourism. However, while this word is often used it is rarely satisfactorily defined, and it is still unclear whether it is a good or a bad thing. Currently, it appears to have two sides that are very different in nature, as can be seen from Table 10.1.

Some elements of the tourism industry are clearly using 'ecotourism' as a label to attract higher-spending tourists, while others are using it to describe a new form of tourism that is environmentally motivated and sensitive. At the same time, there is a dangerous assumption that ecotourism is inherently small scale and low impact. However, experience shows us that most tourism starts small, becomes popular and then grows. Unless regulations are introduced to control the industry, most forms of tourism grow 'naturally' as they become more affordable and are adopted by the mass market. So there is no guarantee that today's small-scale ecotourism will not become mass tourism. This phenomenon can be seen in relation to safari tourism in some areas of East

Table 10.1 The two sides of ecotourism

Positive and sustainable?	Negative and non-sustainable?
Small scale	Large scale
Low impact (e.g. making use of existing infrastructure)	High impact (involving the development of new infrastructure)
Complementary to nature (e.g. working on conservation projects)	Exploitative (e.g. seeing wildlife as sights to be collected
Informal and/or involving voluntary labour	Formal and commercialized
Part of a government policy on tourism development	Initiatives by entrepreneurs looking to improve their competitive market situation
Tourists who are concerned about environmental issues	Tourists who see ecotourism as just another tourism experience

Africa, for example. As it grows in popularity the concept of ecotourism will assume greater significance, and attract more controversy, as the deliberations over the relationship between wildlife, adventure and tourism continue.

Laarman and Durst (1993), for example, offer a simple definition of the term 'nature tourism', arguing that it take place 'principally on natural resources such as relatively undisturbed parks and natural areas, wetlands, wildlife reserves, and other areas of protected flora, fauna, and habitats' (in Fennell, 1999). However, nature-based tourism can occur in urban locations and artificially created wildlife environments and so the definition becomes limiting. Roe *et al.* (1997) attempt to offer an all-embracing broader set of defining parameters for wildlife tourism, and define it as tourism that includes, as a principal aim, the consumptive and non-consumptive use of wild animals in natural areas. They say it can include high-volume mass tourism or low-volume/low-impact tourism, generate high or low economic returns, be sustainable or non-sustainable, domestic or international, and based on day visits or on longer stays. Whilst Roe *et al.* specifically refer to wild animals, Shackley usefully broadens the concept still further to include flora as well as fauna. Newsome *et al.* offer a very practical three-pronged division of tourism in the environment (adventure tourism), about the environment (nature-based and wildlife tourism) and for the environment (ecotourism).

Laarman and Durst (1987) suggest that adventure might be part of a wildlife experience, and define nature tourism as tourism where the traveller is drawn to one or more aspect of natural history found in the destination, and where the visit combines elements of education, recreation and adventure.

The visit combines education, recreation and often adventure' (in Fennell, 1999). Newsome *et al.* comment that adventure tourism and nature tourism share similarities but suggest they are simply different aspects of tourism. They state that adventure tourism is 'tourism that is focused on the activity in a natural area. It involves physical challenge, education and contact with nature, and can be one of three types: small scale, with many ecotourism characteristics (e.g. birdwatching, scuba diving); medium scale and sports oriented (e.g. canoeing and rafting) or large scale, and an aspect of mass tourism (e.g. safaris)'. Roberts and Hall (2001) comment that 'exhilaration, challenge, thrill and fantasy represent some of the experiences sought by those opting for adventure travel as their holiday choice. Imagination appears to be the only limit to the diverse and exciting activities that make this one of the fastest growing tourism sectors'. Fennell also refers to the definition of the Canadian Tourism Commission who, in 1995, defined adventure tourism as 'an outdoor leisure activity that takes place in an unusual, exotic, remote or wilderness destination'. We will see later how wildlife adventures can have all these features.

Thus nature tourism, ecotourism and wildlife tourism are all terms used in the tourism industry where nature is one of the main product ingredients. The experience might have differing degrees of interaction with nature, a variable educational content and differing approaches to the sustainable use of the local natural resources, but also varying levels of thrill or excitement with some experiences being offered purely for entertainment. From zoos and safari parks, wilderness trekking, marine aquaria and wildlife sports to whale watching and working holidays, the range of products is extremely diverse and increasingly difficult to categorize. Wildlife adventures are also continually evolving; balloon safaris, for example, are now popular in Africa, combining the adventure of ballooning with wildlife watching.

Adventures with wildlife are of course key ingredients in wildlife adventure tourism, yet few writers seem to acknowledge the truly adventureous side to wildlife interaction. Natural history, habitats, flora and fauna, protected landscapes and education are hardly adrenalin-linked terms that allude to adventure. However, wildlife adventure tourism can involve much more than this, including conspiracy, jealousy, politics and obsessive behaviours. Wildlife tourism can be as much about the intrigue behind such human behaviours and backstage 'adventurous antics' behind the exploration of natural history.

What, then, are the most salient features of the wildlife adventure tourism experience? Wildlife has always featured as a substantial part of the conscious and unconscious travel 'experience'. The wildlife part of the experience often consists of the more visible and sought-after animals, such as lions, dolphins or snow leopards, yet it is significantly sustained by the less visible backcloth of the habitat and the less obvious wildlife, such as the sounds of cicadas and frogs on warm tropical evenings. Wildlife adventure tourism is therefore very much a separate market niche as well as an all-pervasive part of tourism markets, with wildlife and nature images used to adorn most market products. Using a simple definition of 'to travel and enjoy and appreciate nature', Fillion et al. (1992) estimated that 40–60 per cent of tourists are in fact nature tourists and 24–40 per cent are wildlife-related tourists. But why is the wildlife itself generally seen as adventurous?

Commentators on adventure travel all too often use a rather traditional view of 'adventure', seeing it as outdoor pursuits or extreme sports and other adrenalin-raising physical activities, rather than endeavouring to understand the adventurous side of plant and animal tourism. The underlying excitement in wildlife adventure so often receives little attention, and it is this that we focus on. Some 'wildlife seekers' are indeed no different from any other form of adrenalin-hungry adventurers; they are no different to tornado chasers, or people looking for an eclipse or the northern lights – they are all participating in 'holidays with a difference'. Often wildlife adventurers will seek the buzz of fear and uncertainty, and the unpredictability of the wild animals. However, as with most other adventures on the mass market, the danger is mostly (but not entirely) a perceived one. The risk experience can also sometimes be a rather voyeuristic foray around the periphery of danger, as white Europeans for example venture into Africa to glance at the dangerous wildlife and return home to safety. Whilst danger is indeed one obvious component of the wildlife experience, the relationship between danger, rarity and economic value in wildlife is currently being reappraised.

The fear of wildlife is reduced, and we now think we are more in control. This is the case with most species at least! Risk-free adventure develops largely as a result of the drives of commercialism and the spread of litigation societies, but the dangers of wildlife adventure do not always lie in the obvious form of large popular mammals. It is often the small, unseen threats that present real and less controllable danger. Jonathan Young, in his article 'Don't feed the animals', refers to the very real dangers of wildlife adventure and advises unwary travellers how to avoid being nibbled, bitten or swallowed. The threats that lurk in the natural world are mostly due to the power of the predators. Young refers to the 'International Shark Attack File' (ISAF), run by the Florida Museum of Natural History and the American Elasmobranch Society, and estimates that each year there are between 70 and 1000 attacks and between 5 and 15 deaths. Black bears in North America are known to have killed 35 people in the twentieth century, and grizzlies were responsible for 88 deaths. In America 8000 people are bitten every year by poisonous snakes, of whom 9–15 die; in Australia 3000 people are bitten each year and only 1–2 die. Worldwide, bites from venomous snakes are believed to cause the deaths of 50–100 people each year. However, the minute mosquito causes 300–500 *million* cases of malaria each year, of which 1 million are fatal, and malaria kills 3000 children under the age of 5 years every day.

Adventures with wildlife are clearly not simply about risk, awe or fear. The adventure can be concerned with the collection of prized 'trophies' or photographs, or with swimming with, sitting next to, learning about or searching for new species, exploring, and adding to personal 'tick lists'. Many travellers now prefer to shoot wildlife through camera lenses, and collect and share exciting wildlife stories and tick-off prized checklists. Ticking off rare birds from a checklist is known as 'twitching', and Bill Oddie, in *Bill Oddie's Little Black Bird Book*, humorously describes and characterizes the 'twitcher' subculture of language, habits and clothing, and refers to the cardinal sin of 'dipping out on a lifer' – which, roughly translated, is a person missing out on a once-in-a-lifetime opportunity to see a rare bird!

As we become more in tune with nature society moves towards increasingly empathetic strategies, so removing some of our ancient and basic fears about nature. Western fairytales, for example, paint a picture of nature as foreboding and dark. 'Natural' places are where Hansel and Gretel got lost, and where Sleeping Beauty was surrounded by thorn bushes and immense forests. 'Nature' was a place with 'wild' animals and 'savage' people, both requiring taming. The psychological origins of such negative mindsets are rooted in folklore, history, law, policy and industrial practices, and they are explored by Beard (2000), who offers interesting ways to reframe our thinking about the natural environment by altering our inner script – changing 'metaphors', 'images', 'labels' and 'functions'. This reframing is exactly what happens with the re-branding of wildlife. Shackley, for example, talks of the poor public image affecting the tourism rating of wildlife interest, and refers to the North American timber wolf as such a victim as it is often portrayed maliciously in film. According to some, the wolf is clearly in need of an image makeover. As society significantly tames wildlife, the sense of being in control of the wildlife adventure is reinforced by the anthropomorphic and often humorous marketing language that is used to reshape the public image of animals. 'Escape to "The Greatest Show on Earth". . .' was the theme of one Sunday travel paper. In 'Natural wonders of the world', Sarah Turner describes flamingos:

> . . . the supermodel of the animal kingdom, the flamingo is an exquisitely pointless creature, whose life is largely devoted to feeding on algae that gives it its distinctive colouring. It is the ultimate fashion victim – its spindly legs and non-aerodynamic body make it enormously attractive to predators. As a result, flamingos are forced to live in vast packs up to a million strong (looking not unlike a giant pink duvet); but create one of the most beautiful spectacles in the world at the same time.

In the same article, wildebeest are described as 'animals that can make the London rush hour look like a catwalk', manta rays are said to be 'not exactly beautiful because they were designed on a 1970 style spaceship', and the whale is described as giving birth in the 'world's largest birthing pool' off the shores of California.

Packaging wildlife adventure tourism

Limited numbers of high-profile animals are much prized and sought after by an increasingly regulated number of limited tourists: exclusivity can be applied to animals and tourists alike. Whilst Africa promotes the much sought after 'big five' must-see checklist of elephant, rhino, buffalo, lion and leopard, the Galapagos islands promotes its own famous five wildlife adventure 'package deals' consisting of Boobies, Frigate birds, giant tortoises, marine iguanas and tacky souvenirs (Neil Robinson, 2001). Robertson made reference to a five-star entry into 'birdsville' by going to the Galapagos islands:

> . . . situated 600 miles off Ecuador they have become one of the most tightly controlled tourist zones in the world, and the talk is of cutting numbers rather than increasing them, an interesting reversal of every tourist trend . . . almost everyone on board is transformed into a wildlife enthusiast, thumbing through guidebooks. . .

Wildlife 'events' attract tourists the world over, from the dawn chorus of birds to bat and swallow roosts at dusk, and mass gatherings of fireflies and marching ants. These performances gather crowds in increasing numbers as a result of prudent marketing. Whilst rare wildlife often attracts tourists, the destination or the uniqueness or exclusiveness of the experience are also important. The Midnight Zoo in Singapore, for example, is an alternative approach to passive–interactive wildlife adventure tourism. Here a Philips specialist lighting engineer has manipulated nature and designed illumination systems that do not upset the biorhythms of the animals in the dark of the tropical evenings, yet allow them to be brightly illuminated for the visitors. The night-time adventure inside small open carriages takes passengers close to docile animals that are aware neither of the light nor of the closeness of their visitors. Similarly, exclusivity features in other forms in wildlife adventure tourism. The Lindblad Explorer, an ex–research and exploration ship later purchased for adventure tourism, roamed exotic locations in the 1970s and 1980s. Continuously travelling around the world, tourists flew out to the boat for exclusive and expensive luxury adventure holidays, ranging from the forays into the jungles of the Amazon to landings in the frozen wastes of the Antarctic. The safari market also has its exclusive luxury niche, with venues like Kleins Camp (situated on the edge of Kuka Hills just outside the Serengeti National Park). The main building was once a private hunting lodge and is now a wildlife sanctuary set within 10 000 acres leased form the Masai community by Conservation Corporation Africa. No more than twenty guests are allowed at any one time; advertisements state that there is no camping involved and the bathrooms sport showerheads the size of dinner plates; the promotional material comments that the trek to get there as being 'well worth it' and part of the adventure, and this costs approximately US$500 per night.

The animals themselves are clearly only a part of the unpredictability of nature that creates real or perceived danger. The distance between people and wildlife can vary considerably, as can the degree of animal freedom and captivity, or tameness. The extent of the animal interaction can vary too; sitting quietly with feeding gorillas is a much deeper and more meaningful close encounter than viewing from a safari jeep. In most cases wildlife tourism involves observation of, rather than a significant interaction with, wildlife. However, in some cases the wildlife is also an active participant in the experience on an involuntary basis, for example:

■ In hunting and fishing, where the pleasure appears to derive from the chase and the quality of the 'fight' put up by the creature being hunted
■ In adventures where wildlife provides transport, such as husky sled trips in the Arctic or elephant trips in Thailand or India.

Whilst television programmes help to develop the characterization of animals that adds considerably to their popular appeal, live TV shows have more recently encouraged a new form of passive rather than active wildlife adventures. Live television is merged with the wildlife documentary format, and live footage can be beamed across the world from the big game in the African bush. A UK-based company called Horizons embarked on an ambitious experiment in live television in spring 2001, and sent daily live reports from camps across South Africa, Botswana, Namibia and Zimbabwe in an attempt to bring the safari experience into the living room. High on the agenda were intimate portrayals of the life of Africa's so-called big five (elephant, rhino, buffalo, lion and leopard), and viewers were able to ask questions by e-mail.

Many species of 'dangerous' wildlife are pushed to the verge of extinction, with the ironic result that the species becomes so rare that it becomes a key tourist attraction and a valuable sources of income generation for the host nation, so generating more commercial return than if simply 'left' for people to observe. Some species, however, enter the tourist regime through positive protection schemes such as the Red Kite project in Wales (see Box 10.1).

What we see from the kite story is that although wildlife can present itself as a relatively free resource on which to found a tourism business venture, the unpredictability appreciably affects the commercial value of wildlife in the tourism marketplace: species used in tourism attractions are vulnerable to shifts in status, brand image and rarity labelling. This is true if, for example, the species become success stories in terms of parallel conservation efforts to increase their numbers and secure future ecological stability. There are numerous cases of commercial operators using wildlife to develop major business attractions for tourists yet failing to return any part of the profit to the conservation of the natural resource as the source of wealth. This failure to acknowledge its commercial value and contribution and so take some responsibility for its supply and protection is illustrated in St Davids, the smallest city in the UK, located on the coastline of South Wales, where several boat operators use the logo of the Royal Society for the Protection of Birds to attract tourists to take boat trips to see the bird colonies and aquatic mammals, but offer little or nothing of their trip fees to the bird protection charities.

It is not just wildlife rarity or indeed its potential threat to humans that forms part of the attraction. Ecologists have for some time rated the importance of wildlife as part of the regional, national or international framework of protection and management planning by using categories that can also provide a useful tourism checklist framework for examining wildlife

Box 10.1   Kite tourism

Human persecution of vertebrates, especially the larger ones, forms part of the story of the ancient need to dominate the natural environment. The last wolf was killed in the UK in Scotland in 1643, and in Ireland in 1770 (Tubbs, 1974). Records also exist of the payment for the 'heads' of birds as incentives for people to control those species that were seen as vermin and thus threatening agriculture or hunting, and it was through this system that the red kite was hunted extensively in the late seventeenth century. By the late 1800s it had been reduced to the verge of extinction, with a small population remaining in central Wales.

Now it is seen as one of the rarest and most beautiful birds in the UK. Distinguished by its forked tail and majestic heron-like flight, there were some 27 pairs of breeding birds in central Wales. The bird population has fluctuated over the centuries, and at one time in the UK it was so common it scavenged on rubbish tips in London. Its decline was due to hunting, as the bird was thought to be a killer of young lambs, farmyard poultry and rabbits. A small population remained in rural Wales where conservation programmes, funded by the Royal Society for the Protection of Birds, have helped the kite to make a comeback.

The attraction of the red kite is due to a number of factors: its status as a rarity, the fact that it is an impressive and large bird of prey, and clever marketing. Over the decades the Black Mountains have witnessed the gradual transformation from hunting to kill, to adventure hunting to see and observe. The adventure applies to the other side too, i.e. the kite protectors, as the wardening work for the RSPB is partially shrouded in mystery. Living in wooden sheds and caravans, RSPB staff are advised to watch out for known egg thieves, and lists of car numbers regularly arrive from the special investigation department at headquarters. People asking too many questions in the pub are to be treated with some degree of caution, and staff are asked to be careful about using maps that show the whereabouts of nests of birds such as the buzzard, the merlin and the red kite. Thieves will take many risks to steal eggs or young birds for falconry, and the financial rewards for the latter were significant in the past owing to the overseas demand for birds. In many Arabic countries such birds are now specially bred thus reducing this demand.

A peregrine falcon was seen one season in the Black Mountains after years of absence due to persecution, only to have its eggs taken within days of laying. One valley was robbed of all the buzzard eggs, and the police caught the known collector in the West Midlands several hours later.

The significance of the red kite to the tourism industry is now being investigated in more detail, and it has been estimated that there were some 250 000 staying visitors and some 750 000 day visits to rural mid-Wales in the late 1990s. The adventure lies in tracking down this elusive bird: between 101 000 and 107 000 different people visited the Red Kite Centres during 1996 (Rayment, 1997). The red kite is being used as a powerful tourism marketing tool; *A Green Guide to Kite Country* was produced to encourage sustainable tourism, and various kite merchandise is produced and promoted. Schemes such as 'Stay on a farm in Kite Country' and 'Business in Kite Country' have been launched to attract more tourists and business interest in the kite. The former scheme involved some 130 farms by the mid-1990s, and was launched to link the kite 'benefits' more directly to the local economy. Businesses in the area of the red kite were asked to sign up to a discretionary 'Green Levy', and this scheme was launched to attract more funding for kite research and protection.

Rayment (1997) argues that 'the conservation benefits of Kite Country are more difficult to monitor than the economic impacts, because the project itself involves little habitat management and seeks to achieve conservation gain through education, awareness raising and strengthening links between the kite and the local economy'. The continued breeding success of the kites is clearly evident, with the birds increasing from 27 to 120 pairs (fledging 112 young) in less than 20 years between the mid-1970s and the mid-1990s. No nests were robbed in 1995, but this might be due to secret permanent cameras at some undisclosed sites.

The red kite became extinct in Scotland over a hundred years ago, and was reintroduced in the Black Isle in 1989. Research by Rayment (2001) outlines the economic significance of these species to the visitor spending and visitor motivations. The Highlands of Scotland Tourist Board (HOST) promotes the Black Isle as a naturalists' paradise, with reserves and visitor centres for viewing the red kite, seals and dolphins. Closed circuit television cameras allow visitors to watch live footage of nesting red kites. Whilst the nest sites are kept secret, tourists can follow a red kite trail around the main roads, reducing disturbance to the birds.

The kite-breeding programme is a major success story, and thus might result in a degree of decline in kite tourism in Wales. The red kite has now been reintroduced in Southern England, and is becoming very common in Berkshire, Buckinghamshire and the Chilterns. It remains to be seen if visitors still seek out the bird if it is no longer rare. In this instance, the market does not dictate supply and demand!

issues as part of an adventure tourism market. Ecological habitat categorizations, for example, illustrate their environmental value and include rarity, size, diversity, naturalness, fragility, typicality, recorded history, potential value and intrinsic appeal.

However, larger and fiercer animals have not become rare purely through past human persecution. *Why Big Fierce Animals are Rare* (Colinvaux, 1980) explains the significance of the Elton pyramid to the tourism industry. Charles Elton, observing life on the Arctic tundra, noted how the smaller things were common and large things were rare – something that had been known but unexplained since the dawn of time. What he discovered was that discrete sizes came about because of the science of eating and being eaten. He created the famous 'pyramid of numbers' that simply shows that with every jump in size there is a significant loss in numbers in order to sustain larger biomass. To sustain large beasts there must be copious small things for it to eat. Therefore, quite simply there will always be few big fierce animals! Add to this the destruction of the natural habitats of these animals around the world and we have even fewer large beasts to locate and then marvel at. Rare and big animals add to the tourism attraction whether they are fierce or not.

Whilst the wildlife most frequently referred to in marketing literature include whales, big cats, the great apes and birds, numbers and mass and other criteria can also be important determinants of popularity and economic value to the tourism industry. Classic Journeys, for example, concentrates on wildlife adventure in Asia and notes that whilst the Himalayas are home to the legendary snow leopard, musk deer and ibex, the Indian subcontinent as a whole is home to over 365 species of mammals, 1200 species of birds and

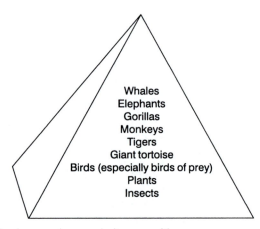

Figure 10.1 Tourism species popularity pyramid.

13 000 species of flowering plants. If we construct a tourism species popularity pyramid, it closely reflects the Elton pyramid of numbers (see Figure 10.1).

The adventure and excitement of plants

The tourism industry is increasingly recognizing that for many people the same fascination can exist for plants as it does for animals. There are many plant-seeking tourists today, and some travellers wish to trace the journeys of famous explorers. Whilst the adventurous exploits of plant-seekers have been documented for many years, *One River* (Davies, 1997) is a relatively recent story of Richard Evans Schultes, one of the greatest 'botanical adventurers' of the nineteenth century, who explored lands no outsider had seen before. The book narrates the epic story of one of the most pre-eminent ethnobotanists in the world, 'a man whose own expeditions a generation earlier had earned him a place in the pantheon along with Charles Darwin, Alfred Russell Wallace, Henry Bates and his own hero, the indefatigable English botanist and explorer Richard Spruce':

> Filled with colour and danger, the story is also one of extraordinary discoveries as Schultes sought to understand the psychoactive plants of the rainforest and how the native shamans used them. In addition to his research into hallucinogenic plants that sparked the psychedelic era, Schultes' search for wild rubber led to one of the most important breakthroughs in the history of cultivated plants.
>
> (Davies, 1997)

The book is filled with plant intrigue. The stories of botanical adventure are globally significant, and the following extracts illustrate so well some of the reasons why plant adventure can be so appealing. The book reports on one plant fanatic who had studied mushrooms for over twenty-five years with his Russian wife, Valentina Pavlovna. The man was Gordon Wasson, a banker and vice-president of J. P. Morgan & Co. of New York. Wasson noted that societies could simply be divided into those that revered mushrooms and those that despised them. On 13 May 1957, Wasson published an article in *Life* magazine about his exploits with sacred mushrooms that affected the mind; the article was to have a profound effect. The editor, in seeking to capture the spirit of the article, titled it 'Seeking Magic Mushrooms'. The book notes that neither the editor nor Wasson could have anticipated how the article would mark 'a certain watershed in the social history of the United States, the beginning of the psychedelic era'.

The political global significance of one single topical plant is also exemplified:

> Every hose on every ship, every valve and seal, every tire on every truck and plane . . . it's wrapped around every inch of wiring in every factory, home and office in America. Conveyer belts, hydraulics, inflatable boats, gas masks, rain gear, it's all rubber.

One River also includes details of the search for and discovery of rubber in the Amazon – said to be one of the greatest breakthroughs in the history of cultivated plants. Brazil was the original home of the rubber trees that now adorn hundreds of thousands of acres of Asian soil that was once rainforest. As a result of the so-called 'theft' of many thousands of seeds from the rainforests of Brazil, which were collected by British botanical adventurers, the Brazilian rubber wealth declined drastically as commercial plantations developed more successfully in Asia.

What also astounded Schultes was the use of natural drugs by, for example, Amazonian indigenous people – not so much their effect, but for the 'underlying intellectual question that the elaboration of these complex preparations posed'. The Amazonian flora contained tens of thousands of species, so 'how had the Indians learned to identify and combine in this sophisticated manner these morphologically dissimilar plants that possessed such unique and complementary chemical properties?'.

Brazil is named after a single species of tree that produces a bright red sap (*pau do brasil*), and *brasile* is from the Latin word for red. Significantly, Europeans wanted the sap for dye for clothing, and this eventually resulted in the first large-scale invasion of Brazil, by the Portuguese. This in turn led to the destruction, domination and slavery of many of the indigenous peoples – all for a tree. The book also describes in detail the intellectual property gained from indigenous people that resulted in significant medical progress from these botanical adventures, especially those into the rainforests of the Amazon basin.

Equally fascinating stories describe the extreme adventure of plant discoveries. One botanical scientist spent his entire career investigating the chemical responsible for killing thousands of people, making noses fall away from faces, and toes and fingers drop away from feet and arms. This occurred in the Middle Ages, and many people suffered horrific hallucinations and many were hung as they were thought to be possessed. The culprit was a simple fungus that grew on rye and caused blood vessels to constrict in humans; only dedicated botanical scientists would think about the promising medical potential of such a phenomenon, and they relentlessly pursued the chemicals involved for many years. It was thought that the chemical in the plant could, for example, help to stem excessive bleeding after childbirth. Plant scientists thus sought to discover the chemical involved, and one man, a Dr Hofmann, was doing just that when one Friday he felt dizzy and set off home on his bicycle. Unknown to him he had indeed discovered the chemical, and small traces had been absorbed through his skin. The chemical was lysergic acid diethylamide-25, LSD for short – the most potent hallucinogenic ever discovered! The book rather matter-of-factly comments 'On his way home Dr Hofmann went on the world's first acid trip'.

Plant adventurers and explorer naturalists exist in many forms, and they continue today to push new frontiers that might affect new tourism initiatives in the future. Botanists and zoologists identify with this natural inquisitiveness that can eventually drive people to extreme behaviours in search of species. Plant lovers and their antics are described in *Orchid Fever* (Hanson, 2001). One international orchid grower summed it up on the rear of the book by commentating that 'You can get off alcohol, drugs, women, food and cars, but once you're hooked on orchids you're finished. You never get off orchids . . . never'. Eric Hanson is a well-known travel writer who, entering the world of plant obsessives, describes the bizarre and compelling tales of corruption, murder and plant politics, uncovering some of the underlying adventures behind the hobby of collecting, breeding and exhibiting plants, giving insight into the drives, impulses and urges of some tourists. The first few lines of the book describe the adventurous side of plant hunting and make it clear that it is potentially much more risky than bungee jumping, or indeed any other extreme sport:

> There is something distinctive about the sight and sound of a human body falling from the rainforest canopy. The breathless scream, the wildly gyrating arms and legs pumping thin air, the rush of leaves, snapping branches, and the sickening thud, followed by an uneasy silence. Listening to that silence, I reflected on how plant collecting can be an unpleasant sort of activity.

Plant exploration continues unabated even today. Claiming a place in the history books is another key driving force in wildlife adventure tourism. On 29 June 2002, *The Times* reported in the UK that (Browne, 2002):

> Explorers have nothing left to discover, but all botanists need is a plane ticket to leave their names in the history books. Whilst the whole of the

world is mapped in the tiniest detail, plants, often big ones, are still being discovered everywhere ... Almost any trip to South America or South East Asia with a trained botanist will reveal dozens of previously unknown species, but they need to go to the remote areas.

'The Scentsation seekers' too are modern adventure scientists, and were discussed in an article in *ZEST*, a health and beauty magazine for women, in May 2001. The article describes how perfumers are looking to the rainforests to find more smells, and says that people want more perfumes for different moods. The article quotes the Director of Fine Fragrances at Quest International as saying '... we've found some genuinely new essences in Madagascar, not just coral and waterfall but delicious fruits, rich, peppery vines and resins that no one has used before'. Quest International also sponsored Oxford University research on rare Madagascan sea turtles, and has invested generously to protect rare ecosystems. Madagascar is home to 200 000 species of plants, 85 per cent of which are endemic. Scientists go on adventure expeditions to capture smells, placing glass bell jars over the leaves or flowers to capture molecules of smell, and then try to replicate them in the laboratory. No flora or fauna are destroyed or removed in the collection process. How long it will be before such adventurous smelling expeditions are created for the travel market?

The ticking of locations – habitats as destinations

Wildlife and nature form the core product for many tourist destinations worldwide at a number of different levels, including the following:

1 Countries that in spite of having diverse attractions are categorized by the industry and are stereotypically seen by tourists as almost solely wildlife attractions, such as Kenya and Botswana. This can be a real obstacle if these destinations wish to develop other forms of tourism.
2 Regions and areas where nature is the main attraction although the country may have other attractions. Examples include the Iguassu Falls in Brazil and the national parks of South Africa.
3 Places where the main product is not wildlife-based but where wildlife attractions are important secondary attractions, such as San Diego with its zoo, and the night safari in Singapore.

Many destinations have attracted wildlife tourists for generations. However, some places are seeking to use wildlife to enter the tourism market as new players, and wildlife attractions are being used to spearhead attraction-led urban regeneration and rural development initiatives. For instance, aquaria have been used to this effect in Boulogne-sur-Mer (Nausicaa) and Brest (Océanopolis) in France, Barcelona in Spain, Baltimore in the USA, and Birmingham in the UK.

However, wildlife tourism can become a problem in destinations if the scale of it begins to overwhelm the host environment, whether this is a forest or a coral reef. Just as with plant and animal species, habitats as 'destinations' have also become fashionable places in the adventure travel industry. The uniqueness lies in searching for new locations – a form of geographical or habitat 'twitching'. Shackley refers to the Galapagos Effect, and comments that even the Antarctica as a new destination has seen a rapid increase in tourism over the last two decades. The 'been there . . . done that' attitude does exist among some adventure travellers. Thus the same pyramid or league table might be constructed for natural habitats in terms of rarity or popularity, and this could look like Figure 10.2.

Figure 10.2 Hierarchical pyramid of natural destinations.

There might be some awesome adventure 'tick-lists' in the future – it is reported by Wright (1996) that there are some 2700 National Parks in 120 different countries!

Apart from the location and wildlife league tables, and the light-hearted characterizations that form the basis of a species 'image make-over', there is a much deeper, more spiritual and genetically anchored connection of people to nature, and this is now explored in more detail.

Curative nature

The outdoor natural world offers a tremendous range of variables, including unpredictability, which can be used in designing and marketing the wildlife adventure experience. Pringle and Thompson (2001), both with significant experience with the advertising agency Saatchi and Saatchi, offer an analysis of the use of cause-related marketing (CRM) to build brands, and they talk of the three waves in branding history. The first wave, the 1950s, is described as the rational era of marketing, whereas in the 1970s the behavioural psychologists were more involved in advertising, and the concern focused on the emotional image and the lifestyle benefits of the product and services in the consumer landscape. This was the second emotional wave. In the 1990s the third wave commenced, as a spiritual or ethical wave:

> If anthropomorphy is one of the fundamentals in branding then it was inevitable that sooner or later the analogy with human behaviour and psychology would be pursued to its logical conclusion. It would lead marketers to having to provide the ultimate dimension in brand personality and brand character in order to complete the presentation to the consumer: the brand's 'soul'.

These issues remain very significant to wildlife adventure tourism industry today. Current lifestyles offer more security and routine for many, and people increasingly experience nature as reconstructed and contrived in a new safe format. Yet it remains to be seen to what extent this new form of the controlled 'nature experience' and our interaction with 'new nature' remains an essential subconscious human need for a satisfying, quality life. Identity and self-fulfilment may well still depend on, and be heavily influenced by, our interactions with nature. Interestingly, a strong set of opposing emotional affiliations occur in the human interactions with nature, and adventure tourism embraces these very different approaches. One is the dominionistic need to master nature – the combative approach (conquering and taming wildlife and the natural environment) – and the other is a more empathetic approach (an affinity and empathy to wildlife and natural habitats). Different forms of adventure can be located in both approaches. Holiday stories often include wildlife adventures, and in one narrative analysis we completed of a UK gap-year young couple travelling in Australia and New Zealand, we found wildlife storytelling commonly consisted of contrasting scary stories or near misses with stories that related to feelings of being at home in nature. The dominant stories were of a scary type, such as swimming with sharks, spiders under the tent and frogs in the toilet, with the occasional reference to the cuddliness of, for example, koala bears, and to lovely sunsets. The contrasting beliefs of Native American and Western civilizations are compared in an article called the 'Spirit of the Earth', by Georgina Peard, who offers a simple analysis from the two perspectives on nature:

Native American	Western civilization
At home in nature	Fear
Belonging	Ownership
Community	Individualism
Spiritual	Capital
Sustainable	Exploitation
Freedom	Domination

Despite the ancient origins of some negative feelings towards nature, it has long been recognized that the natural environment has curative properties for humans and our understanding of such phenomena is rapidly increasing. The natural environment has an extensive history as a place for healing, for repair and for personal development, and the human need to affiliate with life and life-like processes is known as biophilia (Kellert, 1993). 'Wilderness walks' are also now being given serious consideration as an option for doctors' health prescriptions! Research carried out long ago by Ulrich (1974) set out to measure the attractive and aversive human physiological responses to natural phenomena. Some early research was carried out on postoperative patients in hospital, and early indications showed that patients who overlooked natural green space had shorter postoperative stays, fewer post-surgery complications, and required less medication and less analgesics.

The person–environment relationship is of course a two-way process, and this subtle impact of the natural environment on our health and well-being is both physiological and psychological. Kellert (1993) suggests that spending time in green space causes the following physiological responses:

- Reduced heart rate
- Reduced blood pressure
- A decrease in circulating stress hormones
- An increase in cognitive functioning, performance and creativity
- Alterations in brain activity in the alpha frequency range
- Relaxation of stress-induced muscle tension.

These responses, he suggests, are due to a number of stimuli, including colours, textures, natural smells, decreased 'noise pollution' (or more interesting sounds such as running water), and exposure to the elements (wind, rain, heat, cold, etc.). Interestingly, this presents a juxtaposition of calm and cure against adventure and excitement, but is these two very opposite sets of emotional responses that, when combined, can create the thrilling 'Peak experience' described by both Shackley and by Fennell, and explored in depth by Beard and Wilson (2002).

Historically there have been many protagonists of the view that there is not a single social ill or physical problem that would not respond to a course of treatment in the outdoors (Charlton, 1992). In the worldwide Scouting and Guide movements it was long ago considered that exposure to wilderness and adventure was a potential cure for everything from flat-footedness to 'bad citizenship'!

In a more recent study, *Sacred Nature*, Adrian Cooper (1998) explored how 150 travellers reconcile their spiritual faiths with the challenge of interpreting wild, natural environments, from tropical rainforest to frozen lands and deserts. He collected information for eleven years, and in a section called 'Turning points' he describes how wildlife adventure had a very significant therapeutic impact upon a woman who was diagnosed as HIV positive and, two years later, was living in Bristol in a derelict warehouse, drinking very heavily and sharing her life with four other homeless women. She found a rain-sodden magazine blowing across the warehouse floor with a picture of a mother and baby elephant in Amboseli National Park in Kenya. A week later she hitched a lift to London and bought a one-way ticket to Nairobi. In the airport in Africa she met a group of American youngsters about to go on a camping expedition, and was invited to join them:

> For hours on end, I was lost in complete contentment watching the elephants living their lives, and supporting each other. And I'd often find myself hearing someone say the time. And I'd realize that I'd gone almost all day without thinking about HIV. It was incredible. But it was the gentle elephants and the gentle people I was with.

Cooper comments that the woman's healing came intuitively, and her study of elephants turned into weeks of close observation and involvement. This rare and precious fellowship among people and elephants became an adventure that completely re-directed her life. Through her church in London she became a social worker, eventually completed a law degree, and worked for two charities advising young homeless adults. This illustrates how the wildlife adventure experiences can so easily straddle the world of adventure of mind and body – an embracing therapy. Adventure therapy is indeed a specialist field that uses nature and outdoor experiential activities for individual, group or family psychotherapy or counselling (Beard and Wilson, 2002), and wildlife can often form a significant ingredient in the therapeutic process.

The 'outdoors' conjures up many other words, such 'nature', 'earth' and the 'environment'; all of which are used interchangeably in the literature. It is useful to explore this confusion about the nature of the term 'outdoors' if we are to think laterally about the components that make up the term. Many people experience an avalanche of over 1000 consumptive advertising stimuli every day from television, radio, notices, packaging, street advertisements and so on. This creates a blinding over-stimulation of our visual senses, creating personal imbalance. Away from all this, in the more 'natural outdoors', this sensory dulling is removed and replaced with completely new stimulation signals. Outside in nature lie dramatic landscapes of different kinds, providing unpredictable extremes of stimulus, where the natural elements are easily felt, visible and accessible. We are bombarded with new, less familiar, stimuli, and the rainforests represent the extremes of such exciting stimulation. In the forest people listen attentively to thousands of animals that continuously send out signals, such as warnings of encroaching predators. We alert the senses and read the changes in light, humidity, wind, colour and shadows. We can feel a storm coming although we cannot see it – it is a place to sharpen observational and sensing skills (Beard & Wilson, 2002).

Natural surroundings and 'fresh air' energize and revitalize us, as well as beckoning us back to our primitive roots (Consalvo, 1995). Consalvo introduced her book on ready-made games for trainers with the following comment that enriches the imagination:

> Blue sky, red sunsets, white puffy clouds, green fields speckled with flowers, pine-covered paths, moonlit meadows, crickets chirping, birds singing, snow crunching underfoot, the smell of the spring thaw, summer sweetness, autumn decay, a salty breeze, burning leaves, the squish of mud, the sting of hot sand and the cold of snow are just a few among the plethora of sensory images we experience while outdoors. These sensations often tap emotionally and spiritually uplifting memories.

This quotation conjures up so many backcloth facets of the wildlife adventure experience that we cherish in adventurous experiences in the outdoors. Indeed, numerous natural ingredients are available to enhance sensitivity to the wildlife adventure experience, including:

■ The natural rhythms of life
■ Remoteness

- Changing seasons
- Wetness, humidity and dryness
- Heat and cold
- The ebb and flow of tides
- Day, night, dawn and dusk
- The elements and their unpredictability (e.g. storms and winds)
- Dramatic landscapes
- Flora and fauna
- Natural artforms
- Spiritual sensations
- Natural sounds.

(Adapted from Beard and Wilson, 2002.)

Reed (1999) describes five key elements – earth, air, fire, water and spirit – and explains how these elements interact with people. He suggests that these five are important symbols and may hold the key to learning and discovery in adventure. Fire, he suggests, is a symbol of action and creativity, and of destruction and new life. Water can symbolize feelings, emotion, dark undercurrents. Air symbolizes ideas and intellectual pursuits, but also insubstantial dreaming and lofty idealism. The fifth element, spirit, pervades all, but he noted that 'the ether is invisible, insubstantial but ubiquitous'. Watching fire, listening to the flowing water and noticing the silence are powerful experiences. Breathing the clean morning air, savouring and appreciating basic shelter and food, and experiencing darkness are less common everyday experiences for increasing numbers of people. For stressed people these can be very welcome experiences. However, they must be treated like the volume control when listening to your favourite music: too loud and the stimulus can be painful, too low and it has little impact. The ideal stimulus for learning lies somewhere in between, but can vary according to our needs and moods. Physical 'highs' are not always necessary to achieve emotional 'highs', and this is where an understanding of the environment is essential.

These ingredients can be broken down yet further into their subcomponents – e.g. the use of remote wilderness time creating solitude, space, quietness, and mental 'sorting-out time', especially following adrenalin-based adventure. The leads to the idea of creating 'adventure waves' (Beard and Wilson, 2002).

The future is exciting for adventure tourism, as the outdoor arena can give rise to endless experiences when people interact with the terrain, the natural elements and the spirituality associated with it.

Clearly wildlife adventure tourism is a vast and complex subject, as is shown in Figures 10.3–10.5, which summarize the types of wildlife tourism, the levels of interest in such tourism and the forces that can influence demand for it.

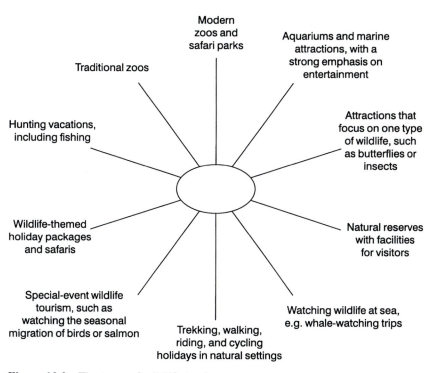

Figure 10.3 The types of wildlife tourism.

The tourism industry exploits all the forms of wildlife tourism shown in Figure 10.3 all over the world. However, while some wildlife 'promoters' such as whale watching or safaris can attract visitors to a destination from all over the world, others like traditional zoos often have a largely local day-trip market only.

Figure 10.4 shows us that different groups of people have different levels of interest and participation in wildlife tourism.

Figure 10.4 is clearly a sweeping generalization, but it is not too inaccurate overall. However, reality is more complex, with shades of levels of interest within each of these categories and, of course, some people who have no

Small   High

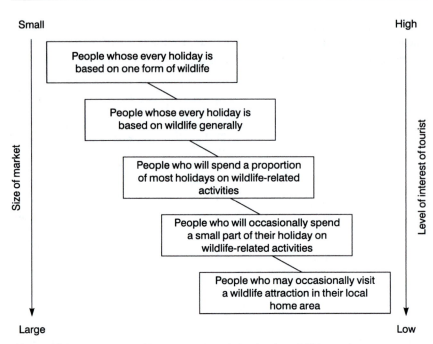

Size of market

Level of interest of tourist

Large   Low

Figure 10.4 The range of interest and participation in wildlife tourism.

interest in wildlife-related tourism whatsoever. At the other extreme you have a tiny number of obsessives whose whole life is dominated by their interest in wildlife.

It is also important to recognize that the motives of wildlife tourists also vary, and may include:

- The desire to study wildlife scientifically
- Entertainment with animals seen as 'funny', such as monkeys
- A wish to commune with nature as a recuperative activity
- The desire for status through collecting experiences involving rare wildlife.

Figure 10.5 shows some of the key factors that influence the demand for wildlife tourism.

However, this model can only be put forward tentatively, as little real research has been conducted on the way in which wildlife tourists make their purchase decisions.

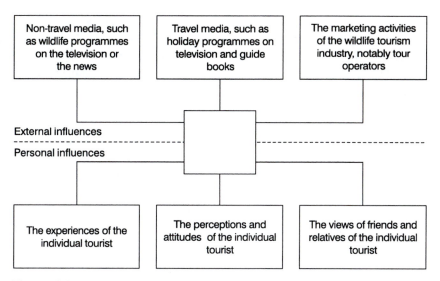

Figure 10.5   Factors that influence the demand for wildlife tourism.

Summary

Nature is an essential component of most tourism products, and thus future tourism initiatives will need to have less negative impact on the environment than many other industries. Otherwise, tourism and wildlife will become involved in a damaging conflict rather than having a symbiotic relationship. At the same time the tourism industry will experience greater regulatory forces that might encourage a distancing or 'moving away' and separation from nature, so that nature might be more protected. The relationship between adventure, nature, product and experience in the tourism industry requires further discussion. Wildlife tourism has a range of potential impacts on the wildlife itself, from hunting, where the form of tourism may well lead to the death of the creature, to those forms of wildlife adventure tourism where the creature may not even be aware of the presence of the tourists. Between these opportunities are a range of impacts from short-term minor disturbance to large-scale destruction of habitats and disruption of feeding and breeding patterns, with severe long-term implications. In this chapter we have paid less attention to these issues of direct impact as they are addressed elsewhere in the literature, although many of these issues remain unresolved. What we have done is to examine in some detail the impact of wildlife on humans, not least the less manageable dangers of some smaller animals.

This chapter has looked at the fashionable, rapidly developing field of wildlife adventure tourism and its emergence from and similarity to ecotourism and nature tourism. However, we have seen that defining this field is problematic, as wildlife adventure tourism is full of many contradictions and is a complex subject. This chapter has extensively explored the deeper interactions of people and wildlife that have received little attention elsewhere. We have explored some of the key salient features that make up the wildlife adventure experience, and examined how issues of rarity, size and diversity have commercial significance to the tourism industry. We have looked at political intrigue and plant politics, as well as other obsessive behaviours, and have considered future new forms of wildlife adventure 'package deals' and 'travellers' checklists' that extend beyond current ideas such as the 'Big Five' game in Africa and the 'Big Five' of the Galapagos Islands.

We have also scrutinized how nature and its constituent elements creates a plethora of underlying therapeutic sensations and feelings in people, such as the escape from over-stimulation that occurs in busy city lives, the biophilic relationship with nature, the physiological and physical impact of outdoor exercise, spiritual feelings, freedom and self-fulfilment. We have also explored how such issues align with the current third wave of branding, involving the spirit or soul of nature.

Nash (in Redclift and Benton, 1994) argues that as societies develop economically they appreciate 'nature' more and 'civilization' less. Our view is that nature will ironically continue to be valued more as it disappears, but societies will also seek to replicate it, mimic its powers, and will eventually find it irresistible to go beyond nature. These are the issues that will spawn a significant debate for the tourism and other outdoor industries in general in the future, as manicured nature increasingly has significant commercial advantages. Nature is unpredictable, and the 'right' experience cannot be guaranteed or indeed easily 'read' by people. This leads to the commodification and commercialization of nature, yet nature itself does not fit easily with or abide by traditional economic models. Economy and ecology follow different rules. As a result, the experiences of nature are increasingly being artificially manufactured and regulated. There are many environmental, social, technical and commercial advantages to this process, but there are also many disadvantages as we become estranged from and lose touch with real nature. Choices concerning the consumption of nature and our relationship with nature are crucial if tourism is to coexist alongside conservation.

Nature will speak for itself, but as we go beyond nature few might hear its voice:

Nature has become imbued with so many virtues that the term 'natural' no longer confers unambiguous meaning. We have refashioned nature, in our minds, as well as in test tubes and fields, transforming ecological processes into political axioms . . .

(Goodman and Redclift, 1991, in Redclift and Benton, 1994)

Exploring nature is clearly an adventurous business.

Discussion points and exercises

1 Discuss the ethical dilemmas involved in wildlife adventure tourism.
2 Discuss the factors that have led to a growth of wildlife tourism in recent years.
3 Select two examples of the types of wildlife tourism product illustrated in Figure 10.3, and compare and contrast them.

11

Artificial environment adventure

Introduction

This chapter explores the key defining parameters of artificial adventure and its future
potential within the tourism industry as a leading
area of income. Here we explore definitions and
boundaries, review market trends in the development and use of artificial adventure, and create a
practical typology. Whilst the creation of artificial adventure sites is not a new phenomenon,
exciting possibilities lie ahead for yet more
innovative developments in the industry.

'Tall Stories' is one of an increasing number of
adventure holiday companies offering all the
excitement of adventure activities for tourists
under seductive product headings such as 'adrenaline junkie', 'radical experience', 'extreme addic-
tion' and 'ultimate adventure'. These clearly
identify some of the needs of the consumers.

Similarly, many other leading tourism companies are also offering exciting adventure opportunities for their clients to experience alongside more traditional holidays, through partnerships with other specialist adventure activity providers. Behind the scenes, however, the prevailing technological developments are beginning to drive the market in less transparent directions, and exciting prospects lie ahead for the tourism industry with a range of new adventure products.

> The Rock is a simulated two-person climbing wall that tilts, spins and rotates in a 105-degree radius to mimic real mountain climbing. You can select famous climbs via the computer console such as Everest, K2 and the Eiger. To add to the challenge we can adjust the speed and incline/decline depending on your ability or the difficulty of the climb. It remains quite safe, as you are never more than four feet off the ground. Moreover your safety is ensured by an operator in attendance at all times. The Rock can be used both inside and outside, and in adverse weather conditions has its own impressive events station. There is no need for special clothing, ropes or helmets.

It is the world of artificially constructed adventure that now represents the new frontier in adventure tourism, for a number of reasons. Besides the technical advancements in new surface materials and the invention of devices and gadgets, environmental protection, space, health and safety concerns and product organization also play a key role. As we will explore later in this chapter, some of these ingredients contrive to make the future of artificial adventure very commercially attractive. Throughout the world we are seeing the emergence of an ever-increasing array of adventure products that use some degree of artificiality or simulation, and this gives rise to the need to create something of a typology in order to understand the market more clearly.

Defining terms

In the late 1980s artificial adventure was given a basic underpinning definition in the USA. Attarian (1999), in an examination of artificial climbing environments, referred to a 'man-made structure, device, or environment that simulates a natural setting, which can be used specifically for teaching or participating in outdoor activities'. This definition implies that artificial equates to 'man-made' and outdoors, and suggests that it is anything 'not natural' – ranging from a small gadget or 'device' to a whole 'environment', which might take the form of a sizeable location.

Such a seasoned view of 'artificiality' is now likely to be more problematic, as a tension exists between artificial adventure and traditional views about what constitutes 'real' adventure.

Real adventure is often perceived as being outdoors because the natural outdoor environment is where there is exposure to wilderness and the associated dangers of natural forces or elements. It is these that represent the core of the challenge. It is perceived as being unpredictable and 'pure', in the sense that it is not contrived. In contrast, when adventure is constructed or contrived it can be perceived as somehow 'not authentic' – not indigenous. The perception of what is natural in terms of the environment and what is natural in terms of the individual endeavour is epitomized in longstanding debates about, for example, climbing natural rock faces with safety bolts, or summiting mountains without oxygen. But does it really matter?

At one end of the adventure tourism dichotomy we might have Theme Parks and Pleasure Parks, as they have long been artificially constructed locations with a focus on popular, packaged excitement and fun. 'Real' adventure might not include such adventurous rides at the fairground, in white-water rafting simulators, or racing driving in an amusement arcade machine. However, the boundaries between real and virtual or simulated environments are becoming ever more indistinct, making it increasingly difficult to distinguish adventure from amusement or entertainment. Furthermore, the high levels of risk-free safety, external inspection, regulation and monitoring associated with the commercialization of these fun-adventure environments is increasingly being transferred to the other end of the spectrum: the extreme adventure challenges. Many companies now offer the ultimate in adventure tourism, providing people with a chance to be 'guided' to summit the highest mountain on earth, Everest, for a significant fee. The challenge is to experience and survive in what is commonly known as the Death Zone (Dickinson, 1998) and to summit Everest. This upper area is rescue-free, and the body is continually breaking down and deteriorating. Despite many people being aided by experienced leaders and highly skilled Sherpas, and being supported by advanced technology and pre-laid ropes and ladders, the death rates are high. Yet the degree to which such an extreme adventure is viewed as a 'product', where paying clients are artificially supported and parts of the environment reconstructed for their safety, is continually changing. Increasingly if things go wrong the lawyers are called in, and the commercialized elements of adventure then take on a new appearance. 'Adventure' tourism is then highly scrutinized and is exposed to the glare of the media coverage regarding blame and responsibilities.

Adventure in the mind

Although adventure is essentially a state of mind, artificial adventure offers a particular type of adventure with the distinct advantage that the focus on mimicry or inventive creation can allow providers to produce the very best environment, or the most challenging natural conditions. This represents a real advantage for large-scale commercial use in tourism or recreation, as the relationship between risk and challenge is fundamentally changing. Products that incorporate natural forces are always difficult to manage and control commercially, and adventure activities themselves often impact negatively on the natural environment. These factors can be immensely significant market drivers.

If the development of these adventure products is to be successful in tourism markets, manageable and variable levels of challenge are needed, without the 'real risk'.

There are also other interesting psychological issues. In the practice of creating adventure in Outward Bound schools around the world there has long been a central debate about instructors 'letting the mountain (experience) speak for itself'. Artificially constructed sites are lacking in this latent meaning; the artificial stone of constructed climbing has no true evolutionary significance, no historical pedigree. The walls cannot speak for themselves, as they have little history to tell. What then is the essential composition of artificial adventure? It can take place in an indoor or outdoor environment, but the two locations can differ greatly in many respects as the boundaries are often not clear-cut. When we use the term 'outdoor adventure' we tend to think of a place outside, in the 'natural' environment, where many adventure activities are conducted. However, a cave is neither indoors nor outdoors, and many forms of artificial indoor caves are now being created to mimic natural caves. This brings us to the point where a much more detailed investigation of the characteristics of a series of practical examples can generate a classification of the nature of 'artificiality', which might be helpful. However, first we will examine a very brief history of artificial adventure in order to observe some basic evolutionary trends.

Historical perspectives

In 1941 the first-ever artificial climbing wall was said to have been built in Seattle, Washington, and in the 1950s the French extensively used adjustable wooden walls, especially for military training purposes. The first successful indoor climbing wall in the UK was at a school in Cumbria in the early 1960s.

In 1970 in Arizona the 'Big Surf' was created on an island lagoon. This was the first artificial surfing environment, though much has happened since those early days and mobile surf machines can now be found adorning indoor adventure exhibitions around the world. In 1972 the first major artificial kayak slalom course was built for the Munich Olympic Games, and many more have followed since. BMX sites, skate parks, roller-blading sites, artificial white-water rafting sites, portable high-ropes courses and many other artificial adventure sites all started to take the form of major commercial ventures in the late 1980s and early 1990s. They continue to proliferate around the globe, and more research is needed into the nature of these developments. In 2001 a million-pound project off the coast of Scotland proposed the creation of the world's largest experimental artificial reef from a million concrete blocks, designed to attract fish and crabs as well as boost the spawning habitat of the Scottish West Coast Lobster (Judd, 2001). This creation of whole islands can also be realized in the name of adventure tourism. Such artificial environments may not be any less 'real' to climbers, surfers or tourists than the natural outdoors.

Beach volleyball is not after all significantly different from indoor volleyball. The old debate among outdoor specialists appears to have focused more on what was considered pure, uncontrived and unpredictable adventure, where a degree of real risk pervaded.

The new contention is centred on technological developments and the continued levels of technical challenge. The artificial–real mix is thus subtler than first appears, as providers continue to mimic or alter or reproduce natural ingredients with a view to enhancing selectively the 'experience' of adventure, play, education, recreation or leisure.

The roots of artificial climbing walls lie in the indoor gymnasium, initially with the careful placing of bricks – sticking out bricks or missing bricks created the basis of a simple rock face. However, technological developments have enabled the emergence of many new artificial adventure activities within the tourism market. From bio-mimicry in clothing to pre-packaged climbing kits, from artificial caves and simulated ramps and hand-holds to bends, burns, snow and ice, there will continue to be many more technical development in the provision of artificial adventure in the future. Light and dark can be regulated (floodlights), thus allowing the provision of simulated adventure to take place when darkness might otherwise prevent it from happening. Artificial wave-making machines can be located either indoors or outdoors, they can be made mobile or fixed in one location, or even be placed out at sea, all creating near perfect surf when and where it's wanted.

The first artificial ski slopes were built in the 1960s, and by 1990 Europe's largest artificial ski resort had been completed in the UK. This attracts many tourists each year. The resort is located on an old industrial site in Sheffield. Called The Ski Village, it has snowboarding, tobogganing, and ski-jumping into water. A popular promotion is the Winter Sports Break, where the package includes luxury accommodation in a hotel, full breakfast, eight hours on the ski slope, equipment hire, and lesson options.

Nearby, converted from semi-derelict buildings, is The Foundry, which originated when students transformed an idea from their undergraduate dissertation into reality. This was the first of a new breed of fully commercial indoor climbing walls. It attracted 60 000 people in its peak in 1996, and was host to the first European indoor climbing championships. There are now over 60 indoor artificial climbing walls in the UK, and many are adding new artificial environments.

Adjacent to the Foundry is Jagged Globe, an adventure travel company specializing in high mountain adventures and with a good reputation for successful client summits on Everest. Just down the road is The House, created by resourceful young skateboarders in an old abandoned warehouse when they were forced off the streets and into the indoor environment by new laws. Now these young skateboarders operate a highly successful business, providing opportunities for skateboarding and roller-blading for many young people. The House was built with very little funding, and it brings with it a whole subculture of clothing, music and language – it appears to some extent to present a replacement of the 'youth club', emerging in the form of an adventure club. These facilities, so easily created, are transferable to tourism locations.

Unofficial motorbike scrambling also occurs on nearby slopes, and mountain bikers are now trying to enter this adventure zone with their own proposals to create an artificial site. A few miles away at Sheffield's Rother Valley Country Park, a recreational site developed on old coal spoil heaps, the British Championships of a new type of board sport called 'all-terrain boarding' were held in 1998. This boarding is similar to snowboarding but the boards have pneumatic tyres and suspension, so it is possible to ride all the year round on grass, through trees, on dirt tracks, even on tracks and roads. At nearby Doncaster, the world's first environmental theme park – the Earth Centre – mixes tourism adventure with visitors' education and experiential learning about the environment. It too has been developed on the site of an old coal mine. Quite by chance these new adventure zones are emerging in urban fringes around the world, replacing old industries and the world of production 'work' with recreational businesses involved in the world of leisure, tourism, training and coaching, learning, and new forms of adventure (Beard, in press). The development of these sites offers interesting perspectives on urban development; they have flourished and created some important fundamental changes from:

- Factory sites to places for adventure, play, leisure
- Potential workers to business owners and managers
- Dereliction to regeneration
- Damaging/polluting to reducing pressure on natural habitats
- Old industries to new forms of work.

Old urban spoil heaps now provide new places for scrambling. Walls and ledges provide places to abseil and climb; and new terms such as 'bouldering' (Proudman, 1999) are emerging (where climbers 'boulder' along a building or wall rather than on natural rock, in a horizontal climb not far off the floor). Of particular interest is the role of urban youth in the origination and design of new adventure activities, who employ their sense of stunt-play and creativity to develop business opportunities.

Urban adventure programmes can provide many personal development opportunities similar to those of traditional adventure wilderness expedition programmes, and the resemblance can be remarkable. The urban jungle can be a very adventurous place to explore; it can be very challenging and will in future present rich opportunities for the design of adventure tourism for people of all ages. Natural urban woodlands, parks and waterways can serve as places for adventure, as well as the physical environment of buildings or other structures. The city can be exhilarating and exciting, but it can also be frightening and intimidating and is often seen in a negative light.

Innovation in adventure developments

Much of the European and American literature on simulated adventure environments was written in the late 1980s, before a number of key technical breakthroughs occurred in some outdoor adventure industries – collectively termed the 'technical revolution'. Since the mid-1980s technical developments have had a significant impact on the diversification of both outdoor and indoor adventure. A traditional indoor environment has walls, floors, ceilings, doors, stairwells and many other features and objects. All of these can be enhanced and used in many creative ways to generate an adventure experience.

The indoor environment can become a climbing wall, a cave or an underground tunnel and, significantly, some features can be either real or imaginary. New materials and surfaces have played a central role in this technological revolution. The climbing surfaces are increasingly 'realistic'. Stone surfaces in climbing walls can simulate either limestone or grit-stone, and so mimic the natural feel and grip of the rock. Artificial ice can also be created from wall materials that have a toffee-like consistency that reshapes itself after the climbers have moved on. Similarly, artificially created indoor snow offers a commercial opportunity to replace the hard-surface approach to artificial slopes.

In mountain biking, the creation of obstacles, burms (high-speed banking corners) jumps and bridges can all mimic natural conditions, but design can theoretically proceed beyond the natural to ultimate environmental perfection for high adventure challenge or skill development. The advantage is that the conditions can be changed and controlled. Mobility too is emerging as a strong design feature. As motion is the key to aircraft simulators, so now we see the creation of rolling climbing walls and of more portable adventure sites. Artificial adventure can also be seasonally synchronized with real adventure activities (e.g. ski slopes operate in the same season as snow-covered natural slopes) or may provide unsynchronized adventure (such as climbing walls in winter). We are likely to see many more of these technical developments in this field.

Rocks caves and snow

In 1994 in Birmingham, a company called Rockface created a much broader leisure environment – again from a derelict warehouse in the city. Whilst the climbing walls form the foundation of the centre experience, there are also bars and restaurants. The centre offers a range of experiences for different visitor groups, including programmes for people with disabilities, training for executives, children's activities, and family fun and adventure. The climbing walls are adorned with a range of artefacts, such as artificial drainpipes and toilets, which amuses many of the teenagers. The walls and ceilings house abseiling platforms, rope bridges, a Jacob's ladder, a tower game and an artificial cave. The cave has been created using wooden panels to form a box structure around the rear of the climbing walls. Painted black to create almost total darkness, the cave also houses climbing holds, chimney breasts, ramps and circular tunnels of various dimensions, and the routes change levels by using trapdoors in the floors or ceiling. In darkness people experience many sensations, some 'natural' and some artificially stimulated. In places masses of thin rope dangle down from the ceiling onto people's backs, and some floor areas are made from crunchy natural gravel. Small bells tinkle to give delicate sounds, which the designers have built in especially for people with various levels of sensory disability. The site is continually evolving, and it is difficult to know whether to classify it as a teaching classroom, a recreational site, a funfair or a leisure centre. It is this multiple perception that underlies its unique success.

On mainland Singapore, six shipping containers have been linked by welded metal tubes to form a long adventure tunnel/cave/maze. The site itself is managed by Outward Bound Singapore as a children's adventure training camp; in Singapore it is compulsory for ten- to eleven-year-olds to experience 'outdoor education'. Each of the six containers has different features and challenges for young people to experience in their introduction to city adventure. The children enter the caves with light sticks or headlights, and the first cave is filled with small balls – creating an atmosphere more like play than adventure. As the children progress through the caves the environment changes. Some caves have pine logs to create a forest maze, whilst others have layered floors that have to be navigated (see Figure 11.1).

Figure 11.1 Future tourism developments? Artificial caves in Singapore, courtesy of SPARKc, Children's Adventure Training Centre.

There is a great deal of untapped potential to attract interest in artificial adventure from the tourism community, perhaps especially so in places where there are few or no large wilderness areas, such as Belgium, Denmark, or Singapore. More adventure zones are likely to benefit the tourism experience, as well as adding more excitement to the transformation of the image of the urban jungle for the tourist of the future (see Table 11.1).

Full-blown adventure resorts are also being created in many places. The Ubin Lagoon Resort is located between the coasts of Singapore and Malaysia. Pulau Ubin is a small natural island lying in the Straits of Johor with about 200 inhabitants, and it had largely remained underdeveloped until recently. Sometimes known as the Adventure Island, it is a ten-minute boat ride from the beautiful green and carefully manicured island city of Singapore, where few natural resources now exist. The island has abundant wildlife and still has traditional wooden village kampongs, and over 2000 visitors troop there in local bumboats at weekends – over 10 per cent of these are now non-Singaporean tourists. The island is an idyllic short-hop retreat for both Singaporeans and tourists, where the vast majority hire a bicycle for the day to roam around the many jungle roads and tracks.

Locals involve themselves in small-scale agriculture, fishing, boat building, and in sundry provisions for tourists. Bicycle rental, drinks and fruit stations have booming small businesses over the years, with more visitors wishing to experience the island's 'great outdoors' by pedal power. Despite the island being very small (a mere 8 km long by an average 1.5 km) there is a huge variety of bird life, and the once extinct Southern Pied Hornbill is making a comeback and is a key wildlife attraction. Over 179 species of birds have been recorded there, along with a total of 382 species of vascular plants. The wild boar still exists, as does the small-clawed Oriental otter. The existence of indigenous wildlife constitutes a key part of the adventure for many people.

A large part of the island, some 549 hectares, is designated as the Pulau Ubin Recreational Area by the Singapore National Parks Board. Amenities include a Tourist Information kiosk, seated shelters, look-out points, beach camp sites, picnic and barbecue sites, and interpretive storyboards. However, there are some tensions under the tranquil surface; according to Chua Ee Kiam (2000):

> Ubin's popularity as an outdoor retreat and repository of wildlife may be what saves the island from being developed for residential purposes. But Ubin runs the risk of being a victim of its own popularity. Outdoor activities, if not managed properly, can actually lead to great destruction.

Table 11.1   The advantages of simulated adventure recreation to the tourism industry (Beard and Wilson, 2002)

Social	*Commerical*
Can take part regularly – high levels of accessibility by walking, public transport. For the urban and rural population	Potential to increase the number of participants and beginners – creates a new market of participants
Potential for greater social interaction – crowds, spectators, cafés, clothing, music, youth culture etc.	All-season participation possible
	Suitable for experienced participants and beginners
Reduced trespass – e.g. by mountain bikers	Suited to experiential development programmes for managers, youth groups, children etc.
Reduced conflict with other users – e.g. public on streets, as in skateboarding, and in National Parks, as in mountain biking	Equipment and clothing sale/provision at location
Located off the 'streets'	Café/bar and tourism functions
Time and space zoning	

Environmental	*Technical*
Controlled environmental conditions	Mimic the 'best' bits – features and obstacles
Less susceptible to the unpredictable elements of the natural environment	Local natural environment may not contain the necessary features in one place
Less travel impact – people and equipment	A valuable training resource
Potentially less environmental impact – less direct physical environmental damage, less pollution and less ecological damage	Creating new champions in sport and recreation
Less environmental unpredictability	Added safety for schoolchildren/youth groups/ managers etc.
Elements on tap – e.g. light, snow or wind	Artificial flood-lighting provides winter opportunities in the UK
Less environmental risk	Controllable conditions
Can create unique/unnatural challenges – those totally new and *not* found in natural conditions	

Hopefully, these offerings will be kept as spartan as possible so that one has time to experience what Ubin has to offer.

Both public and private bodies and their interests are vying for space and resources, and wildlife and nature exist alongside agriculture and fishing and adventure and recreation, with large-scale tourism emerging recently alongside locally controlled tourism development. It is a unique combination, but future harmony is uncertain.

The impressive Outward Bound Singapore (OBS) centre is also located on the northern end of the island. Outward Bound embodies the spirit of public adventure. It started in 1967, and the organization and management were taken over by the People's Association in 1991. It is self-sufficient, with its own power and water supply and sea transportation. Outward Bound Singapore covers approximately one-third of the island, and it is fenced off from the tourist areas on the rest of the island. With its 130-plus staff it has instructed more than 153 000 participants between 1997 and 1999. Outward Bound Singapore has developed many development programmes for the nation's young people, and increasingly provides corporate training and development courses.

The island location was specially selected for the outdoor activities, which use the local rainforests, cliffs of granite quarries, mangrove swamps, surrounding seas and offshore islands. Outward Bound Singapore is one of the best equipped centres in the world, having 66 000 square metres of well-designed centre buildings, a large swimming/training pool in the tropical jungle, a gymnasium, an Indiana multi-element challenge and commitment course, the tripod and summit course, the inverse tower challenge course, the Ubin rescue system, numerous rock climbing walls, cutters, and many other facilities, including one of the largest zip wires in Asia. A vast majority of young Singaporeans will visit the island at some stage in their early lives and stay over in jungle accommodation blocks or in tents and carry out expeditions, treks, and many personal adventure challenge courses.

Further south on this small island is a more recent private venture. The development appears partially to replicate the Outward Bound 'experience', but it is designed for an altogether different audience and has very different accommodation. The Ubin Lagoon Resort is for tourists. It opened in May 2000, when over $S25 000 million was invested in it to make it the ultimate adventure tourism experience in Singapore. Alongside the resort is the Adventure Training Centre, designed by Adventure Training Systems of Australia. One climbing tower sports a large Nike logo, and the resort caters for Singaporeans and overseas tourists seeking either 'adrenaline-quenching pursuits' or simply quiet relaxation away from the hustle and bustle of the mainland. With kampung-style chalets, the resort offers a back-to-nature holiday concept with a focus on outdoor activities. The resort is family orientated and management say it now attracts some 8000 visitors a month. The brochures state that the resort offers a 'comprehensive holiday destination ... and we are proud to say Ubin Lagoon Resort has it all'. The resort also offers corporate training and claims to have gained a large share of this market, having trained 10 000 corporate clients in 2000.

Significantly, in adventure tourism terms, the resort has artificial whirl-pools, an artificial lake with an artificial waterfall, trampolines and high-ropes courses. Tourists can buy adventure by the activity, and the list of activities on offer is impressive. Archery, discovery cruises, fishing, sea-kayaking, swamp-kayaking, a kelong trip, snorkelling, day and night swamp and rainforest trekking, island explorer trips, 'the great leap of faith', a 'flying fox', rock climbing, abseiling, water skiing, mountain biking, simulated parachute jumping and dangle duo are some of the adventure experiences on offer. There is also a 22-metre international standard Extreme Sports Tower and a Challenge Pyramid. The Resort was host to the Ubin climbing championships in 2001. Membership to the Club Endeavour offers people exciting and daring escapades in other places besides Singapore. Other exotic locations for such adventure resorts include the islands of Bintan, Battuta and Phuket, and other destinations in Australia and Canada.

Whilst the Singapore government has postponed decisions about the future of Pulau Ubin developments, one potential solution to the problem of multi-use of small islands was reported in *Action Asia* magazine (August/September 2001). The article remarked that the famous Lion City of Singapore intends to promote tourism by an inventive scheme of 'reclaiming nature', by infilling the land between three offshore islands for resort development whilst leaving the 'natural' islands undisturbed.

Towards a classification of artificial adventure

Some simple practical typologies are created here in order to investigate more fully the diversity of artificial adventure. Whilst practical typologies are helpful in delineating some boundaries of 'adventure activities', the exact nature of artificiality varies and the term 'artificial adventure' might refer to all or some of the following ingredients:

- Devices (e.g. bolts, gadgets, equipment)
- An activity (canyoning, coasteering, roller-blading, indoor climbing)

- The natural elements (artificial snow, artificial lights, simulated wind, simulated waterfalls)
- The structure/location (an indoor climbing wall, roller-blade 'courses')
- Whole environments (resorts, adventure zones, adventure islands).

The biosphere matrix (Figure 11.2) offers an ecological division of the four basic elements in which adventure takes place (adapted from Beard and Wilson, 2002). Each segment can be subdivided into natural and artificial elements used in adventure programmes. For example, natural adventure environments include the land-involving habitats such as jungle, moorland, desert and mountains. Semi-natural environments refer to parkland and highly cultivated sites. Artificial locations include alleyways, subways and tunnels, walls, bollards, bridges or human-constructed islands. Eighty-two per cent of UK climbers, for example, now use artificial indoor climbing sites, and there are more than 60 artificially constructed skate parks in the UK.

In terms of activities, bungee jumping represents an interesting adventure topic when considering whether an activity can be classified as natural or

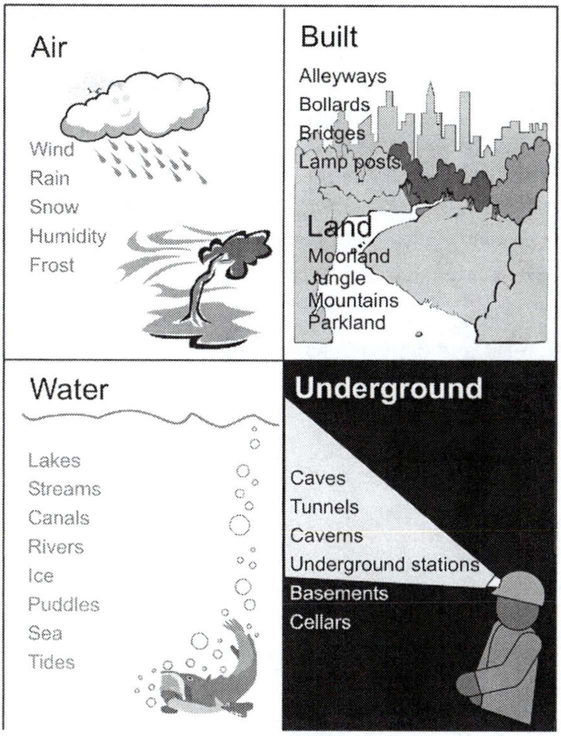

Figure 11.2 The biosphere matrix.

241

artificial adventure. The activity occurs as a tourist attraction in many natural locations, and is popular in New Zealand. It is popular in Europe, too, and there is a European Bungee Sports Association. The activity itself, whilst being exhilarating, is generally the ingredient that seems less natural, in that people throw themselves head first off a high point whilst attached to a strong elastic rope that should engage and halt the fall not too far from the ground. However, this adventurous activity also uses artificial structures to leap from, although it is a variant of a ritual carried out long ago by Polynesian Islanders. Base jumping is also essentially jumping from very high objects – 'base' being an acronym for Bridge, Antenna, Span and Earth. These are the objects that these adventure seekers launch themselves off, and hence it is still a largely an illegal operation. It is undertaken by experienced skydivers who tend to perform at least 250 jumps before moving to try base jumping.

Another exceptional activity is extreme ironing, where people iron clothes in extreme locations. Absurd as it sounds, the activity is very popular and there were over 100 participants in 2001. The sport's worldwide governing body, the Extreme Ironing Bureau, received well over 20 000 hits on its website in 2001. The craze, which has now spread across France, Germany, the USA and New Zealand, evolved from humorous stunts and is said to be a post-laddish activity for new men, invented by Philip Shaw of the UK. He is known by his fellow ironists simply as 'Steam'!

This also leads us to the question as to whether the 'newness' of activities gives rise to a perception that they are less traditional and less natural. Are the newer activities tending to become more contrived and extreme in their artificiality? Technological developments make for more artificial gadgets and

Table 11.2 Natural and artificial activity and environmental adventures

Natural environment	*Artificial environment*
Sky-surfing	Base jumping
Barefoot water skiing	Extreme ironing
Fun-yaking	
Coasteering	
Sea kayaking	Artificial slalom white-water rafting
Cliff diving	
Climbing	Skateboarding
Running	Roller-blading
Walking	Indoor climbing

surfaces, but extreme invention makes for fun and adventure in devising a new breed of activities for the thrill-seekers. This is a subject requiring more research. Thus we see another simplistic classification starting to develop. Table 11.2 shows which activities are natural and which are artificial with respect to whether the location or environment is natural or artificial.

Instant adventure

Certainly the adventurous element of tourism products increasingly has an elevated status, by popular demand. In St Davids in Pembrokeshire, Wales, a company called TYF No Limits has been offering adventure 'on demand' since the early 1990s. 'Instant adventure' decisions are possible for holidaymakers who haven't already planned the details of their holiday and want to be able to make the most of the weather and the choices that they see when they arrive in Pembrokeshire. Another major drive has been to increase TYF's ability to service other accommodation providers as well as provide improved ease of booking for existing clients. An e-commerce-enabled booking system was recently installed, which allows hotels, guest houses and attractions to act as booking agents for activities running the same afternoon or later the same week. The same system makes it possible for families or individuals who do plan ahead to make their own bookings without reference to charts, forms, books or any other paper paraphernalia.

TYF pioneered the sport of coasteering in the 1980s and, through a highly successful PR campaign, raised awareness of the sport. Coasteering involves travelling around the coast by scrambling, swimming and cliff jumping into the water. Coasteering was accepted as a registered trademark in 2000; to protect the investment and 16 years of intellectual property, TYF created a set of safety and environmental standards (SES) for coasteering with input from other centres. These are run on a 'not for profit' basis, with any surplus revenues donated to Surfers Against Sewage, a UK-based pressure group that campaigns for clean water. To make the stories from coasteering sessions more memorable and more easily recounted, sections of each route have been branded recently with new names such as Dambusters, Babylon Bay, Great Plains, Jabberwocky, Soho and many more. Five per cent of TYF's pre-tax profit is committed to environmental charities, and staff have an optional 5 per cent 'timebank' of one day every two months to be used for community development activities.

In the competitive world of retailing, traders have also taken advantage of artificial adventure technology. The Outdoor Experience superstore in Scotland has developed a unique sales environment to stay ahead of the competitors. The superstore has its own indoor ice wall, climbing walls, mountain bike paths, a waterfall and rocky footpaths, all freely available for customers to try out new equipment and clothing before buying. It does not stop there. The temperature can be lowered to minus 20 degrees centigrade, wind speeds can be increased to 30 kilometres per hour, and a tropical rainstorm turned on in an instant!

Conclusion

In this chapter we have revealed the nature of the continuous evolution of new adventure technology, new artificial adventure activities and artificially constructed adventure locations. The transition towards this increasing use of 'artificialness' has, in some cases, been episodic, shifting from simplistic structures such as brick shapes used for climbing coaching through to complex equipment and large specialist adventure resorts. Some artificial sites have had considerable investment, whilst others have involved small sums of money. Some evolving adventure products have an emerging new adventure subculture (youth culture, indoor climbers, music, clothes) and language (coasteering and bouldering) associated with them.

In this chapter we have also explored the changing mindsets associated with the relationship towards traditional versus artificially constructed adventure. The nature and degree of risk and challenge and fun appears to differ fundamentally in artificial adventure, where the challenge and or environment can easily be altered and regulated to suit consumers. Highly commercially controlled activities can still take people beyond their comfort zone, but their psychology plays a key role in their experience and acceptance of the contrived product. Risk is simply perceived as not being real. Commercial pressures in force predominantly influence the risk reduction: it is inherent in business law and practice.

Finally, we have explored many other commercial, environmental and social advantages and disadvantages for artificial adventure. Artificial adventure, it appears, is increasingly likely to play a key role in the future of the tourism industry.

Discussion points and exercises

1 Discuss the reasons why artificial adventure tourism has grown substantially in recent years.
2 Critically evaluate Table 11.1.
3 Create your own typology of artificial adventure, together with a rationale for your chosen typology.

Part
F

The future of
adventure tourism

12

Adventure tourism in the future: the new frontier

Introduction

This chapter attempts to look into the future and forecast developments in the adventure tourism industry and assess the main issues it will face. It is divided into three sections.

The first section examines background trends. The initial stage of prediction is to draw out the underlying factors influencing the trends in adventure tourism, and in particular we will consider:

- Demographic factors, such as population size, age structure, and family structure
- Socio-economic factors, such as employment patterns, attitudes to ageing, and lifestyle trends including consumerism and health and fitness
- Technological developments, such as the Internet, new materials and transport
- Political and macro-economic trends, such as the role of developing countries in the world economy, policy and legislation, political stability etc.

The second section looks at the impact of these trends on the adventure tourism industry, and attempts to predict:

- How the characteristics of participants in adventure tourism might change
- What new adventure tourism activities and products might emerge
- Which destinations will become increasingly involved in the adventure tourism business
- How tour operators will manage their adventure tourism businesses to ensure their sustainability.

Section three concludes by identifying major issues for the adventure tourism industry, and by suggesting areas for further research.

Key background trends

The development of adventure tourism is dictated by demographic, socio-economic, political and technological changes. Of course it is risky predicting social, political and technological changes and how quickly they will develop, but these trends are the foundations upon which forecasts are built. Considering them therefore gives us a more informed basis for the predictions that follow later in the chapter.

Some of these trends have been referred to briefly in previous chapters. However, here we have drawn together and summarized what appear to be the most significant contextual trends for the tourism industry in general, and adventure tourism in particular.

Demographic trends

To begin, it is worth reminding ourselves of key demographic factors – principally population size, age distribution and family patterns. In most developed and post-industrial countries the population is reaching its peak in terms of size, and will shortly enter a period of decline. In the UK and many other developed countries, the largest cohort of the population is of those people born between 1945 and 1970. Over the next 30 years these post-war 'baby boomers' will be a very large potential market – much larger than their younger counterparts. The oldest of the baby boom generation are now in their mid-fifties, and the youngest are approaching their mid-thirties. This population structure means the number of 'empty nesters' (adults whose children are leaving home) and middle-aged 'no family' couples will increase over the next few decades. A more detailed look at all cohorts, over a shorter timescale, is also important for niche marketing. For example, the number of 15–24-year-olds in the UK will increase by 8.4 per cent from 7.2 million in 1998 to 7.8 million in 2005 (Mintel, 2001a). This is the age group most likely to indulge in sporting activities.

Another demographic characteristic of developed countries is that women are not only having fewer children, but are also often having them at an older age. Family and household structure is also changing. More single-parent families, more childless couples and more single-person households are revising expectations of a typical family structure.

Many of these demographic trends are a result of changing social attitudes and financial capacity, which brings us neatly onto socio-economic factors.

Socio-economic trends

Socio-economic changes tend to create lifestyle trends and, as lifestyle is one of the key determinants of consumers' choice of tourism experiences, we will consider some of them here.

Employment patterns

Employment and work patterns have seen considerable shifts over the last 30 years, and these will continue to influence tourism activities. Working conditions are increasingly regulated by legislation. Throughout Europe paid holiday entitlement has risen, and is generous compared with that in the USA. More professionals are taking early retirement, with good company pensions. Working practices such as flexi-time mean that workers can more easily create 'long weekends'. However, whilst in general holiday entitlements have become more generous, many workers find they are working harder and longer than ever. The era of 'a job for life' has gone, nationalized and public sector industries are increasingly becoming 'privatized', and the risk of job loss exists for many employees. The shift from manufacturing to management and professional jobs and the increasing numbers of self-employed mean a considerable sector of the population sees work as the focus of life. Professionals feel under pressure to spend long hours at the office, protecting their reputation and outputs. In the UK, a survey by Buzz, the low-cost airline, estimated that employees lose a staggering 49 million days holiday entitlement per year (published in the *Sunday Times*, Jan 20th, 2002). The development of a '24/7' culture means that service sector workers don't escape this pressure, and are often working unsocial hours. One of the results of these current employment patterns is that short breaks are becoming much more popular.

Career patterns are also changing. The proliferation of 'gap years' directly before or after university, and adoption of 'work–life balance' HRM policies mean that it is becoming increasingly acceptable for workers to take a career break at any time.

Changing attitudes to ageing

There is no doubt that attitudes to age are changing, and this is going to continue to have a major impact on future trends in adventure tourism. Whilst 'youth culture' continues to thrive, plenty of baby boomers are refusing to act their age! They no longer feel they have to adopt the behaviour and attitudes of their parents' generation. High-profile examples of this attitude abound in middle-aged rock musicians, who once epitomized youth and rebellion and now refuse to retire on the grounds of age. Better personal and professional health care is also helping people maintain high physical activity levels.

Lifelong education

In the UK, lifelong education and broader access to education and training are widely promoted. A wider range of young and not so young people is being encouraged to enter Higher Education. Mintel (2000b) suggests that, as the population becomes more mature and education standards rise, leisure will be seen as a broader process of personal development. Travel and cultural and intellectual pursuits will be undertaken during leisure time for self-development and to improve lifelong learning.

Consumerism and fashion

Lifestyles continue to be dictated by fashions and fads. Millington *et al.* (2001) observe that travel is becoming a fashion accessory, and this is reflected in the media, with a number of glossy travel magazines and increased coverage of travel experiences (particularly adventurous travel) on the TV. A whole channel is dedicated to 'extreme' sports on Sky. This media attention is making certain destinations and activities more popular.

Culture and counter-culture

Mintel's *2020 Vision* report (2000a) suggests the next twenty years will see major changes in consumer lifestyles. It particularly highlights the development of an 'entropic society', which is more fragmented, less socially cohesive and more individualistic and personalized. Mintel suggests established social and economic institutions and traditions will be regarded with less reverence, and society will split into subcultures that reflect personal interests. The drivers behind this development are identified as the ageing population, the increase in single households, the trend towards later marriages, a rise in cohabitation, and increased divorce.

Self-reliance will become more important, and consumers will create their own world and sense of belonging from the disordered and confusing array of choices that an increasingly hectic information environment will create. Mintel (2000b) suggests the consumer will actively seek out lifestyle brands that identify the individual and give a stable point of reference that reflects their values. This will apply to young and old alike.

Hand in hand with an increasingly consumerist society we can expect to see an increasing disillusionment with materialism, which does not always bring the fulfilment that many people anticipate. Subcultures ranging from low-key alternative lifestyles to anarchical countercultures will continue to have a presence in the marketplace.

Health and fitness
A growing interest in healthier lifestyles is evidenced by increased participation in active leisure pursuits, membership of gyms and health clubs, sales of diet and detox books and so on. Mintel (2000a) reports an increase in participation in non-competitive sports, suggesting that participants take part out of a desire to keep fit and healthy, look good, and meet other people socially. Outdoor activities are perceived to promote a sense of well being, whether through the benefits of exercise or by reconnecting with the self through contact with nature, and increasing numbers of visits to the countryside are being made (Countryside Commission, 1998).

Under-represented groups in tourism
Some groups of consumers do not participate in tourism as much as other groups. There are a number of barriers to participation in leisure activities, including adventure tourism. Lack of time and lack of disposable income are two barriers that are easily recognized. Patmore (1983) has identified a typology of barriers to participation, which include 'social' barriers (where some people consider certain types of activity are 'not for them') and 'physical' barriers (where physical obstacles prevent some individuals from participating).

Two groups in particular are increasingly participating in leisure tourism activities as these barriers shift. People with disabilities have been confronted with many man-made obstacles in tourism – for example, the design of buildings and transport has often created barriers. They have also been faced with discriminatory attitudes and social barriers that make a tourism experience less enjoyable. Pressure groups have helped develop a growing awareness of ways to accommodate people with disabilities, and technical advances in specially designed or adapted equipment have enabled participation in lots of adventurous activities, such as skiing.

Ethnic minority groups have also been under-represented in certain types of tourism activity. For example, in the UK they are under-represented in countryside recreation and outdoor activities (Agyeman, 1990). A number of projects have been set up to encourage participation in countryside and outdoor activities by ethnic minority groups, and these, along with the UK current policy focus on 'social inclusion', may augur change in participation rates in this type of adventure tourism.

Technological trends

There are a number of areas where technological trends will have impacts on the adventure tourism industry.

The information environment will continue to grow more complex. The increasing cheapness of technological goods such as e-mail, voicemail, video conferencing, and portable PCs will have a number of impacts, including information overload and an increased sense of pressure. This will in turn impact on the tourism industry as more people wish to escape these pressures.

Electronic communication and data management will have an impact on how consumers find information and make bookings, and on how operators manage their businesses. The Internet has already had a huge impact on the tourism industry; for example, it has been the big technical innovation behind low-cost airlines (further illustrations can be found in Chapter 7). In the future, voice-based computer systems may save time for businesses and tackle the reluctance of some members of the public to use IT. Virtual reality will be used in new ways, perhaps as a marketing tool.

More sophisticated data handling systems will enable businesses to target micro markets. Mintel (2000a) suggests that the era of mass communications (and advertising) will come to an end, as increasing individualism means consumers will plug into channels designed specifically for their interest.

The development of new materials and new manufacturing methods will make some activities accessible to a wider range of people, through cheaper production, enhanced safety control and lighter, stronger materials.

Technological changes in the world of transport are going to affect tourism in general. The Channel tunnel has cut down journey times from the UK to the

European continent, whether by car or Eurostar. High-speed catamaran ferries, tilting trains and faster air flight are also predicted to make an impact (O'Connell, 2002). It is a commonly held perception that journey times of more than two and a half hours put people off making a trip, and reducing travel time opens up new destinations to the weekend break market in particular. Fast-track travel, with personalized electronic ticketing systems, will also play a part in reducing journey times. Environmentally friendlier alternatives to petrol engines are being researched and tested by the motoring industry, and their introduction could benefit the environmental reputation of the tourism industry.

Technological developments that improve the safety of passengers, particularly security scanning equipment in airports, will be developed. Restoring confidence after the terrorist turmoil of 2001 and 2002 is been a priority for the airline industry.

Both transport initiatives and electronic communication will create a global market that will be easier to access than ever before, at least for those who have money and power. These last two factors bring us to the issues of economic and political trends.

Economic and political trends

We can speculate on what individuals and businesses may or may not be able to do, but their activities are very much constrained by the economic and political contexts in which they exist.

It is already clear that many of the early-industrialized nations are moving into a post-industrial era, where the economy is not so reliant on manufacturing and is more dependent on service, technological and information/knowledge-based industries. Where manufacturing remains, it is for specialized, high-value products. There has been an increase in the proportion of 'white collar' workers and, whilst there have been real problems with unemployment amongst the displaced manufacturing workers, in general standards of living and personal disposable income have consistently risen and look set to continue to do so over the short term. One of the results is that there has been an increase in spending on leisure and tourism products.

Developing countries have picked up the manufacturing and production role that industrialized countries have lost, often using high-tech methods of production. The location of production near the intended market is no longer a practical issue, as transport and communication make access to a global market easy. Much of the investment needed to set up manufacturing and production plants in developing countries comes from foreign investment. This also often means that a lot of the profit generated by the business leaves the country. Multinationals in particular hold a great deal of economic and political power.

There are growing concerns and tensions about this kind of investment, and the foreign policy of powerful western governments and the actions of multinationals may come under closer scrutiny. The relatively low wages paid to most workers in developing countries will make it difficult for them to match the affluence of their western counterparts. Nonetheless almost all forecasts predict a global rise in standards of living, and consequently in developing countries an increasing proportion of people's disposable income will be spent on leisure and holidays, initially based in their own region. Whilst it is unlikely that developing countries will become larger generators than receptors of international tourists, there will be a growing number of newly wealthy individuals in developing countries who will look beyond domestic tourism opportunities.

A number of the remote and exotic destinations that attract adventure tourism are affected by political and social unrest. Some destinations have not yet developed a tourism industry because of concern over safety; in other places tours are put on hold when levels of crime, civil unrest and military action escalate. However, once the levels of risk to travellers become 'acceptable', often the first returning tourism activities are adventure tourism activities. Mintel (2001b) identifies overland expeditions as being the first to lead tourists to destinations that are emerging form a period of war or social instability. Overland tours do not require sophisticated accommodation and transport networks, as they are relatively self-sufficient. Indeed, it is their speed at moving into new areas makes them an attractive activity for adventure tourists.

It is hard to predict which areas will be 'out of bounds' for tourists in the future. Current conflicts in Israel, Palestine, Kashmir and Afghanistan are impacting on the tourist trade, as are concerns about crime and personal safety in countries such as Bolivia and Papua New Guinea. The Machu Pichu Trail has suffered from a number of attacks on tourists recently. In some instances terrorist activity purposely targets tourists, who are viewed as representatives of the countries and policies that terrorists are fighting against. Visible and identifiable groups such as adventure tourists, especially those who have expensive adventure gear and vehicles with them, also run the risk of being resented for their privileged and consumerist lifestyle. The destinations where such tensions against western developed countries are likely to arise are often prime destinations for adventure tourism, being less developed and remote. Terrorism has the potential to impact significantly on the development adventure tourism business in these locations, especially where the North American market is involved. Of course the adventure tourism sector is the one sector where this type of risk might act as an attractor rather than a detractor, but these consumers will be in the minority.

Sometimes self-imposed restrictions, based on objections to regimes with poor human rights records, deter many tourists from visiting destinations such as Burma or China.

The opening of borders and the government policy on tourism are of course hugely influential. Developing countries are aware of the potential socio-economic benefits of international tourism, and this is generally resulting in the opening up of more borders and the promotion of more destinations.

Policy and legislation influence the tourism industry in a more sedate but equally far-reaching way. For example, European legislation forced deregulation of the UK airline industry, which enabled the launch of low-cost, 'no frills' airlines. These now look set to become the chosen beasts of burden for medium-distance travel.

The political agenda is manifested in policy as well as legislation. Policies relating to environmental conservation and sustainable development provide an example of how policy can influence developments in tourism. Since the 1980s, international strategies, conventions, resultant national policy and growing public awareness have ensured that the concepts of sustainable development and eco-ethics have penetrated all types of business and activity. However, because sustainable development is more of a policy matter than a legislative one, some companies and authorities take it on board more than others. This is as true of the tourism industry as any other.

Currently, in the UK at least, history, culture and heritage are high priorities in terms of policy, as well as being popular topics of interest amongst the general public. The fashionability of culture and heritage has created a large market of customers who are interested in discovering more, and this demand bodes well for discovery-based tourism.

Future developments in adventure tourism

This section looks at the implications of these trends for the future development of adventure tourism. It is structured around future developments in four aspects of adventure tourism – participants, activities and 'products', destinations, and operators.

Table 12.1 Main discussion points

Participants	Activities and products	Destinations	Operators
Older Youth Family Women Singles Nationalities Changing motivations	Extreme adventure Activity and multi-activity holidays Family adventure 'Benefit' adventure Technology-mediated activities Prestige adventure travel Non-physical adventure Independent adventure Short breaks	Developing countries and alternative destinations Eastern Europe Domestic destinations Artificial environments Restrictions	Independent Vertically integrated Partnership Standards and certification H&S/risk management Marketing Retailainment

Table 12.1 summarizes the main points in each of these aspects, and the following discussion provides an analysis of each point.

Participants

Adventure tourists are not a homogeneous group, and the profile of adventure tourists in the future will be as wide ranging as it is now. However, we can expect certain segments of the market to grow. Here we discuss the growth of older participants, families, youth, women, singles and certain national markets in adventure tourism. This is followed by an examination of whether we can expect the motivations of tourists to change.

Older adventure tourists

We predict that there will be an increase in the number of older participants in adventure tourism. The baby boomers who are refusing to get old will seek more adventurous holidays. This large market will be relatively affluent, and as each cohort approaches retirement its members will have the time to travel too.

Self-fulfilment rather than escapism will be an important motivator for older adventure tourists, supporting a growth in discovery adventure travel, and 'ed-venture'. Many of these consumers will also aim to maintain their levels of physical activity and skill, which they have not allowed middle age to diminish, and so a growth in physically challenging adventure holidays for this market segment is also anticipated. Millington (2001) states that many adventure companies report that at least one-third of the people who like to rough it whilst on white-water rafting, snowmobile, horse riding and other adventure activities are in their fifties, sixties and seventies. A Mintel (2000a) survey implies many will purposefully avoid the traditional 'senior travel' activities.

Youth adventures

We predict an increase in what Millington (2001) terms 'globe trotting youth'. In the USA student travel increased by 20–30 per cent each year during the 1990s. As more young people enter higher education they will be exposed to the concept and expectation of travel as part of the total education experience.

Another major development will be the increase in teenagers' autonomy as consumers. Individualized lifestyles will affect families too, and there will be fewer shared family activities as children get older. Youngsters are becoming increasingly sophisticated and experienced purchasers, and familiarity with the Internet gives them access to the information they need to make their own choices. There is no doubt this will encompass many goods, and we anticipate an increase in tourism purchase decisions being made by children in the future.

Family adventure

There is an opportunity for an increase in family-focused adventure tourism products as people delay having a family until they are older. By the time adults start a family they have often developed leisure and holiday patterns that they are reluctant to give up when children come along.

The US Travel Industry Association (1997, in Millington et al., 2001) say that 'over 55 per cent of people participating in adventure activities while travelling in the previous 5 years had children in their household, and at least a third of them took children on their trips'. This suggests a huge potential market for adventure tourism for families, which is as yet untapped.

Leisure time is a precious commodity for adults in the middle of the family life cycle. A survey of parents of children aged 0–15 years put family holidays at the top of the list of leisure priorities, beating keeping fit, watching TV, eating out and gardening by a substantial margin (Mintel, 2000b). Time pressure means that many of these customers will pay for services that maximize the intensity and quality of their valuable holiday experience. It also means that 'sure bet' holidays are sought, as holidays that turn out to be mediocre or poor are a waste of precious time. However, cost is also important to families on a budget, and transportation costs (both financial and emotional!) to remote or exotic destinations may be prohibitive for family groups. Concerns about health-care provision often exclude these destinations too.

Women

The growth of the service and information sectors and flexible work practices has increased the proportion of women in the workforce. This trend will continue, and the demands of these financially independent women will influence tourism services. This suggests opportunities for adventure tour operators to develop less 'macho' adventure products that will appeal to a greater range of women.

Singles

The number of single people also looks set to increase, and we anticipate the tourism industry will respond by creating products that assist singles to mix socially. An example of such an initiative can be found in the Activities Abroad 2002 brochure, which states: 'Group trips make up the bulk of our departures and solo travellers will find themselves amongst friends on one of these holidays. In response to requests from our clients we have also set aside certain weeks catering exclusively for families, single-parent families and women only'. Adventure tourism based on group travel or on group activities is very well aligned to meet the needs of these market segments.

Nationalities

It is predicted that established generating regions for adventure travel will continue to provide most of the growth in numbers of consumers of adventure tourism. These regions are principally the USA, Canada, Australia, New Zealand and North West Europe, particularly the UK, Germany, France and Italy.

However, as tourism develops in areas such as East Asia, India and Brazil we can expect a move away from 'initiate' tourism activities, such as organized group trips with set sightseeing itineraries and specially tailored hotel accommodation, to more independent travel and adventurous activities. The younger clients will probably lead the way in these changes; indeed Millington (2001) reports that heli-skiing, climbing in the Himalayas and live-aboard diving trips in remote parts of the Pacific are growth products among high-flying young Asian professionals. The size of the Chinese market is potentially huge, and many companies will be considering how they can best tap into this market.

The rapid change in the economic fortunes of Central and Eastern Europe, including Russia, suggests that participants from these regions will aspire to the same types of tourism experiences as their western neighbours. They will certainly become enthusiastic adventure tourists, and because it will take some time before wealth distribution across Europe is similar, we can expect the development of adventure tourism destinations in Eastern Europe to cater for this demand at more affordable prices.

Changing motivations

It is unlikely that the range of motivations, in terms of tourism pursuits, will change greatly over the next few years. However, the numbers of consumers motivated by particular needs will ebb and flow with societal changes. We predict that the following four motivators will become more significant, and these will drive the growth of adventure tourism:

1 *Escape* – from the stresses of urban living, employment and information overload, and from the materialistic culture of our consumer society. Adventure tourism can provide absorbing activities and a simpler life, close to nature, that meets these escapism needs.
2 *Self-fulfilment* – increasing exposure to the concept of self-development, through higher education, professional development and the media, means this will become a more clearly articulated demand. In addition, Muller and Cleaver (2000) suggest that the baby boomers will experience certain psychological transformations as they approach middle age. They identify two changes that are particularly pertinent to this discussion: the emergence of introspection, which can lead to a re-setting of goals and new challenges, and people's desire to make the best of who they are and what they are capable of, and in doing so find self-fulfilment. These reinforce the likelihood that older participants will become a major part of the adventure tourism market.
3 *Stimulation and intensity* – the consumers' appetite for new and novel experiences seems insatiable. Time pressure demands full and intense

experiences. Things that are 'different' and things with a high 'experiential' quotient will be seen as a valid antidote to the vicarious acquisition of knowledge through an intermediary such as the TV or the Internet, and will fulfil sensation-seeking needs.

4 *Aspiration* – in today's image-conscious world, leisure activities and the type of holiday a person takes are regarded as reflections of their character and values. Adventure can suggest heroism, strength, bravery, individuality, independence, skill, and many other impressive qualities. The TIA (see Millington, 2001: 84) also found, in a recent survey, that 85–90 per cent of all respondents had a positive reaction to adventure travel. We can expect to see more aspirational purchasing of adventure tourism products, and more marketing activity focusing on these aspirations.

Activities and products

New products are being developed and refined in response to the changing market and technological developments. The following is a list of products and activities that we anticipate will take a more prominent position in adventure tourism, ranging from more physical challenges to products at the 'softer' end of the range.

Extreme adventure

'Ask any extreme sports participant and they will tell you that their sport is more than just a sport – it's a state of mind and a way of life. It's about challenge, adventure and pushing the boundaries . . . It's about meeting and sharing your enthusiasm for your sport with a like-minded group of people and it's about fun, challenge and excitement.'

(Mintel, 2001a: 1).

We predict that 'extreme' activities will develop as a significant component of the adventure tourism industry (see Box 12.1). These physically challenging activities will be based on a 'harder, faster, deeper' mentality. As adventure activities become more popular, people will push the boundaries of performance and achievement levels – hence the development of sports such as speed skiing. Many of the activities that form the adventure activity milieu, such as mountaineering, sport climbing, stunt surfing etc., are undertaken by professionals who are sponsored to develop their techniques and prowess as part of the ultimate goal of promoting the sport and equipment. Amateurs are spurred on to achieve similar standards. The competitive aspect of sport is one of the drivers of the development of more extreme activities.

Box 12.1   Extreme adventure

We are beginning to see the first signs of major tour operators expanding their product range into this 'extreme' area. The UK's leading adventure travel operator, Exodus, is an example of a company that is diversifying into developing more challenging forms of adventure holiday. It launched a new brand of holidays called 'Feat First' in 2001, targeted at those people who want to 'test themselves to the limit' (*Planet News*, 2001: 6). Although Exodus already offered six other types of adventure holiday to more than 80 countries – Discovery and Adventure, Overland Journeys, Biking Adventures, European Destinations, Multi-Activity, and Walking & Trekking – and hence catered for many different typologies of adventure tourist, it was keen to develop more extreme forms of adventure. Its Feat First holidays are mainly of a mountaineering nature, with several trips taking clients up to high altitude and on the ultimate of adventures, to the summit of Everest. Other trips include expeditions to destinations such as Greenland and the North Pole, and survival courses in demanding environments – for example, deserts and jungles (Exodus, 2002). Clearly these products are geared towards the more practised adventurer who is seeking out exciting, unusual and challenging experiences.

The Observer Sport Monthly's Guide to Extreme Sports (2001) describes extreme leisure activities, and gives information on how to get involved in them (see Table 12.2). Getting involved often encompasses a tourism experience, in that travel and overnight stays are required for these activities.

Mintel (2001a) identifies some of these, notably skateboarding, inline skating, wakeboarding and snowboarding, as 'lifestyle extreme sports'. These are sports that place more emphasis on clothing, codes of behaviour, music and language. Some of these have less potential as mainstream tourism activities, as they can easily be undertaken at home, but snowboarding and wakeboarding need resources that merit travel. In addition, three emerging extreme sports are identified as having the potential to be the next popular trend: – kite-surfing, street luge and parakarting.

Mintel's survey of extreme sports (2000a) suggests they are of most appeal to the 15–34 age group, with teenagers looking forward to being able to

Table 12.2   *The Observer Sport Monthly's Guide to Extreme Sports* (2001)

Extreme air	Base jumping	Sky diving
	Bungee jumping	Sky surfing
Extreme motor	Rock crawling	Quad biking
	Drag racing	Truck racing
	Motocross/enduro/trials	Snow mobiling
Extreme ski	Speed skiing	Snowboarding
Extreme water	Scuba diving	Sea kayaking
	Free diving	White-water rafting
	Cliff diving	Barefoot waterskiing
	Wakeboarding	
Extreme boarding	Skateboarding	Mountainboarding
	Sandboarding	Downhill skateboarding
Extreme wheels	Inline skating	BMXing
	Mountain biking	
Extreme climbing	Sport climbing	Rock climbing
	Ice climbing	Abseiling
Other sports	Adventure racing	Skeleton

participate in their twenties, and those in their thirties using extreme sport as a way of continuing their youth. As equipment and travel can be expensive, most of those expressing an interest were from the ABC1 socio-economic group, although this is not the case for activities such as mountain biking, bungee jumping and motocross. The image of extreme sports appeals to individualistic, anti-establishment, fitness-conscious individuals – values that seem to be on the increase. The trend for delayed parenthood has created an extended pre-family life stage, and has positive implications for increased participation in extreme sports and adventure tourism based on these activities. However, we also predict a growth in participation of extreme sports adventure tourism for families. Some 'extreme' activities are more suitable for older and younger participants, and the most popular of these are snowboarding, white-water rafting and mountain biking. These can provide all the thrills and spills associated with extreme sport, regardless of the actual level of skill being employed.

Not only will more people participate in these activities, but tourism operators will also promote association with the 'extreme' element of the products, regardless of how extreme or risky what they are offering really is.

This ploy will be used to connect with the 'adventure' aspirations of potential consumers. It should be noted that a significant part of the enthusiasm for extreme sports will not actually result in direct participation, because much of the interest is aspirational rather than realistic. However, this augurs well for products that have some relationship with extreme adventure, such as clothing, locations, media, and soft-adventure holidays.

Tourism operators will find new ways of providing packages for a much larger range of extreme activities. The issue of 'packaging' will be an interesting one to follow. Packaged holidays involving activities such as scuba diving and mountain biking already have a considerable presence in the marketplace. However, many tourism trips involving the pursuit of 'extreme' activities are currently organized by the participants themselves. One of the difficulties tour operators will have to deal with is the risky nature of these activities. Some, such as base jumping, are unregulated and occupy a legal grey area. Also, there is an uneasy relationship between commercialization and the anti-establishment lifestyle and philosophy of many participants of extreme sports. There is some resentment of sponsorship and advertising, and no doubt this will extend to the tourist industry's packaging and appropriation of extreme activities. Nonetheless, we anticipate that there will be an increase in organized holidays based around extreme activities.

Activity and multi-activity holidays

Multi-activity holidays, which provide customers with adventure activity options, are currently a growth area of travel (Millington, 2001), and we expect this sector to continue growing. It's a great way for beginners to find out which activities they like, and also for groups with mixed preferences.

Mintel (1999) reports there has been a steady growth in general activity holidays (walking, biking, horse riding, multi-activity etc.). Of all types of activity holidays, multi-activity holidays and adventure holidays are high-lighted as becoming more prominent. They note it is difficult to disentangle activity holidays from adventure holidays, especially for foreign trips and long-haul destinations. We predict that a greater proportion of activity holidays will rely on an adventure theme, and this overlap will be inescapable.

Multi-activity holidays produced the highest volume of sales for the UK activity holiday market leader, Acorn Activities, in 1999 (Mintel, 1999). This organization's activity holidays are geared towards singles, couples and families, span from weekend breaks to week-long trips, and are held in North Wales and the Lake District. Figure 12.1 illustrates the range of activities

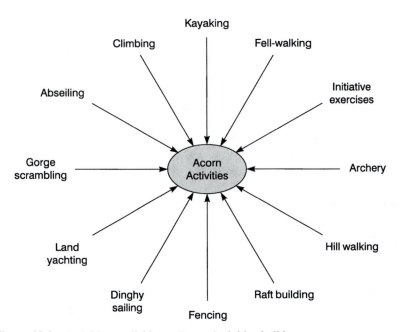

Figure 12.1 Activities available on Acorn Activities holidays.

offered by Acorn, and highlights the link between activity holidays and adventure trips. Whereas some activities require the participant to have an adventurous spirit, for example climbing and dinghy sailing, others could not really be regarded as adventure activities, for instance archery and fencing. The sales of this type of holiday in 1999 superseded sales for other single activity trips such as white-water rafting, air sports breaks and gorge adventures.

The Mintel (1999) survey found that 47 per cent of all people asked would like to go on an activity holiday but had never been on one. This is an encouragingly large untapped market. Potential expansion can be expected in at least three areas; first among the mid-twenties, as the trend for later marriages delays family commitments, and second, among teenagers, who want to do something independent of their parents. The fact that current participation in physical activities and sports is greatest in the 18–25-year-old bracket lends weight to this proposal. Third, the increasing average age of first-time parents provides a more mature, wealthier family market, which we also predict would enjoy adventure multi-activity holidays. There are obviously opportunities to develop very specific micro-niche markets within the 'adventure activity' holiday sector, to meet the very different needs of these three distinct groups of consumers.

A major strength of this market is the endless variations that operators can supply to keep the novelty needs of customers satisfied. Different cycling or hiking itineraries or activities in different locations will help maintain repeat custom.

We also anticipate seeing adventure activity 'add-ons' to 'ordinary holidays'. Mainstream tour operators will add appeal to their packages by offering opportunities for holidaymakers to buy into 'instant' adventure experiences, in much the same way as package holidays try to sell day sightseeing tours or local cultural experiences to holidaymakers at the moment.

Family adventure

There are a number of approaches that adventure tour operators can take with regard to this family market segment. The most common manifestation of adventure tourism for this segment is the adventure activity-based holiday, as mentioned above. We predict that packaged activity-based holidays (particularly multi-activity) will grow in popularity for the family market segment, as parents are relieved of the time-consuming organization and co-ordination of activities that would be necessary if these holidays were undertaken independently. The adventure theme increases the appeal of these holidays to both adults and children.

We also anticipate growth (albeit smaller) in family adventure holidays that do not conform to archetypal family holiday requirements (such as being inexpensive, and having good health care provision, low levels of objective risk and short journey times). Two leading UK adventure tour operators have begun to offer family safaris and a range of family adventure trips that can accommodate children as young as five years. Traditionally companies have been reluctant to provide family adventure packages like these for health and safety reasons.

One approach to dealing with the difficulty of combining the abilities of children with adults when on an activity-based holiday is to provide packages where separate activities are provided for different abilities (or ages), and families are catered for separately from other tourists. Skiing companies have already responded to the demand for family holidays from clients who are unwilling to give up their ski holidays with the arrival of children. They have developed initiatives such as family chalets, where family groups book a small suite in a large, multi-suite chalet. The chalet staff provide communal meals for children in the evening, prior to a more sophisticated dinner for the adults. Nanny and activity supervision services in the chalet mean that children are occupied and parents can go out in the evening. Out on the slope, ski clubs for children enable parents to ski hard and fast in the morning and join their children for family activities in the afternoon. These types of holiday are also relatively affordable because the facilities are shared between a number of family groups. Adventure tourism may well use similar techniques to package and sell products to this growing market segment.

An alternative approach, for families who want to provide quantity and well as quality time together during their holiday, is to have activities that the whole family can participate in. Examples include river journeys, or journeys that include pack animals (llamas, camels etc.) so that some members of the family can walk whilst others ride. In the next chapter, a case study explores the setting up of a small, independent, family adventure vacation business.

'Benefit' adventure

Charity challenges involve travel and adventurous activities, and are undertaken with a higher purpose than purely leisure and recreation. Participants generally seek sponsorship for their adventurous and often arduous task (such as climbing Kilimanjaro or cycling across Egypt). The donation of monies raised through sponsorship is for the benefit of many good causes. Sponsorship-based events are not the only type of 'benefit adventure'. Participation in environmental or community projects also has a donation element, but in this case of time, labour and perhaps expertise rather than money. Humanitarian or environmental compassion is usually a significant motivator, but participants also hope to get some more personal reward and enjoyment from the experience, and the adventure element is one way that organizers can appeal to both sets of motives. We forecast that this type of adventure tourism will continue to grow. We also anticipate that the increasing involvement of the not-for-profit sector as purchasers, and indeed of the clients themselves (who are likely to be ethically minded and conscious consumers), will push ethical and eco-friendly practices in adventure tourism forward. Bleasdale (2000) makes a number of practical suggestions, such as briefing packs, to help organizers limit the negative impacts of the trip on local communities and the environment.

Technology-mediated activities

Of course, technology is already facilitating many aspects of adventure tourism. However, there will be some activities that are very dependent on technological developments or on using expensive technology, and we believe that this will be an area of growth.

Heli-skiing and heli-hiking both involve the use of helicopters to get to remote and almost untouched locations. The nature of the location is part of the adventure, but for many of the participants the helicopter flight, the landing on a narrow, snow-covered ridge and the procedures for disembarking from the helicopter are very much part of the thrill!

New materials and construction methods have already helped revitalize skiing and put a brake on its decline into something of a passé leisure pursuit. In fact, the development of snowboarding has had a large role to play in this story. The construction methods, materials and attitude associated with boarding have inspired the development of new types of ski, which are shorter and wider than their predecessors. These skis are easier to manoeuvre and are shaped to facilitate beginner and intermediate skiers to progress to 'feel-good' carving turns quickly. Perhaps more telling is the development of very short freestyle skis, which help a skier to perform tricks and jumps that catch lots of air, in much the same way as snowboarders do. Ski resort operators now provide terrain parks with half-pipes and jumps for these skiers as well as snowboarders.

One particular example of a technology-mediated activity that deserves a more detailed analysis is space tourism. It seems that leisure travel beyond the earth's stratosphere is becoming a reality at last. As rocket technology progresses, the cost of a ticket will plummet from 'astronomical' to merely phenomenally expensive. Technological developments will be the key to making space tourism an economic reality. It is not simply a question of developing the technology that makes space travel possible, but also of developing a technology that is cheap enough. Even at today's prices, consumer demand far outstrips supply, and the scale of latent demand is unknown and potentially huge. The political barriers that have kept civilians out of orbit are crumbling as government space and defence policies change in response to new world orders. Funding is however crucial for the necessary technological advances, and the relative contribution of government and private sector investment will have to be negotiated if space tourism is to take off sooner rather than later.

Motivations for space tourism include taking in spectacular and ever-changing views of the Earth suspended in the blackness of space. This is one of the most profound and moving experiences reported by space travellers. Stunning views of the moon and galaxy of stars add to the awe-inspiring and magical quality of this sightseeing trip. The physical experience of weightlessness in zero and micro-gravity environments is another fascination, and in the future we can expect facilities where tourists can play and experiment with this novel experience. There is also the excitement of the journey itself, including the sensations of speed and acceleration in the launch. As if these are not enough, there's always that extra little frisson of risk to add to the heady mix! As an adventure experience, space travel has plenty of the 'core ingredients' – novelty, discovery, self-actualization . . . In fact its 'step into the unknown' quality makes it a classic adventure.

Prestige adventure travel

Millington (2001) considers 'prestige' adventure travel as one of the innovative product segments in adventure travel. Space travel is perhaps the most extreme form, but there are plenty of other options that are somewhat easier to achieve. Participants are motivated by the prestige of the destination or activity, which should be unusual or exclusive, and perhaps inspire admiration or envy in others. Adventure tourism can certainly hold its own in terms of one-upmanship! Exclusivity can reside in the price of the product – for example, a luxury safari. This takes an already relatively expensive product (due to the distance travelled and the need for guides and permits etc.) and adds further prestige by ensuring that the accommodation, catering, and service are of luxury standard. Climbing Everest is an example of a destination and an activity that is prestigious because of the difficulty and challenge involved. Gorilla watching is an unusual activity based on a scare resource, a rare species. Numbers of visitors are regulated and limited, ensuring it will never be a run-of-the-mill activity. These latter examples suggest that prestige is not a function of price alone; however, most of these activities will be expensive, if not luxurious, and cost is the major factor that distinguishes the 'prestige adventure travel' sector of both hard and soft adventure products.

We predict an increase in prestige adventure travel products as disposable incomes rise and aspirations widen through the promotion of such travels by the media. Mintel (2000a) forecasts that the divide between the very rich and the very poor will widen. Certainly very affluent consumers will be prepared to pay a premium for holidays that minimize inconvenience, use the shortest journey times and maximize the intensity of the experience.

Non-physical adventure

The authors believe that non-physical adventure tourism will grow dramatically in the future, because of both demand and supply factors.

The demand for non-physical adventure tourism will be fuelled by:

■ The search for new experiences by tourists bored with mainstream tourism products; Mintel (2000a) suggests that limited free time will lead to an active search for life-changing experiences

- Increasing disenchantment with the materialism of consumer cultures, which adds impetus to the search for meaning, fulfilment and self-actualization
- The desire to learn something new while on vacation
- The general growth in international tourism and the development of outbound tourism markets from countries such as India, China, Russia and Brazil – a significant proportion of whom are likely to be interested in non-physical adventure.

Even physical, activity-based tourism has a non-physical dimension – there has always been a strong emotional element to mountaineering, for example. Interestingly, in recent years we have seen a steady blurring of the distinction between physical and non-physical adventure. Consider, for instance:

- Charity challenges where the physical activity is undertaken partly because of the emotional motivation of wanting to help a good cause
- Television programmes where people are left on a 'desert island' (or in another remote environment) to 'survive' – here the challenge is physical but is also emotional in terms of how people cope with new situations and new people.

We believe that this trend will continue to develop in the future.

However, returning to the subject of non-physical adventure tourism itself, we predict that the following forms will experience significant growth in the next few years:

1 Fantasy tourism, where the tourist chooses to enter an imaginary, non-authentic world. This could include virtual reality experiences, trips to artificial environments such as biospheres and 'underwater worlds', or the use of themed hotels where guests can act out their sexual fantasies.
2 Gambling tourism, as new casinos are developed and traditional resorts endeavour to regenerate themselves by developing this market.
3 Short breaks, based on the desire to relieve stress, either to resort hotels that offer stress reduction therapies, or to peaceful, relaxing, stress-free destinations.
4 Spiritual enlightment seeking. It is our prediction that, following previous interest in Hinduism and Buddhism, future spiritual enlightenment seekers

from the West may turn to the native Shamanic religions and Islam. This will change the geography of this type of tourism.

5 Visiting places seen as dangerous. More people will be tempted to 'walk on the wild side' by travelling to these places, whether the danger is due to crime, terrorism, war, extreme climate, or disease.

6 Intellectual adventure seeking. An increasing number of people will travel for intellectual adventure, which includes student exchanges and people travelling to other countries to undertake a course of education or to learn new skills – from a new language to cooking, for example.

7 Backpackers, who will increasingly be seen around the world, always trying to get 'off the beaten track' and away from other tourists. This market will become more heterogeneous, we believe, with an increasing number of older people taking part as well as more and more young people from Asia.

In this list, we have viewed non-physical adventure tourism in terms of particular types of activities. However, if we view adventures as experiences that are simply new to the tourist, where they are not sure of what might happen, then the scope of non-physical adventure tourism is much wider.

For those people who are not experienced travellers, or those from countries where outbound travel is still a relatively new phenomenon, non-physical adventure tourism could include the following activities that might be seen as rather tame by experienced adventure tourists:

- Buying timeshare properties in another part of the world – a financial adventure
- Travelling much further than ever before, to countries that are very different to the visitors' home regions.

At the same time, the authors believe that three groups of people in the future will have greater opportunities to become active participants in non-physical adventure, namely:

1 People with disabilities, as facilities for them improve around the world
2 Children travelling with other children, rather than their families, for non-physical adventures, as children become tourism consumers in their own right
3 Retired people, as company pensions and improved health care allow them to take a growing role in the non-physical adventure tourism market.

We suggest that these three groups will also be participating in greater numbers in the field of physical adventure tourism.

Independent adventure tourism

People are increasingly putting together their own tailor-made packages by booking the flight, car hire, accommodation and activities with separate companies. The development of a more individualistic society is fuelling this trend. Developments in technology have also opened up an Aladdin's cave of opportunity, especially with the advent of the Internet. As mentioned previously, independent travel can be an adventure in itself, stimulating feelings of self-reliance and of going into the unknown. More people are going to experience this particular form of adventure as access to, and confidence in, using the Internet increases. The development of secure payment mechanisms will help reduce some anxiety and suspicion, and better-designed websites will make the experience less frustrating and time consuming. Independent travel is attractive because holidays can be tailor-made to suit individual requirements and substantial savings can often be made, despite the claims that big operators can keep costs down through economies of scale and ruthless application of their purchasing power. In addition to this, some people simply find it satisfying to beat the system and thwart big operators!

More people will undertake adventurous activities on their holidays, which they will organize with independent operators. Networking and exchange of information amongst like-minded individuals (on dedicated websites, such as those for climbers or gap-year travellers) will also aid this trend. In fact there is a long history of independent travel arrangements for adventure trips as, previously, tour operators were not particularly involved in packaging this type of holiday. Adventurers have therefore gained quite some experience in organizing trips themselves, and this experience is easily shared.

Short breaks

The recent reduction in the cost of flights has revolutionized the short break market. It is now financially viable to fly around Europe for a long weekend, as the cost of getting there is no longer the biggest proportion of the cost of the holiday. Added to this, overworked professionals who feel they have too much to do or are nervous about their career prospects are choosing shorter holidays with less time away from the office. A long weekend means that such employees get a four-day break with only two days away from the office. Short breaks for the cash rich/time poor are increasingly popular – this is universally acclaimed as one of the fastest growing sectors of the travel industry. This is sure to be translated into the adventure tourism market, and we predict seeing growth in short packaged breaks, with intense activity levels to create a complete break and ensure value for money and time spent.

Destinations

The destinations that will grow in importance for the adventure tourism industry are those that can offer a new, fresh tourist experience and a sense of personal discovery. These will include 'alternative' destinations that are just starting out on tourism development. In addition, locations with sophisticated or high quality resources and facilities will engage and inspire the tourist. The type of resources required will vary for each of the main sub-sectors of the adventure tourism market.

Developing countries and alternative destinations

The demand for new and novel experiences is going to feed the growth of adventure tourism visits to developing countries. Different cultures and exotic or rare wildlife are two things most developing countries can offer. The less developed transport infrastructure and difficult terrain means that accessing some regions can be an adventure in itself. The economic status of some developing countries makes them relatively cheap for visitors, and the need for foreign income means that tourism is encouraged. Countries such as Namibia or Bhutan have purposefully adopted a policy of low volume, high value tourism. Latin America and Africa are currently popular destinations for discovery adventure travel – the popularity of South America with gap year travellers is testimony to this. Political stability and the ability to create partnerships between local providers and tour operators will determine which of the countries in these continents are winners and which are losers over the next few decades.

Another group of 'alternative' destinations that looks set to grow in adventure tourism terms is that of colder destinations. As holidaymakers' desire for alternative experiences overrides their desire for sun, locations such as the Arctic and Antarctic will become more popular.

Also, as consumers increasingly take more than one holiday a year the winter holiday market (especially that segment based on winter sports) is growing. People are becoming more accustomed to taking at least some of their holidays in colder climates.

Eastern Europe

Central and Eastern Europe provides a closer-to-home destination for most Europeans. Political and economic factors dominate the development of this region. Many former Eastern Bloc countries are currently awaiting accession to the European Union (EU). Their integration into the EU will have economic repercussions for member states. In return they have much to offer, not least vast areas of landscape with a high scenic and nature conservation value.

The speed of development in much of Central and Eastern Europe is phenomenal. A great deal of money is being invested in the development of these countries, both from Western Europe and from internal investors. Entrepreneurial spirit has been set free, for better or worse. We predict that established tour companies from Western Europe will exploit adventure tourism opportunities in Eastern Europe, but small-scale independent operators within these countries will also respond to demand. These will particularly supply the independent adventure tourist, and will use the Internet to advertise and communicate with potential customers. We also anticipate the growth of partnership arrangements between the foreign tour operators and local organizers. As is the case with many developing countries, the exchange rate means that destinations in Eastern Europe are relatively cheap for EU tourists. There will also be a considerable demand from the domestic market, so it appears that this region could support some very buoyant adventure destinations.

Domestic destinations

It is important to remember that most of the participants in current adventure tourism activities are domestic tourists. As most participants in adventure tourism reside in North America, Europe and Australasia, we anticipate the development of adventure-focused destinations in these areas. This is where an impressive range of innovative facilities and high quality resources is advantageous. These help create a sense of novelty and anticipation, and stimulate the jaded palate of the repeat customer. Queenstown, in New Zealand, has shown the world the way when it comes to creating an adventure-themed destination. In the UK, we predict the Lake District, the Southwest coast of England, Scotland, and Wales will develop the adventure sector of their tourism industry. These are the more rugged, upland regions that have landscape features that facilitate outdoor adventure activities, and have obvious nature and cultural interest for those consumers preferring the discovery aspect of adventure.

Artificial environments

Tate (2002) describes the development of very specific facility-based destinations, such as ice hotels and undersea resorts, in a report on alternative tourist destinations. An ice hotel is built each year from blocks sawn from the adjacent frozen river, near Kiruna in northern Sweden. In 2002 it had 60 rooms and 11 000 overnight guests, and over 33 000 visitors made the trip in the 2000/2001 season. The resort is being extended to include an ice adventure park in the nearby forests.

Undersea resorts are not so far progressed, despite a huge interest in marine environments. Full undersea hotels, where an entire stay can be spent underwater in restaurants, lounges and bedrooms with a high proportion of transparent surfaces, are still at the drawing board stage. Mooted destinations include Hawaii, Taipei and Miami (Tate, 2002).

The growth of 'artificial environments', as described in Chapter 11, means that urban locations may see more adventure tourists. Likewise, 'gateway' destinations on the periphery of wilderness or remote zones will develop artificial environments to keep adventurers happy while they are preparing, resting or awaiting better weather conditions.

Restrictions

We anticipate seeing more restrictions employed in destinations where there is a concern about the impact of increased tourism activities on the resource and local culture. Already, sensitive areas such as American National Parks have a bookings systems and ceilings on visitor numbers. Bhutan has adopted a very cautious approach to the development of tourism in order to protect the culture and environment of this small Eastern Himalayan kingdom. Visitors must be either invited guests of the government or designated tourists. Independent travel is not permitted, and visits may be booked only through government-registered tour operators. There is a minimum daily tariff, and government approved accommodation must be used, which costs from US$150–$250 per night. In 2000, the number of tourists allowed to enter the country was 7559 (Tate, 2002). Closer to home, the use of the new open access areas of countryside created by the Countryside and Rights of Way Act (2000) will be restricted for commercialized and organized adventure tourism activities, such as outdoor pursuits.

Restrictions can be used to manage visitor numbers, distribution and behaviour. Consequently there are different forms of 'restriction', which vary in their precision. For example, a strategic tool such as planning control policy can be used to direct the building of facilities in one place, leaving other areas undeveloped and therefore less attractive to large numbers of visitors. High price policies tend to restrict numbers; a booking system restricts them more precisely. Legislation and fines support stricter policies. There are some issues related to the use of restrictive tools – for example, equality of access to places and experiences and the distribution of economic benefits from the limited tourism allowed.

Adventure tourism operators

Independent tour operators

At present specialist independent tour operators continue to dominate the adventure tourism market. According to Millington (2001), the tour operating industry has witnessed the emergence of an increasing volume of small tour operating businesses, many of which are specializing in adventure tourism. Most of these adventure operators report growth rates of between 15 and 20 per cent annually, an indication of the current popularity of packaged adventure holidays and their future expansion. Mintel's (2001) research on UK independent tour operating companies found that as many as one in four operators affiliated to the Association of Independent Tour Operators (AITO) offer adventure-based holidays. The proportion would be even higher if AITO's classification of adventure tourism included snow sports, sailing and diving holidays.

AITO is a trade body that 'represents the collective voice of what essentially are small-to-medium sized holiday operators with just over 150 members producing approximately 245 branded products in 2001' (Mintel, 2001).

The market position of these operators seems to be secure in the foreseeable future because many of the adventure tourism products that they offer require personal attention, for example in creating individualized itineraries or contacting local guides and hoteliers. This means that it is difficult for such operators to achieve economies of scale; their success depends more on achieving economies of scope. Therefore, up until recently the adventure tourism market has not been particularly attractive to large mainstream tour operators.

However, adventure tourism is obviously a very attractive area for portfolio development for specialist tour operators, and we can expect to see a growth in the number and range of adventure products they offer. We can also expect to see more newly established operators entering the fray, especially as predictions for growth in the adventure tourism market are so encouraging.

Vertically integrated tour operators

Although smaller independent operators are currently the dominant players within the adventure tourism industry, large, mainstream, vertically integrated operators are starting to challenge their dominance. For example, First Choice

Holidays – 'a leading European leisure travel company comprising main-stream and specialist tour operations' (First Choice, 2002) – recently acquired one of the leading specialist tour operators, Exodus Travels. First Choice also offers activity holidays through Flexigroup, its ski operator, and Sunsail, its yacht charter and water sport club operator.

An increasing number of mainstream tour operators are following First Choice's acquisition and diversification strategies. For example, Thomas Cook, 'the third largest integrated travel group in Great Britain' (Thomas Cook, 2002) has moved into the activity holiday market through the setting up of its sister company, Neilson Holidays, a snow sports and water sports specialist.

It could be argued that the two aforementioned mainstream operators offer conventional, well-established adventure tourism products (e.g. skiing and sailing) whereas the smaller specialist operators are focusing on emerging products that fit into the broad umbrella of adventure tourism. This aside, it is important to note that the mainstream tour operating industry appears to be committed to developing the adventure section of its portfolio, and this trend looks set to continue.

Mintel (1999) reports a mixed response from independent activity holiday operators to the presence of 'large, general tour operators', with some feeling threatened and worried. However, most concur that there is also a plus side, and agree that the entry of large operators would help to expand the market for activity holidays and raise its profile.

Partnership

We anticipate the development of partnership working between organizations in the destination and tour operators in the generating regions. As sustainable development ethics become more embedded within the tourism industry, it will become less acceptable to bypass native operators in developing countries. Developing countries themselves are also becoming more experienced in international tourism and the generation of foreign income, and we expect this to mean that benefits and involvement will be re-negotiated.

Standards and certification

It is predicted that as adventure tourism becomes a more prominent niche holiday product, an increasing number of tourism organizations will employ the concept of adventure as a marketing tool. Evidently, some of these organizations will be offering true adventure products whilst others may merely be 'jumping on the bandwagon', taking advantage of the fact that the adventure phenomenon is presently in vogue. The increased usage of the word 'ecotourism' by numerous tourism organizations is proof that fashionable tourism terminology can lead to the successful promotion and selling of products. Buckley (2000) notes that 'for tourism marketers, almost any form of nature-based tourism is advertised as ecotourism, irrespective of environmental management, education or conservation'. Tourism Concern (2002) further corroborates this idea, suggesting that 'there are in fact a variety of tourism "ecolabels" around, but without one standard for industry to conform to, working out the green from the greenwash is tricky'. These statements suggest that some tourism organizations do not adhere to ecotourism principles yet claim to be offering ecotourism products. This problem may well emerge within the adventure tourism sector as organizations start to recognize the growing potential demand for adventure experiences. As it is clear that the growth of adventure tourism has been driven largely by the tourism industry, the likelihood of this happening is strong.

One way that ecotourism organizations convince consumers that they are offering authentic ecotourism holidays is through their membership of certification schemes. Such schemes usually assess whether an organization has met certain tourism standards, and relate to the company's contribution to the environmental management of a destination. They help to protect the consumer and assist their decision-making. However, there are over 100 of these schemes in operation and they vary in standard. Some are complex environmental management systems, whereas others are promotional umbrellas and unsubstantiated awards (Sallows; see Tourism Concern, 2002). If similar schemes were set up for adventure tourism organizations they would inevitably be variable in quality, with some merely acting as marketing tools whilst others serve the purpose of ensuring that their members are genuine adventure tourism organizations. One obstacle that may hinder the successful operation of these schemes is that adventure tourism embraces such a wide range of activities and niches (e.g. ecotourism, special interest tourism, wildlife tourism, charity challenges) that it would be virtually impossible to encompass all these under a single certification scheme.

Health and safety/risk management
We predict that there will be increasing emphasis on the health and safety and risk management side of adventure tourism operations. The implementation of more formal procedures to protect clients is also highly likely.

Despite the importance of risk management, it is not a well-established area of the adventure tourism industry. Although most adventure tourism organizations will have their own risk reduction and avoidance methods, these are often inconsistent across different companies and different sectors (see Chapter 8 for further details).

This inconsistency could be due to a lack of national legislation concerning adventure tourism and/or recreation in some countries. For instance, in the UK the Adventurous Activities Licensing Bill legislates only for children under the age of 18 who participate in water sports, caving, climbing and trekking. This bill does not take into account other adventure sports, and equivalent legislation for adults does not currently exist.

Guidelines and opt-in schemes do exist; for example, in Ireland the Association of Adventure Sports (AFAS) has worked in collaboration with several national governing bodies and adventure sports providers to design and monitor safety standards that have become benchmarks for the Irish adventure sports industry. The Irish government has accepted these standards as minimum safety requirements. The standards are primarily concerned with staff qualifications, instructor to participant ratios, equipment requirements and activity locations. The guidelines apply to a range of adventure sports, including rock climbing, mountaineering, canoeing, kayaking, surfing, sailing and snorkelling. Any organization that supplies these sports and wants to conform to these standards can register with the AFAS Centre Standards Board (CSB). Members are subject to a previously announced annual inspection as well as 'on the spot' inspections, and these are carried out by qualified sports instructors with industry experience (CSB, 2002).

However, Queensland's Diving Industry Taskforce, a government body (see Wilks and Davis, 2000: 594), suggests that voluntary codes of conduct don't entirely work:

> Unfortunately, experience over the 1990s has shown that it cannot always be assumed that all employers and self-employed persons in the recreational and snorkelling industry have been or are willing to voluntarily adopt safe systems of work in the absence of regulatory controls prescribing minimum workplace health and safety standards.

It seems that minimum safety standards may only fully be achieved through the development of legislative measures. One of the difficulties with legislation is that it is generally national rather than international, and this leads to even more inconsistency. Hibbert's (2001) work (see Chapter 8) highlights several inconsistencies in the safety measures used by mountain adventure tour operators that offer international trips and expeditions. For instance, companies employed different systems for grading their trips and assessing their clients, not all operators transferred risk to third parties in the same way, and emergency plans sometimes differed according to destination.

Some of these inconsistencies could be ironed out if legislative measures that imposed a uniform set of safety guidelines on this type of adventure operator were enforced.

We anticipate risk management strategies to be further refined as more research and experience is shared. Research carried out on New Zealand's overseas visitors to establish the nature and extent of adventure tourism injuries provides some useful recommendations on reducing the risk of injury (Bentley *et al.*, 2001). Table 12.3 presents a summary of a selection of measures that could be implemented.

Table 12.3   Possible interventions to reduce the risk of adventure tourism injuries in New Zealand (adapted from Bentley *et al.*, 2001: 334–336)

Tourist/recreation authority/service	Adventure tourism operator	Government intervention
■ Make participants aware of the 'actual risk' involved in adventurous activities, plus the level of skill and experience needed to participate safely	■ Ensure clients are equipped with adequate knowledge, fitness levels and understanding of possible risks and how to deal with these	■ Regulatory government intervention for perceived 'risky' sectors of the adventure tourism industry (e.g. horse riding and cycle-related adventure activities)
■ Promote safe adventuring specifically to independent tourists who participate in tramping in wilderness areas and mountain recreation without guides	■ Make sure clients fully understand key safety instructions before the activity begins	
■ Discourage independent overseas tourists from engaging in new activities in unfamiliar environments	■ Maintain activity equipment and ensure this and clothing are carefully matched to the client	

Although the recommendations identified in Table 12.3 have been designed specifically for the adventure tourism industry in New Zealand, most are generic to almost any country or destination.

Marketing

Marketing is one of the major activities of tour operators, and it is bound to see some changes in the future. We have already drawn attention to the fact that many products will be re-labelled and re-branded to benefit from the current enthusiasm for adventure tourism.

Mintel (2000) predicts that micro-marketing will proliferate with the growth of a more individualistic and fragmented society and the demise of the mass media. Brand managers will have to tailor their marketing initiatives to specific lifestyle groups, channels and, perhaps, points of purchase. We envisage adventure tourism operators, many of whom already use these techniques, honing this type of marketing even more. In this forthcoming era of micro-marketing, with everyone being an individual market segment, understanding the highly personal nature of adventure tourism is essential if marketing initiatives are to be effective.

Mintel (1999) reports that eight out of ten activity holidays (within or outside the UK) are booked directly with the operator or venue. Direct contact between customers and companies can only be intensified by the Internet, which means that repeat business and personal recommendation are going to be the most important means of marketing for these companies. However, despite the growing role of the Internet for marketing, there will still be a place for brochures in adventure tourism. Customers will continue to enjoy browsing brochures at leisure, and taking the opportunity to be inspired and dream in the comfort of an armchair rather than in front of a VDU screen.

Retailainment

In the future retail stores will be competing with on-line shopping, and Mintel (2000) suggests that retailers will entice customers by marketing the environment and entertainment provided by the store. 'Retailainment' and 'Destination Stores' that are convenient and provide added leisure value to the retail experience are seen by many as the way forward. Already this idea has found practical expression in adventure equipment and clothing stores, such as those that provide indoor ice-climbing walls and artificial climate environments, and we foresee this trend being picked up and exaggerated by adventure gear retailers.

Conclusions

It seems that the way is relatively clear for a growth in adventure tourism over the next few years. Demand is increasing, as is evidenced by the increasing numbers of people participating in adventure themed holidays. Positive consumer reactions to the concept of adventure mean that the supply side will promote adventure heavily, to stimulate further latent demand. Micro-marketing of the vast range of different adventure tourism products will be the key to greater participation, as the consumers of adventure tourism are by no means a homogeneous group.

The moving frontiers of adventure tourism

Frontiers in adventure tourism will be attacked both 'head on' and more incrementally. The development of enabling technology and equipment will smash through current barriers to participation in some adventure tourism activities, such as undersea resorts and space tourism. Increasing industry and participant involvement in 'extreme' adventure tourism will help promote adventure tourism as a new and 'happening' development. Radical and exciting artificial or simulated environments will introduce large numbers of participants to activities they would probably never otherwise try, and will fuel the development of extreme and technical adventure.

However, there will be a more gradual sea change that incorporates adventure into mainstream tourism. We anticipate the re-labelling of products we currently regard as other niche forms of tourism, such as ecotourism, discovery, cultural and spiritual tourism, with the adventure theme. Potential demand will also be stimulated by the introduction of optional adventure add-ons to existing holidays. Adventure will be incorporated into luxury products, to enhance their cachet further. Most of these will fall into the so-called 'soft adventure' tourism market. Because soft adventure covers such a wide range of activities, and because participation in these activities is already substantial, the potential customer base is very large. This more stealthy growth of adventure tourism might not be so showy, but it will be important because this is where the highest turnover will be.

The recognition of the adventurous characteristics of non-physical activities will also expand adventure tourism away from the 'standard fare' that we are accustomed to. New groups of participants will also broaden the adventure tourism market.

Adventure tourism will become very much part of mainstream tourism, rather than something on the periphery of the tourism industry. This is for two reasons: first, the adventure element of tourism products will become more commonplace, and second, the tourism industry itself will change. In the future, 'mainstream' will no longer mean 'mass' tourism. The WTO (1997) identifies diversification as a primary trend in the tourism industry, and this means the industry itself will come to regard niche tourism as the norm.

Unconstrained growth?

In the meantime, there is a danger that the type of adventure tourism we have been describing in this book will grow at a rate that is unsustainable in resource terms. The various 'resources' that adventure tourism uses (for example, landscape, biodiversity, remoteness and culture) are susceptible to degradation through overuse, and systems need to be negotiated and put in place to help reduce this. This will require different mind sets, as society has often treated these resources and qualities as free goods. Indeed, the restrictions on commercial use of open access land specified in the Countryside and Rights of Way Act (2000) highlights the issue of whether organizations that use the resource for commercial purposes such as outdoor pursuits should contribute to its upkeep. Despite the active debate on sustainable tourism, it is our belief that the philosophy of sustainable development will constrain growth of adventure tourism in only a relatively minor way in the short term.

Further to this, on an individual level, the WTO (1997) suggests the consumer will experience a growing personal conflict between a socio-environmental conscience and the urge for travel consumption. The awareness-raising activities of organizations like Tourism Concern have helped to make consumers much more conscious of their impacts and responsibility. Adventure tourists comprise one of the groups most likely to have to face up to this dilemma. They are often the first tourists into newly opened up areas, and the world is littered with examples of how the 'recreation succession' that follows this incursion can spoil the very qualities that once made the place so attractive. Like the adoption of sustainable tourism practices, we sadly anticipate this discomfort will only motivate behavioural change for the majority of adventure tourists in the longer term, rather than the short term.

The development of artificial adventure environments will be a crucial release valve for this type of pressure. We also believe, in the longer term, that adventure tourists will grapple with the moral obligation to maximize the benefits that accrue from visiting remote and unspoilt adventure destinations. The education and personal development agenda will come to the fore, adding value to an already privileged opportunity.

Will the concept of adventure tourism stand the test of time?

Adventure tourism is a topical idea. The phrase fulfils a purpose at this moment in time because it captures the essence of prevailing desires and developments. As a method of categorizing tourism activities it relies on the common theme of adventure, which pulls together a rather unwieldy range of experiences. In many ways adventure tourism is more of a 'meta-category'. Almost every single product we have examined could just as easily be defined by another label. However, although it's awkward, it remains undeniably irresistible! One of the major benefits of the concept of adventure tourism is that it articulates something fundamentally important for both the consumer and the supplier.

In the not too distant future, niche tourism and micro-marketing will predominate and one of the biggest barriers for adventure tourism, the difficulty in using it as a way of 'pigeon-holing' tourism products, will become largely irrelevant. Being able to pin down the category a product belongs to will not be as important as being able to pin down the target market sector.

Nonetheless, in the short-term future we expect 'adventure tourism' to be embraced by the industry and the public as both a phrase and a concept. In many respects, its use marks a shift in the nature of tourism products and activities.

However, adventure tourism will only really develop, achieve recognition, and be effectively managed if it is well understood. We therefore end this book with a plea for more research.

Towards a research agenda for adventure tourism

It is clear to the authors, based on their experience of writing this book, that there is a great need for more empirical research to be carried in this rapidly growing field. Below is a proposed research agenda to help us better understand the phenomenon of adventure tourism as it has been defined in this book.

1 In contrast to the field of physical adventure, there is very little research on spiritual or intellectual adventure tourism. We know too little about the scale, motivators, and tourist behaviour in sectors as diverse as westerners seeking spiritual enlightenment in Asia to tourists who take holidays to learn a language or a new skill.

2 More research is also needed on what we might term emotional adventure tourism, such as the hedonistic holidays discussed earlier in this book.

3 Another neglected area requiring researchers' attention is urban adventure tourism, including red light district tourism and visits to dangerous cities and neighbourhoods.

4 There is clearly a need for us to find out more about cross-cultural differences in perceptions of adventure and adventure tourism. This is a very important subject as the tourism market becomes ever more globalized.

5 We need to know more about the impacts of adventure tourism on both the tourist and the destination.

6 It would be interesting for the industry to know more about the perceptions, attitudes and motivators of adventure tourists, and how they make their purchase decisions.

7 Adventure tourism is an ideal sector in which to study entrepreneurship, given that many operators are small businesses, often started almost as 'hobbies' by enthusiasts with little or no experience of running a business.

8 Work needs to be done to find out how people view the concept of adventure, and how this view may differ depending on their age, culture, gender, personality, and past experiences.

9 It would help the adventure tourism sector to be taken more seriously if international agreement on definitions could be reached so that data could be collected world-wide on a comparable basis, and if governments could be persuaded to see this sector as a discrete field worthy of research as a separate entity.

10 More research would be welcome on the ethical dimension to adventure tourism, covering everything from pricing policies to human resource issues.

11 The media clearly plays a major role in influencing consumer behaviour in adventure tourism, but it would be useful to have empirical data to show the relative impact of guide books, the Internet and television, for example, on the behaviour of adventure tourists.

12 It would be interesting to see the Delphic Oracle technique and focus groups being used to try to predict likely future changes in the adventure tourism market.

However, currently it looks unlikely that this research agenda will be implemented because:

■ Adventure tourism is not generally perceived in the way suggested in this book; it is largely confined to the rather restricted idea of physical adventure, usually in remote areas or wilderness

- The industry is highly fragmented, with no real professional bodies focusing on adventure tourism rather than either adventure activities or general tourism
- Adventure tourism is growing and changing so rapidly that conducting any research on it is perceived as too difficult and costly to be worthwhile
- Governments still do not recognize the value of adventure tourism to their national economies.

Yet this research is vital if we are to manage effectively this growing but potentially damaging form of tourism.

Discussion points and exercises

1 Discuss the factors that will influence the future development of adventure tourism.
2 Select several adventure tourism organizations and interview representatives of each organization about how they feel adventure tourism will develop in the future. Compare and contrast their views.
3 Discuss the benefits and costs of implementing the research agenda outlined in this chapter for adventure tourism.

Postscript: 11 September 2001 – the dawn of a new era?

On 11 September 2001, the terrorist attacks on New York and Washington stunned and shocked the world. At the time of writing, it is impossible to predict what the long-term implications of these events will be for the world as a whole, and adventure tourism specifically, partly because we do not know if this was a one-off event or just the first manifestation of a phenomenon that will go on for years. However, they could have the following impacts on adventure tourism:

1 Adventure tourism as a whole could suffer a general decline, as with other types of tourism, as people become increasingly concerned about the risks of travelling.
2 Countries that attract adventure tourism but are seen to be near to the destinations with the greatest perceived risks could experience a reduction in inbound adventure tourists.
3 Because of voyeurism, or because people feel sympathetic towards New York, there may be a trend for people to visit the city, almost as a form of adventure tourism, even if the city is subjected to further terrorist attacks.

4 If these events herald a new era of urban terrorism, it may change our attitude towards 'adventure' forever. If the everyday act of living ordinary life in a city becomes more risky than trekking in the wilderness, then the motivation for the latter may diminish. On the other hand, urban terrorism could stimulate the demand for wilderness adventure tourism as a 'safer' tourist destination than cities.

Alternatively, maybe nothing will actually change once the original immediate impact passes, and things return to 'normal'. However, at the moment of writing, it is hard to believe that the events of 11 September 2001 in the USA will not have a long-term impact on tourism in general, and adventure tourism specifically.

Second postscript: terrorists targetting tourists, Autumn 2002

In the few months since the first postscript was written further tragedies have directly affected tourists. In Bali and Kenya terrorists deliberately targetted venues which they knew would be full of tourists. The victims in Bali were largely young backpackers, particularly from Australia. Thus, adventure tourists have now become targets for the actions of terrorists.

Interestingly, many people believe these recent attacks will encourage tourists to avoid well established, high profile destinations. This could boost 'off the beaten track' adventure tourism or it could reduce the volume of adventure tourism.

Only time will tell what the future holds.

Part
G

Case studies

13

Case studies

Introduction

This book suggests that adventure tourism has several characteristics, including the following:

- It encompasses both physical and non-physical adventure
- The concept of adventure tourism varies between different cultures, countries and individuals
- Adventure tourism is growing, evolving and mutating all the time, with new forms developing constantly
- Adventure tourism involves complex inter-relationships between the tourists, suppliers and destinations
- Increasingly, some types of adventure tourism raise serious ethical concerns.

The following selection of case studies is designed to illustrate some of these points, as well as demonstrating the breadth and diversity of adventure tourism.

Case study 1   Family adventure tourism

Active Family Vacations

Active Family Vacations is a small company that provides 'outdoor adventure-based vacations for families on the go'. It is at a transitional stage in its development, where a concept is becoming a real business. The company was set up in 2002, essentially in the directors' 'spare time' to reduce the investment risk. At the time of writing it is too early to tell whether it will be successful or not, but the company directors say that if the company continues to stimulate interest and business, and build critical mass, this will signal the need for full-time career commitment.

The company is run by a married couple who have long had an interest in, and extensive personal experience of, activity-based adventurous holidays. The arrival of their own children helped focus their business concept. As this happened at a time when the couple were firmly committed to corporate careers and study, it also deepened their understanding and empathy towards the needs of busy parents when it comes to planning family vacations.

An excerpt from the 'company history' section of the Active Family Vacations website describes some of the thinking that lay behind the formation of the company:

When it came to family vacation planning, we always made sure that our vacations had two main components: (1) fun activities in a unique setting, (2) family inclusion – good quality time for the entire family. That is the environment we aim to create for you. All you need to provide is the enthusiasm.

In establishing Active Family Vacations, we sought to offer our clients what we had wanted, but could never find:

1 vacation planning from beginning to end – including arranging accommodation, car rental, hiring of gear and the adventures themselves,
2 locations away from the masses and over-crowded tourist destinations,
3 an itinerary or individual tour to fit your own pace (no concern about the 'pace of the others'),
4 a vacation that you could enjoy at your leisure,
5 assurance that the tour provider was well established, knowledgeable and experienced in meeting the needs of families.

Vacationing with us means you get to enjoy your family and the activities without the stress and time pressure required to arrange all the finer details.

In many respects, this company is an example of the type of small, independent operator that predominates the adventure tourism market. It also echoes some aspects of Mintel's (2001b) observation on overland expedition companies: '... almost without exception these companies were started up by people who, having made an overland trip to an unusual destination, have come home and set up tours to take other people on the same route'. Like these companies, Active Family Vacations is deeply grounded in personal experience and interest.

The company has attempted to define its own niche and differentiate itself from other 'family adventure' providers. One of the main differences is that it is not trying to replicate the most common manifestation of family adventure holidays, where a company provides separate programmes for adults and children. Instead, there is more emphasis on offering products for parents who want to spend both both quantity and quality time with their offspring whilst on holiday. Family Active Vacations also offers to make arrangements for individual families, which means that a family group can have its own itinerary, at a pace and with activities that suit the family. It also means they escape the pressure of having to join a bigger group and fit in with other people's needs and agendas. Each family can have its own guide, which maintains the intimacy of the family group and lets members focus on developing their relationships with each other, rather than with other holidaymakers. To sum up, one of the most distinctive characteristics of this company is that it is targeting families who want to spend time together and experience what it means for the whole family to get involved in their own adventure-based holiday.

The main accent is on holidays involving physical activities rather than, say, historical tours. However, non-physical activities do feature within some trip itineraries. Peppering a holiday with a few of these activities can work well with families, as even non-physical activities can keep children busy and active, and most children have a natural need for variety. One of the challenges facing Active Family Vacations is providing activities that all family members can participate in together and find adventurous, despite different abilities. They have tried to overcome the potential difficulties by:

- Selecting activities that are not extreme or highly dangeous in nature but are still exciting and enjoyable, such as rafting
- Working closely with suppliers who are willing to provide the individual attention and added support that could make a family adventure more enjoyable, i.e. bicycle trailers, tag-a-longs and backpacks
- Using qualified and skilled guides who are sensitive to safety needs and are able to switch between different 'guiding/instructor' styles to suit different levels of ability within the family
- Including vehicle-related activities within the itinerary, to rest weary limbs.

A range of different types of holidays is offered. Some, for example 'multi-sport adventures', may be programmes run in one location, where guests can undertake a different activity every day and return to the same ranch or hotel every evening. Alternatively, some holidays are 'point to point' – perhaps three days river rafting followed by two days in a jeep or on a mountain bike, with a pick-up at the end. Accommodation varies, and can range from backcountry camping to ranch or inn accommodation. There are also 'single theme' holidays such as family rafting, horseback holidays, biking or hiking. Local suppliers, with whom Active Family Vacations have built up a relationship, provide these programmes. Todd Heskett, the Company Director says: 'It has been difficult finding suppliers who comply with our philosophy and provide good family tours. Many of them say they do, but can't substantiate the difference between an ordinary tour and a tour that really is suitable for all the family to do together. Field research has been invaluable in helping us find local suppliers we are confident in'. Destinations for these holidays are primarily the USA, Canada, Puerto Rica, Belize and Europe, and are based in areas of inspiring landscape. Most of the holidays on offer are five days to one week long. This reflects the needs of cash-rich, time-poor parents, who may not be able to take extended holidays (this applies to the USA market in particular).

These parents also benefit from the time-saving and hassle-reducing 'packaging' service offered by Active Family Vacations, who will organize everything, including transport and gear hire. In general the prices range from US $2500 to $8000 for meals, accommodation and most transportation (excluding the airfare) for a family consisting of two parents and two children.

One of the chief strengths of Active Family Vacations is in researching and putting together a holiday to suit a client's needs, and to that end they also advertise 'Tailor Made Family Vacations'. Families are encouraged to identify their 'dream holiday'. A list of activities that the company can arrange is provided to help stimulate ideas, and this is illustrated in Exhibit 1.

The company headquarters is currently in the UK, yet 60 per cent of the prospective clients are anticipated as being North American. Information about the product is available on the company's website, although a full-scale marketing drive has not yet been implemented. The Internet has been incredibly important in the way this company has begun, allowing the company to be based in one country, yet target customers in another. It also enables the company to do the research required to arrange tailor-made holidays to specific requirements and budgets relatively easily and cheaply. Setting up a company in this way would not have been feasible ten years ago, without the Internet. The relative cheapness of setting up a website has also facilitated this 'dipping a toe in the water' approach to business development.

A considerable amount of research and analysis preceded the establishment of the company. Todd Heskett, the company director, confirms that a gap analysis between self-catering family holidays, adventure tour companies and the large holiday/tour operators particularly convinced him that family adventure holidays were a viable business opportunity. He adds that research also demonstrated that:

Exhibit 1 Activities at Active Family Vacations.

Adventure training	Dog sledding	Iceberg viewing	Rodeo tours
African heritage	Dolphin research/swim	Ice fishing	Safari/game viewing
Air safari	Dude ranch	Island cottage rental	Sailing schools
Backpacking	Elephant ride	Jeep safari	Scuba/snorkelling
Ballooning	Equestrian riding lessons	Jungle expeditions	Sea kayaking
Barge/canal cruising	Equestrian tours	Jungle lodge	Skiing/cross country/touring
Biblical tours	Expeditions	Kite flying	Skiing/downhill
Bicycle touring	Family heritage trips	Kon-Tiki rafting	Snowboarding
Bird watching	Farm stay	Lighthouse tours	Snowmobiling
Brown/black bear watching	Festival tours	Llama packing	Showshoeing
Bullfighting	Fishing	Mine tours	Spa/hot springs tour
Camel safaris	Fly fishing trips	Mountain bicycle tours	Spelunking
Camping	Fly-in hiking	Mountaineering	Surfing
Canoeing/kayaking	Foliage tours	Multi-sport family trips	Children's sports camps
Canyoning	Garden tours	National Parks tours	Trekking
Castles/palaces tours	Geneaology tours	Native Americans tours	Volcano tours
Cattle drive	Ghost town tours	Natural history	Walking tours
Cave art tours	Glacier tours	Nature reserve	Water-skiing
Caving	Goat packing	Nature trips	Whale watching
Christian tours	Gorilla viewing	Northern Lights viewing	White-water rafting
Christmas tours	Great walks and hikes	Outdoor skills school	Wild horse watching
Church tours	Heli-mountain biking	Penguin viewing	Wilderness courses
Collectors tours	Heli-rafting	Polar bear watching	Wildflower viewing
Conservation	Heli-skiing	Polar expeditions	Wildlife viewing
Country house tours	Heli-trekking	Rafting	Windjamming
Country inns	Hiking	Rainforest tours	Windsurfing
Covered wagons	Historic houses	Ranching/guest ranching	Wine tasting
Cowboy skills	History tours	Reindeer safari	Winter sports
Cultural expeditions	Horse carriage tours	River rafting	Yachting
Cycle touring	Horseriding/packing/trekking	Rock climbing	Yoga/meditation
Desert expeditions	Hot air ballooning		Zoology
Dhow sailing	Ice climbing		
Disabled tours			

... families desiring adventure and time together had limited options if they wanted an intimate, non-threatening and relaxed family setting. Our company is built on this analysis. Market analysis also suggests a lack of competition offering true family holidays. An increase in dual income families, resulting in time constraints for parents, and increasing desire and demand for adventures of this type have also helped convince us that the market is ripe for our product.

As for proposals for future development, the company is currently researching European and UK destinations for the USA market. Todd illuminates further on the company's development plans:

This winter (2002/3) we will be launching our full scale marketing campaign in the US for travel in Europe and the UK. Our marketing efforts are differentiated from classic Internet sites, as we do not equate high volume of traffic through our website with families on holiday with us; we will be focusing on quality of hits as opposed to quantity of hits. During the next three years we will continue to work closely with our suppliers refining the tours, and adding tours run directly by ourselves. We will also concentrate efforts on accreditation through widely accepted travel industry associations. We have a strategic plan that extends to five years and beyond, yet we understand that the market is changing dramatically and will continue to do so. Therefore we expect constant environmental scanning and adjustments to our products and operation to be very much part of our future work.

Case study 2   Women backpackers

In recent years there has been a great increase in the number of female backpackers taking trips across Asian, Africa and South America. More and more women are also choosing to make the journey alone. This trend does not seem to be affected by well-publicized stories of the murder of women backpackers in different parts of the world over the past three or four years.

Most of these women backpackers are in the younger age group, are relatively highly educated, and tend to come from developed countries in Europe, North America, Australasia and – increasingly – South-East Asia.

In the past twenty years, guidebooks specifically targeted at women backpackers have appeared. For example, in 1986 Pandora/Rough Guides published *Half the Earth: Women's Experiences of Travel Worldwide.* (See Davies and Longrigg, 1986.) This book highlighted the risk of sexual harassment faced by solo women backpackers, and over 3000 women contributed articles on around 70 countries for this book.

Today, most guidebooks for independent travel – Rough Guides, Lonely Planet, Lets Go – include sections of advice specifically for women.

The first edition of *Asia Overland*, published in 1998, assessed 35 Asian countries in terms of how 'woman-friendly' they were for solo women backpackers using a scale of 1 tick (very bad) to 5 ticks (very good). The results are shown in Exhibit 2.

However, it must be stressed that the assessment in Exhibit 2 was highly subjective and was prepared by 'western' authors. It may therefore reflect perceptions rather than reality, and misunderstanding (or intolerance) of other cultures.

Some of the commentators can sound stereotypical or arrogant, as can be seen from these few patronizing examples:

South East Asia is not the Middle East – women play an active role in day to day public life.

While most of Indonesia and Malaysia is Muslim, it is not of the fundamentalist variety – you will not be stoned by religious zealots for baring an ankle.

A haughty attitude can work wonders.

On the other hand, women travelling alone in some parts of the world do face particular risks and harassment.

Exhibit 2 Attitudes towards solo women travellers in 35 Asian countries.

Number of ticks	Number of countries	Comments
No ticks – unable to make any judgement	5	Includes Afghanistan and Bhutan
1	1	Pakistan
2	5	Includes Turkey, Iran, India, and Indonesia
3	6	Includes Azerbaijan, Uzbekhistan, and Turkmenistan
4	14	Includes China, Russia, Malaysia, Nepal, Sri Lanka, and Vietnam
5	4	Includes Japan, Thailand and Singapore

Many solo women travellers make use of a wide range of information sources when travelling to reduce the problems. These sources include websites, guidebooks, and the experience of fellow travellers. Women also tend to join up with other women or a male companion when they are about to travel across countries or regions that are considered particularly risky for solo women travellers.

Each year thousands of women travelling alone succeed in crossing Asia and, to a lesser extent, Africa and South America, unscathed.

The profile of solo female backpackers appears to be changing, in the following ways:

- More older women appear to be starting to go backpacking as solo travellers
- Young women from countries where women have not traditionally travelled alone, are starting to be seen around the world as solo backpackers; this is particularly true of women from South-East Asia.

The growth of female solo backpackers is probably being partly stimulated by the travel writings of women who have travelled the world on their own. One example is Dervla Murphy, who has made solo journeys and then written about them in books with titles like *In Ethiopia with a Mule*, *Eight Feet in the Andes* and *On a Shoestring to Coorg*.

It seems likely that social change around the world will further stimulate the growth of the female solo backpacking market in the future.

Case study 3   Disabled people and adventure travel

In recent years there has been a growing demand for vacations from disabled people. In a large number of countries any vacation is something of an adventure for these tourists owing to a lack of specialized facilities and services. Nevertheless, a growing number are seeking to take more adventurous vacations than would have been the case a few years ago.

This growing interest has been reflected in specialist guidebooks for disabled travellers. In 1991, for instance, the Rough Guide published its contribution, *Nothing Ventured – Disabled People Travel the World*.

At the same time, many guidebooks to adventure tourism destinations have started offering specific advice to disabled travellers. However, many of these guides present a picture that is far from encouraging, as can be seen from the examples in Exhibit 3.

From this evidence and other sources of data, it is clear that:

- Facilities for disabled travellers are more sophisticated in developed countries; this is an issue for adventure travel, as much of it takes place in developing countries where there are fewer facilities for the disabled

Exhibit 3 Guidebook advice for disabled adventure travellers.

Guidebook	Selected comments
Lonely Planet Guide to South America on a Shoestring, 7th edn (2000)	'South America is not well set up for disabled travellers.' 'Unfortunately, expensive international hotels are more likely to cater for guests with disabilities than cheap local lodgings; air travel will be more feasible than inexpensive local buses; and well developed tourist attractions will be more accessible than some off-the-beaten track destinations.' 'Careful planning is essential, but there is little detailed information on South America for disabled travellers.'
Footprint Morocco Handbook, 2nd edn (1999)	'Morocco really cannot be said to be well adapted to the needs of the disabled traveller.'
Ministry of Sound, Misguided Ibiza (2001)	No mention of disabled people and no details of facilities for disabled travellers
Let's Go Central America (1999)	'Central America still poses a formidable challenge for the disabled traveller. Though few facilities are accessible to disabled persons, many attractions are trying to make exploring the outdoors more feasible.'
Eyewitness Travel Guide to Greece (1997)	'There are few facilities in Greece for assisting the disabled, so careful planning is essential.'
The Rough Guide to Mallorca and Menorca (1996)	'Despite their popularity as holiday destinations, Mallorca and Menorca pay scant regard to their disabled visitors.'
Trailblazer Publications. *Guide to Azerbaijan and Georgia* (1999)	No specific section on travel advice for disabled people.

Continued overleaf

Guidebook	Selected comments
The Rough Guide to Australia (1997)	This guide has three pages of detailed advice for travellers with disabilities. It provides details of advice leaflets from the Australian Tourist Commission, and encourages disabled travellers by telling them they can go snorkelling and visit the Kakadu National Park with no problems.
Lonely Planet Guide to Norway (1999)	The guide gives details of specialist attractions designed for disabled visitors and also talks about ski events for visually impaired skiers, and disabled athletics; however, it still advises disabled travellers to plan well ahead when travelling to Norway
The Rough Guide to Brazil (2000)	'Travel in Brazil for people with disabilities is likely to be difficult, if special facilities are required.'
Trailblazers Publications. Asia Overland (1998)	This guide has no general specific advice for disabled travellers; there is advice for each country for women travelling alone and for vegetarians, but nothing for disabled travellers
Lonely Planet Guide to Syria. 1999	'Scant regard is paid to the needs of disabled travellers in Syria.'
The Rough Guide to St. Petersburg (1998)	'In the past, very little attention has been paid to the needs of the disabled anywhere in Russia. Attitudes are changing, but there is a long way to go, the chronic shortage of funds . . . doesn't help.'
The Lonely Planet Guide to South-East Asia on a Shoestring (1997)	'Travellers with serious disabilities are unlikely to find South-East Asia very user friendly . . . It is unrealistic to expect much in the way of public amenities.'

- Services for disabled travellers are usually better in big cities and on airlines than in adventure tourism destinations
- Provision is improving, albeit slowly.

One development in recent years has been the great increase in infrastructure and advice for disabled travellers, from two main sources:

1 Organizations for disabled travellers such as RADAR and the Holiday Care Service in the UK, Mobility International USA, and ACROD in Australia
2 Websites for disabled travel organizations, specialist tour operators and destinations, as well as for the experiences of individual disabled travellers.

There are also more tour operators offering packages for disabled travellers.

In spite of all this progress any travel still seems to be an adventure for disabled people, while true adventure travel is too often an impossible dream.

Case study 4   Red Letter Days

Red Letter Days is a UK-based company that sells out-of-the-ordinary 'experiences' to its clients, both individuals and as part of the incentive travel market. In the individual market, many of the experiences are given as gifts by friends and relatives. They either choose the experience for their friends or relatives, or give them gift vouchers valued at between £49 and £1000 in 2000–2001.

Most experiences involve either adrenaline rushes of some kind or luxurious breaks where the consumer is pampered. An indication of the range on offer from this company is given by the following selection, taken from their 68-page 2000–2001 brochure:

- The chance to drive a Ferrari 350 around a 1.7-mile course in Leicestershire, UK (£225 for four hours)
- A half-day 4×4 off-road driving adventure at a range of locations in the UK (£120 for four hours)
- The chance to spend 20 minutes at the controls of a F4 Phantom jet simulator (£149)
- A balloon trip over London with champagne (£185 per person)
- A four-day visit to the Yuri Gagarin Cosmonaut Training Centre in Moscow, including ten 30-second weightlessness experiences in an Ilyushin 76 aircraft (estimated cost £4750!)
- A four-day vacation in Russia including a 25-minute flight in a MIG-29 fighter with the chance to take the controls (estimated price £8500!)
- A week's holiday in South Africa that includes the chance to come face to face with a Great White Shark, albeit from the safety of a cage (around £1250)

- A day of SAS-type military training in the UK (£165)
- A nostalgic flight of 40 minutes duration in a classic old biplane (£120)
- A unique opportunity to descend in a submarine to the wreck of the Titanic, off the Newfoundland coast (£30 000!)
- A two-day package in the UK, learning to handle eagles (£225)
- A one-day yacht racing course in the UK (£165)
- A luxurious weekend break for two at a stately home in Scotland (£1200)
- A three-night cookery course, with 13 hours tuition at the Raymond Blanc L'École de Cuisine in Oxfordshire (£800)
- A full personal makeover in London, including photographs, taking a day (£199)
- A three-hour recording session in a professional studio (£149).

While very different from each other, all of these experiences can be seen as adventure travel because they are usually new or very unusual experiences for the consumer. The price of the experience includes free cancellation, personal accident, and public liability insurance.

While Red Letter Days pioneered this kind of tourism package just over ten years ago, new companies are appearing in this growing market all the time.

Case study 5 GREENFORCE

This case study examines GREENFORCE, a company that organizes and runs conservation expeditions in various countries around the world. The case study also focuses on the experiences of two people who worked as part of the GREENFORCE team, first in Uganda and then later in Zambia. Sue Norbury and Julian Harlow started out as volunteers on a ten-week expedition to Uganda, and were able to extend their stay as staff trainees for a further three months. After briefly returning to the UK, Sue and Julian were selected as part of the Zambia project set-up team, a truly fantastic experience for them. After a further two years of fieldwork they were selected for the MSc sponsorship programme, and are very grateful to GREENFORCE for launching both their careers.

GREENFORCE was set up in 1996, and is a non-profit organization that operates environmental conservation expeditions in developing countries around the world. Its mission statement is:

> To assist in the conservation of wildlife and the natural environment through the provision of interpretative biological information regarding species within or using protected areas. In doing so to integrate with existing programmes and collaborate with like-minded institutions for mutual benefit and to ensure the sustainable development of the aforementioned protected areas.
>
> (GREENFORCE, 1996; see GREENFORCE 1998).

To this end, GREENFORCE works for the host country's National Trust or Wildlife Commission and yields useful environmental data to assist these organizations in producing management plans that endeavour to protect or rebuild endangered ecosystems. In order to carry out such work, GREENFORCE utilizes volunteers and employs paid staff to work in the host country over a period of time. Field-staff who originate from the host countries also work on the projects. Other stakeholders also become involved in the projects – for example, Peace Corps Volunteers.

GREENFORCE's inaugural project was set up in Uganda in 1997. The director of the Uganda Wildlife Authority invited the organization to carry out a biodiversity inventory of Karuma Wildlife Reserve, an area of land that acts as a buffer zone for Murchison Falls National Park in southern Uganda. The country was subjected to civil war and unrest throughout the 1970s. Consequently wildlife populations were decimated, leading to a loss of wildlife diversity and uncertainty about which species still existed within the national parks. Though the conservation value of conducting the species inventory acted as the

Exhibit 4   GREENFORCE's environmental projects (adapted from GREENFORCE, 2001).

Environmental project	Destination	Project overview
Marine projects	Bahamas	Assessment and monitoring of two coral reef areas that will shortly become marine 'no take' (no harvesting of any marine organism) zones
	Borneo	Conducting baseline surveys of the flora and fauna of coral reefs
	Fiji	Carrying out an assessment of coral health and fish populations to assist with community-based conservation
Terrestrial projects	Zambia	Producing species inventories and population estimates for all species, from large mammals to birds and reptiles
	Peru	Conducting research on birds, mammals and tropical trees in the Amazon rainforest

main impetus for this work, other benefits were also achieved from this project. The project team helped to identify areas within the Park that could be developed for tourism purposes. In addition, they set up links with local schools and carried out workshops at the GREENFORCE base camp to encourage children to learn about the importance of conservation in the area.

As illustrated in Exhibit 4, GREENFORCE's current projects are either marine- or land-based and take place in a number of global destinations.

GREENFORCE staff

The organization 'provides opportunities for conservation enthusiasts to gain practical experience, essential for building a career within this competitive and fast growing sector' (GREENFORCE, 2001). GREENFORCE recruits up to fourteen fee-paying volunteers per project four times yearly. In addition, paid staff work as research co-ordinators, research assistants, expedition leaders and country co-ordinators. The organization also helps volunteers and employees who are keen to develop careers in conservation through funding their postgraduate studies in relevant subject areas. Most people start off working with the organization as volunteers, and as such have to raise sufficient funds (approximately £2550) to finance their trip. Volunteers generally undertake a project for a period of ten weeks, although some stay out in the field for a longer duration. For example, Sue and Julian worked as volunteers in Uganda for six months in total and gained relevant work experience through the organization's training programme in order to become field staff in Zambia, where they spent eighteen months. This programme offers individuals the means to build up their fieldwork, teamwork and organizational skills, as well as gaining experience in running an environmental project.

GREENFORCE provides volunteers with full training, 'so no previous experience is required, however living conditions in the field are basic so you must have enthusiasm and a desire to provide a positive contribution to this vital conservation work' (GREEN-FORCE, 2001). The type of work that volunteers get involved in depends upon which project they choose (see Exhibit 5). Most projects run over a much longer duration than ten weeks, and therefore some volunteers will not see the end results of their efforts.

Volunteer training

Four months prior to embarking on an environmental expedition, volunteers participate in a comprehensive training programme at the Bowles Outdoor Centre (Kent, UK). This takes place throughout the course of a weekend. During this time volunteers are given information about the history and culture of the host country, the National Park where they will be based and the overall aims of the specific project that they are to be involved in, and also basic training in orienteering skills. Another important part of this training

**Exhibit 5   Examples of GREENFORCE's conservation activities
(source: GREENFORCE, 1998).**

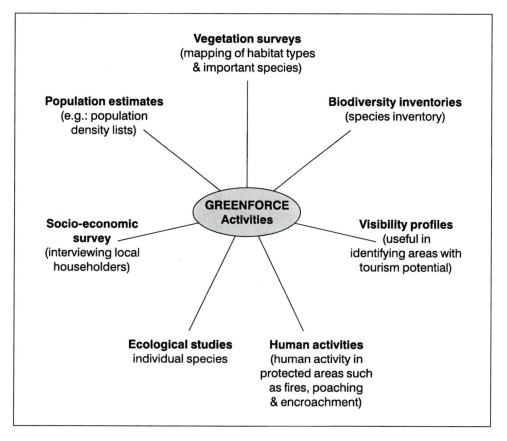

session is to communicate to volunteers the conditions they might expect whilst working in the host country. In the initial few weeks of their time spent in Uganda, Sue and Julian comment on their pre-expedition expectations and how different these were to the actual expedition experience itself:

> We were permanently warned it would be very basic. They [GREENFORCE] try to place some negative thoughts in your mind rather than it all being completely positive. Obviously they don't want it to sound too negative but the aim of that is just to prepare you for some of the extremes that you're going to face. So, you have your own expectations that you see on TV and in the newspapers, then they help you to shape your expectations throughout the training weekend. When you actually arrive there [the developing country] it's nothing like you expected it to be, and yet you

don't know why it's not like that. You go there and think that some things are just like you expected but most of it is not.

It was all so new and exciting. Every small detail about being in another country on the equator was just so exciting. I remember being absolutely petrified of walking to the pit latrine. I wouldn't go on my own because I thought there would be snakes. I remember lying in my tent and I could hear the termites underneath, I was so pathetically terrified that I was my own worst neighbour.

There were times when we had to go out and collect our own water, as our vehicle broke down so often. It really made you think. Local people have to do that all the time, cycling with water containers on the back of their bikes. You see people cycling along, no problem. It was impossible! They were killing themselves laughing, watching us trying to cycle down the road carrying water.

Such comments illustrate the uniqueness of GREENFORCE's expeditions in providing individuals with highly exciting adventurous experiences that no amount of pre-expedition training can prepare them for. It is apparent that the organization's training sessions and the volunteers' expectations built up during these sessions result in only the most determined of individuals ultimately working on GREENFORCE's environmental projects.

Volunteer profile

Although volunteers embark on GREENFORCE expeditions primarily because of their interest in conservation, there are also other reasons. The volunteers range from those with only a limited interest in conservation work to those with total enthusiasm for the subject. Many express a need to do something that is worthwhile and valuable to the environment and to society. Talking about their experiences in Zambia, Sue and Julian comment:

It was quite amazing how diverse people's reasons for coming out were. There were people like us who'd just finished their degrees and wanted an experience and wanted to feel they were doing some good as well as going to a country they'd always dreamed of going to. You'd get people who were on career breaks – one of the women was earning an absolute fortune and she had just decided to come away for ten weeks and she didn't know whether or not she was going to come back to it. People want to have something that will stop and make them think. Other people who came out wanted to view large mammals. They didn't seem to have much interest in conservation and that's very difficult as the basis of what we do is conservation work. If you saw wildlife as well, then that was absolutely fantastic.

Volunteers' expectations are also wide-ranging, and whilst some people are quite realistic about what to expect whilst working for GREENFORCE others seem less willing to accept that their work will be largely routine in nature with only intermittent bursts of excitement:

> Some would see conservation as something spectacularly exciting and think 'what a job. It's going to be brilliant!'. But a lot of it is routine, tedious, incredibly boring, repetitive (vegetation surveys especially) and it's not always permanent excitement. Occasionally you witness something and you think 'Oh my God, I can't believe I've just seen that'. Three weeks of solid sweat and toil is absolutely and completely worthwhile. Some people expected to see things all the time – people who perhaps weren't experienced. Some other people came out to try to do a research project and saw it as an opportunity to get practical experience.

It is evident from the above that a diverse group of individuals make up the volunteer team, and that these people are looking to fulfil various needs whilst on GREEN-FORCE expeditions. On further examination, it becomes clear that some of their needs and motives are indistinct when compared with other groupings of adventure tourists. It has already been noted that an important part of adventure is risk, and the opportunity to engage in an experience that will lead to excitement, thrills and ultimately an 'adrenaline high'. GREENFORCE volunteers are no exception, placing themselves in situations where some degree of risk is often inevitable – for example, working in a country where political instability is rife. Their personalities and lifestyles may also reflect the need to take part in risky activities on a regular basis, as demonstrated in this quotation:

> I was looking for something adventurous, something different to do. If you liken it to bungee jumping and white-water rafting, that's always been something I've loved doing and jumping out of trees when I was a child etc. There's always something different to look for that's exciting.

A range of other motives and benefits are experienced from participating in GREEN-FORCE expeditions, and these are illustrated in Exhibit 6.

People who participate in GREENFORCE's expeditions appear to do so in part for adventure and excitement. The various expeditions offer challenging environments for individuals, no matter what their level of experience of living in the bush. Although carrying out conservation work in developing countries is the primary goal spurring GREENFORCE's work, from the volunteer's perspective there are a whole host of other reasons. Importantly, people are interested in doing something that is going to be a memorable and perhaps life-changing experience. Adventure most definitely forms an integral part of this experience, and is encountered on a day-to-day basis whilst conducting the field research and living in base camp. For instance, when Sue and Julian

Exhibit 6   Benefits and motives – the GREENFORCE experience.

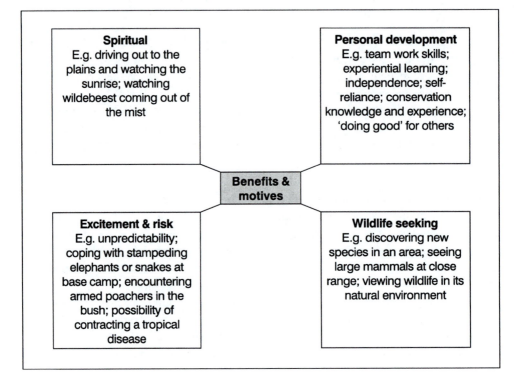

were asked about their feelings towards the risks when working as GREENFORCE staff, one of their responses to stampeding elephants in Zambia was:

> It was great! Sometimes you'd be driving the vehicle and your legs would be shaking so hard that you could barely press the accelerator and they'd just charge towards you.

Conclusion

This case study attempts to illustrate connections between adventure tourism and the conservation expeditions offered by GREENFORCE. Although the latter may not be conventionally viewed as a form of adventure tourism, or indeed any form of tourism, its participants work throughout an expedition and often spend extended periods of time away from their home environments and thus links can clearly be seen. The most obvious similarities can be found through drawing comparisons between the adventure tourist and the GREENFORCE participant; both appear to be primarily driven by risk, excitement and the need to do something new and different.

Case study 6   Adventure tourism magazines

The growth of adventure tourism in recent years has been both reflected in and stimulated by a plethora of new glossy magazines focused on this area. Here we will analyse just two UK examples, *Adventure Travel Outdoors* and *Wanderlust*, based on an individual issue of each magazine chosen at random.

Adventure Travel Outdoors appears six times a year, and was launched in 1996. It is a full-colour magazine with an editorial : advertising ratio of approximately 75 : 25 per cent. However, it should be noted that a number of pages are not advertisements but are editorial features that review all kinds of products produced by individual companies, from package holidays to walking books, guidebooks to weatherproof clothing.

For the March/April 2001 edition, the breakdown of the editorial aspect is shown in Exhibit 7.

Other interesting features of this issue were as follows:

- Only one article was focused on the UK, the remainder being largely international in flavour
- Several articles focused on health issues, including deep vein thrombosis on long-haul flights, mosquitoes, and food hygiene

Exhibit 7   Analysis of the editorial content of *Adventure Travel Outdoors*, March/April 2001.

Type of content	Approximate percentage of editorial content
Destination features	33
Stories of individual travellers' experiences	11
Reviews of adventure holidays offered by tour operators	12
Equipment reviews	13
Articles on issues of interest to the adventure traveller	24
News items and factual information	7

- Sections had titles such as 'Stuff', 'Tales from the trail', 'Yes grasshopper' (questions to the editor), 'Do you wanna go', and 'The big trip'
- Most of the advertisements were either large ones for equipment manufacturers or smaller ones for specialist tour operators
- There were two pages of small advertisements where travellers could advertise for companions on future trips.

Wanderlust is also produced six times a year and was launched in the early 1990s. It describes itself as a magazine 'for people with a passion for travel'. While this could in theory include people taking, sun, sand, sea and sex holidays on the Costas or coach tours in the Benelux countries, it is clear from the content of the magazine that it is largely about adventure travel. For example, the April/May 2001 issue contained features on Azerbaijan,

Exhibit 8   Analysis of the editorial content of *Wanderlust*, April/May 2001.

Type of content	Approximate percentage of editorial content
Destination features	27
Stories of individual travellers' experiences	3
Reviews of adventure holidays offered by tour operators	0
Equipment reviews	6
Articles on issues of interest to the adventure traveller	30
News items and factual information	9
Miscellaneous, including book and music reviews, letters pages, details of world travel related tourism programmes etc.	15
Special features	10

tree house hotels in Kerala, Uganda, Hong Kong and South America. Even its feature on European cities featured more offbeat places, such as Rotterdam, Trömso, Split and Vilnius.

Nevertheless, *Wanderlust* is more mainstream and is concerned with all types of tourism, not just the active pursuits tourism covered by *Adventure Travel Outdoors*; it also looks at urban tourism, culture tourism and wildlife tourism.

The content of the April/May 2001 issue is analysed in Exhibit 8.

Of the 136 pages in the issue, around 30 per cent consisted of advertising whilst the remainder was editorial.

The interesting features of this issue were as follows:

- Ten pages were devoted to a 'Travel photos of the year' special, featuring 38 photos from over 3000 submitted by readers; of these photos, none was taken in the UK and only five in Europe as a whole
- There was a broader range of advertisements than in *Adventure Travel Outdoors*, with advertisements from airlines and national tourist boards
- About 6 per cent of the editorial related to health and safety issues
- Travel photography was the focus of around 5 per cent of the editorial and advertising content of the magazine (excluding the 'Travel photos' special)
- Readers' letters and small advertisements designed to allow one reader to communicate with another represented 8 per cent of the editorial content
- Cultural tourism was well featured, with an article on Branson, USA, famous for its music heritage, and one on six unusual city break destinations in Europe.

It is clear that both magazines are aiming at somewhat different markets, but both concentrate on types of tourism that are 'out of the ordinary' and represent some kind of adventure experience for the tourist.

Case study 7   Walk on the wild side – travelling to the world's most dangerous places

A small but growing number of people seem to enjoy travelling to places that are perceived to be dangerous for some reason. 'Dangerous places' (DP) travel has clearly become an obsession for its aficionados, and there are now guidebooks just for them. For example, in 1997 Fielding World-Wide published the second edition of its *The World's Most Dangerous Places* guide (Pelton *et al.*, 1997), which claims it helps its readers to:

- Stay alive in the world's most dangerous places
- Find hidden or forbidden areas, including war zones

- Explore the dark side
- Find 'hard-core' adventures.

The following extracts from the preface to this book indicate the nature of this market and the motivations of such DP tourists.

The DP thing

To say that DP has become popular would be an understatement. In less than a year we have gone from laid back travellers visiting the world's cesspools and hot spots, to minor celebrities, complete with offers of TV and movie deals. Throughout all this, we have the bizarre sense of being Peter Sellers in *Being There* or Tom Hanks in *Forrest Gump*. 'Dangerous is as dangerous does' might even be our motto. We didn't set out to be the post boys for thrill seekers and professional adventurers, but things have changed since the first edition was published. Coskun now has one of the top television shows in Turkey, Wink keeps getting mistaken for Mel Gibson in Saigon, and I endure the hundreds of questions reporters throw at me in an effort to find out just what is so appealing about this book.

Along the way, we have chatted and broken bread with some interesting characters – from the leaders of Hezbollah to the warlords in Liberia, to the Moros in the Philippines to the taliban in Afghanistan. We also have hit the books and tried to keep track of, and make sense out of the rapidly changing world.

Is DP a macho thing?

Some adventure magazines have tried to portray us as tough guys cruising the world looking for trouble. I can't think of anything that is further from the truth. I now consider myself a seeker of knowledge, a far more cerebral occupation than my previous title of professional adventurer. I can admit that we may be adrenaline junkies, but none of us has ever been bungee jumping, rock climbing or even windsurfing. I collect art, write books, love nature and have two beautiful twin daughters. Coskun likes to cook, Wink likes to play blues guitar, and together, we don't exactly fit the hairy-chested, cigar-chomping adventurer profile.

What is the most dangerous situation you have been in?

I truly can't answer this. It might be as mundane as surviving a plane crash in Borneo, Coskun hitting a land mine in Afghanistan, or Wink riding his motorcycle through war-torn Cambodia. We really never set out to do anything overly dangerous, but we do pride ourselves on knowing how to handle ourselves in dangerous situations, and we have done a lot of fast talking at gunpoint.

A message to fellow adventurers and seekers of knowledge

The response to the first edition of this book has been overwhelming. Governments have expressed their outrage, and readers have sent in their heartfelt thanks for creating a book that 'tells it like it is'. If this book can save one life or change a misconception, we did our job. As for the many readers who gave us the benefit of their experiences in dangerous places, we are very grateful and they now own a free book and a cool T-shirt. If you have any pearls of wisdom that may save another traveller from misfortune, please send it in and if we use it we will gladly send you a DP book and one of our politically incorrect (but heavy-duty) T-shirts.

The authors are very candid about their views on travel to dangerous places. While claiming not to be classic macho adventurers, their words make them seem very different people to the ordinary tourist. While they claim not to be in the business of promoting tourism to dangerous places, the book does attach a certain status to such travel, which may make it attractive to some people.

Pelton, writing as publisher as well as author, seems to be suggesting dangerous place travel really is a new adventure tourism market when he says:

Despite early predictions of folly, DP has become Fielding's fastest-selling travel guide and the rallying point for a new type of traveller. A traveller who is a lot like the authors: curious, intelligent and sceptical of the sound-bite view of the world's least travelled places – people who trust other travel guides as much as we trust infomercials.

Many people ask how we do the things we do. The answer is simple. We just do it. We may not always be successful in our quest, but we always have a good time.

Some sections of the book have headings that suggest that the authors believe this a sector of adventure tourism will grow and become formalized in the future, including:

■ 'Coming attractions', where the authors predict which destinations will become more dangerous places to visit in the future
■ The 'Adventure guide', which gives details of related issues and types of vacations such as expedition planning, volunteer vacations, adventure travel publications and survival training schemes.

The 1997 guide rated Afghanistan, Algeria, Angola, Burindi, Colombia, India, Israel, Liberia, Pakistan, Sierra Leone, Saudi Arabia and Lebanon as the world's most dangerous countries to visit, but its list of dangerous places also included popular tourist destinations such as Egypt, Sri Lanka and Turkey.

Interestingly, the guide suggests that the danger in a destination can be a result of:

- War
- Terrorism and the actions of security forces
- Crime
- Transport accidents
- Disease
- Drugs.

Most worrying for the mainstream tourism industry is that, in the future, the authors predict that several popular destinations may become more dangerous places due to tension, social unrest, war and crime – including Cyprus, Greece, Kenya, Morocco, and South Africa.

Case study 8   Clubbing and party tourism in the UK market

In the UK market, clubbing and party tourism has grown considerably in recent years, becoming ever more sophisticated. An increasing number of tour operators are targeting this market and developing brands to satisfy the party tourists.

The market for this form of adventure tourism is generally men and women under 30 years of age. Such tourists are found in the UK and a number of other Northern European countries, notably Germany, Denmark, Finland and the Netherlands. College students in the USA also have a reputation for enjoying similar vacations when their examinations are over. Furthermore, in the UK market there are hedonistic holidays aimed at an older clientele.

The authors have analysed the 2001 brochures of four leading brands in the UK market: Club 18–30, Escapades, Ministry of Sound, and Twentys.

Club 18–30 was the pioneer of this form of tourism in the UK market, and has in the past attracted criticism for the overtly sexual nature of its advertising. The 2001 brochure promoted packages with phrases such as:

- 'We take you that little bit further'
- 'Stick your fingers up at convention and have the holiday that you want'
- 'If you want stimulating, you have come to the right place'
- 'You can guarantee that at our accommodation "there are no screaming kids or whinging old people to complain about you enjoying yourself"'
- 'Come again – wouldn't we all love to?'

The brochure also contains details of the annual reunion for Club 18–30 holidaymakers in Skegness in November 2001, where it says there will be:

. . . a 2-week holiday crammed into one bloody great party weekend . . . blokes, birds, boozing, bums, boobs, beer, bonding [and if you're lucky, a bit of bondage].

The brochure features holidays in thirteen destinations in the Mediterranean and the Canary Islands. Not surprisingly, the largest single destination in the programme is the party island of Corfu.

Each resort section features a 'diary' quotation, purporting to be from a holidaymaker in the resort. The flavour of the product is contained in these quotations, including:

- 'I'm not sure how I came to wake up on the beach. Chalk that one down to experience.'
- 'I don't believe for one second that Simon got a shag last night. He was so drunk he couldn't have raised a smile.'
- 'All praise to the God that is me. What a fantastic pull.'

Escapades also makes the nature of its offer clear, with the terms at the beginning of its brochure like 'Shocking good holidays' and 'For you – not your parents'. It goes on to add that 'we've picked resorts with wild bars where anything goes and closing time comes when you finally leave'.

Escapades offers not only Mediterranean/Canary Island destinations but also Cancun in Mexico, described as being 'for the fun-loving, sun-loving generation'. It sells all its packages with a message of 'wild days, crazy nights'.

The Ministry of Sound's Clubbers Guide Holidays brochure promises five great features of their Mediterranean packages:

1 The Wave-Larks in Watersports – a combination of water slides, music, and dancing
2 The Beach – beach parties with top music, drinks, and barbecues
3 The Sunset – parties on board yachts and catamarans with music and champagne
4 The Flick – parties with the music of the 1970s and 1980s
5 The Session – nights at the best clubs with big name DJs.

It also offers a winter 'snow stormin' party, which in 2001 took place from 31 March to 7 April in Mayrhofen (Austria), and weekend clubbing breaks to Barcelona, Berlin and Reykjavik.

With this company the focus is clearly on clubbing rather than sun, as it says twice in the brochure 'F__k the tan?'

Twentys begins its brochures with the words:

Holidays that change the way you walk. Overdo it, love it, drink it, snog it, jump it, have it.

Part of the brochure features 'Straight from the Horse's Mouth', which purports to be the record of a week's holiday of one customer. It features a mixture of hedonistic pleasures, including drinking, casual sex and partying. Helen says she 'ended up shit-faced' on Sunday night and 'ripped to the tits on the beach'.

The spirit of such holidays seems to be summed up well by a description of Kavos on Corfu:

> There are no kids and old gippers so we can do what we want, when we want, with who we want.

These holidays are more than the traditional 'sun, sand, sea, and sex' holidays. The music, alcohol and watersports are also now an important part of the experience. This partying market reflects a distinctive lifestyle lived by this market segment, with its own language and music and set of shared beliefs.

It could be argued that these people are not being that adventurous because they are simply doing on holiday similar things to those they do at home. However, there is adventure, for they can go further when they are away from the constraints of their own home town. And being with new people in a foreign country is an adventure in itself.

If the operators have gauged the market correctly, and there is no reason to believe they have not, then price is very important to this market. They want to pay the minimum price with as many added value features as possible, so they can have the maximum cash available for drinking and other entertainment.

It is also clear that this is a very fashion conscious market, where people want to be seen in resorts that are the current 'in places' in terms of clubs and nightlife, with the best DJs.

There is no doubt that this market has grown rapidly in recent years. However, it has been criticized, largely on moral grounds, as encouraging bad behaviour and leading to problems in resorts. While no doubt lucrative for destinations, there is a fear that this tourism puts other tourists off visiting the same destinations. It has been suggested that resorts where clubbing tourism dominates should 'de-market' themselves to this market, to allow them to attract other, more morally acceptable, markets. This apparent discrimination against certain people and their lifestyle is clearly controversial.

As this market continues to grow, there is no doubt that the arguments surrounding this form of tourism will continue.

Case study 9   Rock climbing in Spain

Spain has experienced relatively recent and dramatic growth in climbing-based tourism as adventure addicts have begun to visit the country's coastal and inland regions to climb on its crags and mountains. One of Spain's most important attractions for climbers is its relatively mild winter climate. The main period for rock climbing in this country is the shoulder season, between the months of October to March, outside the peak tourist season. At this time of year the congenial climate is naturally appealing to Northern European climbers seeking out some winter sun, while during the summer months the Spanish climate usually becomes too hot and humid for climbing. Spain has a wealth of natural resources suitable for rock climbing, and those crags that have been developed for the purpose of climbing comprise only about 20 per cent of the total potential (Craggs, 2001 personal communication). Such a figure indicates that climbing-based activities are merely at the early stages of development and there is considerable scope for further expansion in the future.

Rock climbing in Spain is predominantly of the sport variety, and therefore there is a high proportion of bolted routes (routes that have artificial protection bolted into the rock) as opposed to the traditional/adventure routes commonly found in the UK. One reason for this high propensity of bolted routes is the geological nature of the rock. Most rock found in the climbing regions of Spain is limestone, and such rock typically has sections that do not allow climbers to be protected with climbing gear because of the lack of features and gear placements. It is generally advocated that bolted routes provide a safer environment in which to climb as the bolts are firmly embedded into the rock and will effectively hold a climber should he or she fall whilst leading. Leaders of the more traditional type of climb have to be far more reliant on the effectiveness of their gear placements should they fall.

Rock climbing destinations in Spain

Although a seemingly small proportion of Spain's natural resources have been cultivated for rock climbing, several destinations have recently evolved to become well-established areas for participating in this sport. Many of these destinations – Majorca, Ibiza and the Costa Blanca – are household names in Europe, originally renowned for their mass tourism and coastal package holiday offerings. Other climbing destinations have grown from different types of tourism. For instance, El Chorro in Andalucia (see Box 13.1) originally became famous for the Garganta del Chorro, a spectacular limestone gorge, and El Camino del Rey, a somewhat dilapidated concrete catwalk that spans the length of the gorge.

The mountain of Montserrat, situated in Catalonia, is another example of a destination that attracts people to climb its unusual rock formations, although it is better known for its monastery – one of the most popular visitor attractions in the region. Various individual shapes characterize the mountain:

> ... the towering spire of Bernat's Horse, the huge bulge of the Bishop's Paunch, the shaded folds of the Mummy, the massive trunk of the Elephant and the exaggerated bump of the Pregnant Woman to name just a few.
>
> (Climb Catalunya, 2002)

Box 13.1   El Chorro

The village of El Chorro, situated in Andalucia, is a well-established climbing destination. An impressive yet overwhelming gorge is the main focal point of the village, and every year thousands of climbers gravitate to its towering walls to tackle its exposed routes. The gorge offers a range of single and multi-pitch climbs that cater for various climbing abilities. El Chorro's surrounding natural environment is renowned not only for its rock climbing opportunities but also for walking, cycling and caving activities. Climbers can easily access the village by taking a one-hour journey by car or train from Malaga airport in the Costa del Sol. Cottages, bunkhouses and a campsite are available in the local vicinity, within a short walking distance of the gorge. The campsite was set up in response to the increasing volume of visitors to the area; prior to this 'wild camping' was the norm in El Chorro, although this style of camping exerted certain negative impacts on the area's environment. El Chorro is considered to be one of the first destinations in Spain to attract international visitors for the purposes of climbing. Its popularity has risen partly as a consequence of a readily available climbing guidebook of the area. However, it is thought that any future growth in demand for climbing in the El Chorro region may be restricted by the current lack of accommodation facilities.

(Craggs, 2001 personal communication)

This unusual massif is made up of towering rock formations that contain literally thousands of climbing routes, 'from micro-routes to big wall adventures'.

The Costa Blanca coastline, famous for the resort of Benidorm and notably a settlement area for ex-patriot communities, is perhaps the best-known region in Spain for rock climbing. According to Craggs (1997), It has 'become known as one of the premier sun rock destinations for Britons (and Germans and Scandinavians) wanting to escape the rigours of our grim northern winters'. The region is extensive, and covers the whole coastal area from Murcia in the south to Valencia in the north. Aside from the appeal of its warm winter climate, the Costa Blanca offers a variety of climbing opportunities on its sea cliffs – adjacent to the heavily developed coastal strip – and on its numerous mountains and cliffs located further inland.

Majorca, the largest of the Balearic Islands, is another climbing destination that has grown in popularity over the last few years, drawing in rock climbers from all over Europe and more recently from further afield. Simmonite (1999) describes the island and the many climbing opportunities available:

Mallorca's northern coast is dominated by a rugged mountain range, topped by Puig Major with a height of 4700 ft and criss-crossed by spectacular gorges and ridges that provide a plethora of walks for the energetic. It is also very tranquil with inlets that are only accessible by boat, and lush vegetation abounds.

Further north, mountains give way to impressive sea cliffs at Cape Formentor on the northern tip of the island and are well worth the drive even if you don't climb in the area. The southern side of the island is gentler and less rugged, and parts of it are no less beautiful than its northern counterpart. It is also home to the majority of Mallorcans, and tourism, centred mainly on Palma. The entire island has an abundance of rock with everything from slabs to walls dripping with tufas and the most awesome caves.

There are numerous other climbing destinations on mainland Spain and its islands, such as the well established island of Tenerife in the Canary Islands, the mountain region Los Picos de Europa in La Cordillera Cantábrica, northern Spain, and La Pedriza in the Sierra de Guadarrama, north-east of Madrid. Such destinations are also increasingly attracting the international climbing tourist.

Demand for rock climbing in Spain

Much of the European demand for climbing in Spain has stemmed from the independent travel market. There are also a few outdoor activity organizations and specialist tour operators that offer climbing packages and courses in Spain for those people requiring instruction or guiding in the sport. The Spaniards have been proactive in developing both crags and mountains for traditional and sport climbing ever since the 1930s. Originally this resulted in domestic demand for the sport, but over the past couple of decades the country has attracted an increasing volume of international climbing tourists.

Aside from the domestic market, climbing holidays in Spain primarily attract the Northern European markets. This destination mainly seems to entice 'part-time' or less serious climbers, as well as a smaller number of 'hard-core' individuals who regard climbing as an integral part of their lives. The part-timers are generally less experienced in the sport and interested in doing lower graded routes whilst concurrently being motivated to improve the grades that they climb at. They are attracted by both the abundance and the quality of sport climbing routes available in the region, and the relatively safe environment associated with this type of climbing. A number of these climbers, often on their first climbing trip abroad, select renowned climbing regions such as the Costa Blanca and Majorca for their holiday. In contrast, the hard-core group of climbers prefer less-crowded, more isolated regions that offer new opportunities for climbing (Craggs, 2001 personal communication).

A number of significant factors contribute towards the broad appeal and growth of rock climbing in Spain. The country is easily accessible by road, rail, sea and air from most parts of Europe. Several climbing destinations are situated within close proximity to major international airports – for instance, Barcelona airport and Monserrat, Alicante airport and the Costa Blanca, Bilbao airport and Los Picos de Europa, Malaga airport and El Chorro. Undoubtedly this is advantageous for climbers who prefer to make their own travel arrangements. Likewise, the introduction of European no-frills airlines such as EasyJet and Go have revolutionized air travel through the provision of low-cost airfares to numerous destinations in Spain. Whereas return scheduled flights to most parts of Spain consistently cost upwards of £200, their no-frills equivalents charge a much lower fare of between £50 and £150 on average.

As the Spanish tourism industry is well established and has a prolonged tourist season, climbers visiting various destinations can take advantage of competitively priced package holidays (inclusive of flights, accommodation and airport transfers). For instance, Benidorm, an established inclusive holiday resort, provides an ideal base for people who want to climb in the Costa Blanca region. A key benefit of booking a package holiday is that it is convenient for the traveller: 'people like the fact that they can hand over a cheque and then be met at the airport' (Craggs, 2001 personal communication). For independent travellers there is a wide choice of good quality, cheap accommodation in the form of villas, apartments, campsites and refuges, often located in close proximity to the climbing areas.

Climbing guidebooks seem to have exerted a significant influence upon people's choice of climbing location and hence are useful in providing an estimate of the demand for rock climbing in Spain: 'if it's not got a good guidebook and cheap flights, people are put off' (Craggs, 2001 personal communication). Craggs wrote the first English guidebook to the region, entitled *Costa Blanca Climbs*, in 1990, and a more comprehensive second edition was released in 1997. ROCKFAX's (2001) Costa Blanca, Mallorca and El Chorro guidebook is its best-selling book amongst a plethora of other guides that this company publishes. Over the last few years Craggs has produced several guidebooks to various climbing areas in both mainland Spain and the Spanish islands: *Rock Climbs in Majorca, Ibiza & Tenerife* (1995, 2000); *Costa Blanca Rock* (1990, 1997); and *Andalucia* (1994). Book sale figures have reached 14 000 over a period of nine years. The books are mainly sold through shops, and most of the sales have been to the UK market. Since a website has been established through which people can directly purchase these guides, the volume of sales in Scandinavia and Germany have increased and the North American market has grown slightly.

ROCKFAX has been producing guidebooks on Spanish rock climbing since the mid-1990s, and covers the Costa Blanca, Mallorca and El Chorro areas in just one guidebook (see Exhibit 9) in contrast to Craggs' three separate guidebooks for each different location. Such similar coverage by both producers illustrates the popularity of these different

Exhibit 9 ROCKFAX climbing guidebook sales (James, 2001, personal communication).

ROCKFAX guidebooks for Spain	Total sales	Sales ranking in order of volume (1996–2000)	
Costa Blanca, Mallorca and El Chorro (1st edn 1996, 2nd edn 1998, 3rd edn 2001) *Costa Daurada* (published November 1998)	7200 copies sold between September 1996 and October 2000	1. UK (80–85% of sales) 2. Germany 3. Spain 4. Scandinavia 5. Holland	6. France 7. USA 8. Japan 9. Australia 10. South Africa

regions for rock climbing. Furthermore, both Craggs' and ROCKFAX's guidebooks were published from 1990 onwards, which highlights the relatively recent growth in consumer interest in Spain as a climbing destination. In addition, various editions of these books have been published in short succession. For instance, Craggs' original *Costa Blanca Climbs* (1990) guidebook comprised information on 200 routes spanning nine cliffs. The second edition (1997) contains over 1500 routes on more than 50 cliffs. Such a pattern of guidebook production confirms that the development of rock climbing in Spain is rapidly expanding and new routes are constantly being developed.

Rock climbing organizations operating in Spain

In contrast to climbers who make their own holiday arrangements, some climbing tourists prefer a more structured holiday that includes some form of training and/or guiding from qualified instructors. There are a number of organizations and individuals located throughout the main climbing regions of Spain that offer such provision. The training courses tend to be set up by climbing enthusiasts, originating from the UK or other parts of Europe, who have become residents within Spain's different climbing regions.

Compass West International School of Rock Climbing (ISR) is a small family-run organization, originally set up in Cornwall, England. The organization has been operating rock-climbing courses in Spain since 1982, and is run by Roland Edwards, a qualified international mountain guide. Both the guides and the courses are based in and around Finestrat, a small village situated at the foot of Puig Campana in the Costa Blanca. The school offers tailor-made packages that include seven nights' accommodation, five full days of instruction covering every aspect of rock climbing, equipment (except rock climbing boots), transport to the crags, and airport transfers. It is ideally located amongst a varied range of high-quality limestone crags either situated along the roadside or on mountain routes. Such a variety of crags guarantee appeal to both novice as well as more experienced climbers. Similarly, the courses are designed to suit different standards of climbers from beginner to advanced levels.

There are a number of advantages associated with using Compass West ISR when compared to the 'DIY' approach that most rock climbers tend to adopt when organizing their holidays. This organization has operated in the Costa Blanca region for two decades, and its instructors have an excellent knowledge of the local area and its climbing crags, both popular and more remote ones. They also have substantial climbing experience, and collectively have pioneered approximately 300 new climbing routes in the region. The organization's courses target all levels and abilities of climbers, and the ratio of students to instructor never exceeds 4:1 (Compass West ISR, 2001).

Climb Catalunya specializes in providing tailor-made holidays for rock climbers 'who have limited time and who want to be looked after so that they can concentrate on the fabulous rock found in this part of Spain' (Climb Catalunya, 2002), but also offers holidays for other types of outdoor enthusiast. It is a small organization that usually caters for between two and six people at any one time, with a maximum group size of twelve.

The rationale for this is that clients are guaranteed the personal attention they need in order to make the most of their holiday. Climb Catalunya is based in the Montsec Mountains, at the edge of the High Pyrenees in the north west of Catalunya. It offers various packaged climbing trips to different areas of the region to climb in gorges, on the High Pyrenean granite, and on the Montserrat Massif. The packages include transport transfers from Barcelona airport, transport to and from the climbing areas each day, full-board accommodation in two or three refuges over the holiday duration, typical Catalan meals, experienced guides and expert route advice, and guide books of the area (Climb Catalunya, 2002).

Both of the aforementioned climbing organizations are small scale and cater for small groups of people. It is apparent that larger organizations based in Spain and offering similar packaged trips simply do not exist at present. This could be due to the niche nature of climbing tourism and its specialized appeal to this unique category of adventure tourist. Another explanation is that Spain has only become established as a climbing destination since the 1990s. With the wealth of guidebooks providing detailed accounts of different areas' climbing opportunities, the majority of climbing tourists choose to be independent travellers who do not require the services of such organizations.

It is evident that there is a growing market for rock climbing in Spain, and its natural resources attract both the independent traveller and package holiday market. There have been a number of different factors impacting favourably on this growth. The country has abundant natural resources that can be exploited for rock climbing tourism, and a relatively warm climate throughout the winter months. Several of Spain's rock climbing destinations are situated within close proximity to internationally renowned holiday resorts, and therefore rock climbers can travel to prime climbing areas with relative ease and enjoy well developed tourist services at these resorts. A number of publishers are producing climbing guidebooks to the area, stimulating a growth in demand, and there are organizations in Spain that cater for climbers who are looking for a packaged trip. All these factors present a positive picture for the potential growth of rock climbing tourism in Spain.

Case study 10 Backpacking across Asia

Backpacking across Asia has been fashionable since the 1960s, often being seen almost as a rite of passage for those passing from youth into adulthood. Traditionally Europeans have made the journey from West to East, and Australians *vice versa*. In recent years the overland route across Asia has been disrupted by political upheavals in Iran, Iraq and Afghanistan. Nevertheless, backpacking across Asia is still very popular with young people, and a proliferation of guidebooks exist to help them. This case study is based on the first edition of *Asia Overland*, published in 1998 by Trailblazer Publications, UK. Like most guidebooks, it is written by Westerners who are experienced backpackers. They suggest that things change rapidly and invite readers/travellers to keep them up to date with developments, in anticipation of the next edition.

The authors cover 35 countries in 533 pages, from the point of view of overland budget travellers. The relative attractiveness and popularity of these countries can be partly gauged from the pages devoted to them in this book, which are as follows, although they are countries of very different size:

Afghanistan	10	Armenia	7
Azerbaijan	15	Bangladesh	13
Belarus	4	Bhutan	3
Cambodia	9	China (including Hong Kong and Tibet)	78
Georgia	23	India	33
Indonesia	11	Iran	29
Japan	22	Kazakhstan	12
Krygystan	19	Laos	15
Malaysia	8	Mongolia	8
Myanmar	16	Nepal	18
North Korea	4	Pakistan	21
Philippines	5	Russia	22
Singapore	4	South Korea	12
Sri Lanka	7	Taiwan	2
Tajikistan	5	Thailand	12
Turkey	24	Turkmenistan	10
Ukraine	10	Uzbekistan	18
Vietnam	21		

Taking the size of the country into account, it is interesting to note that:

- Vietnam has more than twice the number of pages given to Malaysia
- Indonesia has only a half as many pages as Pakistan
- China receives more than three times more attention than Russia
- The Philippines receives a third of the coverage of Laos
- Georgia has ten times more pages than Taiwan
- Vietnam receives more than five times as many pages as Singapore.

Just like the Silk Routes in the past, there are well-established routes for backpackers crossing Asia. The book identifies thirteen such routes that cross all or parts of Asia. Factors influencing the route chosen by backpackers include:

- Their country of origin
- Transport problems, including the impact of wet seasons
- Incidence of terrorism and war
- Health risks
- Visa requirements and immigration policies.

On the main routes and at the favourite stopover points for overland travellers an infrastructure of specialist services has grown up to meet their needs, including:

- Guest houses and hostels designed for backpackers
- Cafés, bars, and restaurants, where tourists compare notes on where to go and where to stay
- Ground handlers offering car and bike rental and one/two/three-day tours for those stopping over briefly.

Guidebooks like *Asia Overland* include an eclectic selection of advice for western travellers. In the Uzbek capital, Tashkent, for example, the guide warns travellers about:

- Extortion and unfriendliness by officials at the airport
- Over-priced hotel rooms
- Over-crowded public transport
- Areas in which women travellers feel uncomfortable
- A heavy police presence in some neighbourhoods
- Dishonest taxi drivers
- Hotels that will not accept foreigners
- Poor quality skis and bindings that are rented out for skiing trips to the mountains.

Guidebooks such as those in the Lonely Planet and Rough Guide series greatly influence demand, and inclusion in these guides guarantees visitors will come – or not. However, the Internet and word-of-mouth recommendations from fellow travellers also influence tourist behaviour.

Overland backpacking through Asia does pose some risks, ranging from abduction by terrorists to bus accidents. Occasionally tourists are murdered, and these incidents receive world-wide publicity, particularly when the victims are women. However, the main risks are usually health-related – from stomach bugs to malaria. Backpackers are increasingly using e-mail to remain in contact with home and friends, although some prefer to stay incommunicado, thinking it adds to the experience.

In the 1960s and 1970s, many people travelled to Asia, principally to India and Nepal, in search of spiritual enlightenment. This is still the case today, although the emphasis has moved on now to include Thailand, with its Buddhist tradition. Many travellers over the years have stopped at points on their route and stayed for months and sometimes years.

Overland travel in Asia is often budget travel, and therefore travellers frequently spend most of their time in countries with a low cost of living. As well as the experience, the Trailblazer guide considers that important factors in destination selection for overland backpackers include places where English is spoken, what it is like for women travelling alone, and the situation for vegetarians.

In the past most overland backpackers in Asia were Europeans, Americans and Australians, but in recent years, mirroring the global tourism market in general, more and more Asian people have been making similar trips around or across the continent.

Overland travellers, are always searching for new, off the beaten track, 'non-touristy' places, as these give status. However, this search for new places to explore also puts locations with fragile environments and/or vulnerable populations in jeopardy.

Case study 11   Winter sports in New England

Until recently, winter sports meant skiing, usually of the downhill variety. Now the term covers a wide variety of types of activity of two main types, versions of skiing, and non-skiing activities.

Exhibit 10 illustrates the range of activities available in 2001 in two New England resorts in the USA, Jay Peak (Vermont) and Loon (New Hampshire).

The New England list of 'sports' excludes a range of activities found in other parts of the world, including troika rides and ice-fishing, dog sledding and heli-skiing.

Winter sports in fashionable regions such as the New England resorts is not inexpensive. For example, in 2001:

Exhibit 10   The range of winter sports activities in two New England resorts in 2001.

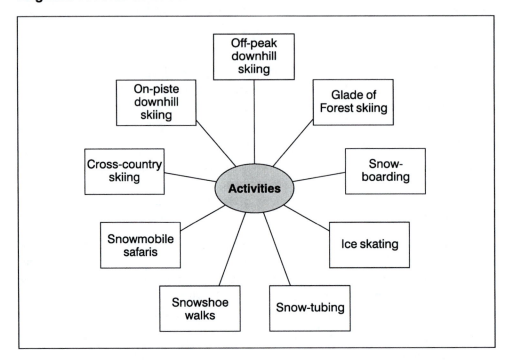

- A three-night half-board package for an adult in Jay Peak, including a lift pass, cost between $607 and $667
- A day's skiing or snowboarding activities for children in Loon cost between $59 and $89
- A five-day lift pass cost $159 in Loon, and $210 in Jay Peak.

Whatever activities visitors engage in they are accommodated in resorts and inns, generally with good facilities. The Northern Lights Resort in Jay Peak is typical of an upscale resort in New England. This is how it described itself in 2001.

Nestled on the mountainside of Jay Peak, Inglenook Lodge provides fine accommodations. The Inglenook is located less than one mile from Jay Peak and features an indoor pool, jacuzzi, sauna, game room and full-service restaurant and lounge. Our tastefully furnished rooms, all with private baths and TV, offer privacy and comfort. The sunken lounge with its giant circular fireplace is the place to visit while taking in the spectacular mountain views.

Trillium Woods English country-style townhouses offer you gracious, comfortable living for long or short visit to the Northeast Kingdom in Vermont. Located one mile from Jay Peak, each eight-room townhouse provides over 2000 square feet of beautiful multi-level accommodations, with the ability to sleep up to eight people. During your stay you will enjoy the many features, such as a den with TV/VCR, a family area with TV and exercise equipment, a large whirlpool tub and sauna, and an open living area with woodstore. All townhouses have fully-appointed kitchens and washers and dryers.

Exhibit 11   Woods skiing policy, Jay Peak 2001.

- When skiing in the woods or when you pass beyond the all area boundary, you leave the area of ski patrol services. You are entering an area that has many hazards and no skier services. Woods are not open, closed, or marked.

- If skiing beyond the ski area boundary, you are responsible for your own actions, for your own rescue and the cost of your rescue, and you waive all claims for injury.

- Woods are recommended for EXPERT SKIERS in groups of three or more only, and should not be entered into in late afternoon (3 pm).

- Woods skiers must enter and exit from an open trail and cannot ski under or around any traffic-controlling ropes or fences.

- Be aware that skiing in the woods may lead you away from Jay Peak trails.

(Jay Peak brochure, 2001)

Exhibit 12   Responsibility code, Loon, 2001.

Your responsibility code:

1 Always stay in control and be able to stop or avoid other people or objects.

2 People ahead of you have the right of way. It is your responsibility to avoid them.

3 You must not stop where you obstruct a trail or are not visible from above.

4 Whenever starting downhill or merging into a trail, look uphill and yield to others.

5 Always use devices to help prevent run-away equipment.

6 Observe all posted signs and warnings. Keep off closed trails and out of closed areas.

7 Prior to using any lift, you must have the knowledge and ability to load, ride, and unload safely.

In New England great emphasis is placed on safety and informing guests of the risks, to protect visitors and, perhaps, to reduce the chances of successful actions for damages by guests! For example, the Jay Peak brochure (Exhibit 11) gives warnings concerning 'woods', 'forest', or 'glade' skiing.

The resorts also encourage responsible behaviour by visitors, as can be seen from Exhibit 12.

In other parts of the world winter sports are not as commercialized or heavily managed as in New England, and nor is the infrastructure as highly developed.

Case study 12   180° Adventures

Introduction

180° Adventures is a South African-based organization that provides adventure services within Sub-Saharan Africa. Two founding directors established the company in August 2000, and their backgrounds clearly illustrate the level of expertise that exists from both business and adventure sport perspectives. Brad Pearse is a qualified and registered chartered accountant with extensive business experience. He also has an avid interest in sports and the outdoors, and represented South Africa in rowing, becoming a finalist in the South African 2000 Camel Trophy event. He pursues a number of outdoor activities, including canoeing, surf skiing, mountain biking and scuba diving. Xavier Scheepers is a qualified and registered civil engineer, although he is an adventurer at heart and has participated extensively in adventure activities. He has also competed in the Camel Trophy, and was a member of the year 2000 winning team held in Tonga and Samoa. The rest of the team comprises spirited adventure enthusiasts who are all from professional backgrounds. 180° Adventures describes its mission as follows:

> 180° Adventures is an adventure company dedicated to providing unique experiences amidst the splendour of Africa's great wilderness. We are committed to providing our customers with experiences they will never forget through the supervision of our skilled and experienced staff and by striving to become the standard in quality and safety in the adventure domain.

Historical background

The company originated in Durban, in the South African province of KwaZulu Natal. At the outset, the founders built up business by tapping into the clientele of large companies such as Unilever and PricewaterhouseCoopers within which they were previously employed. They also exploited existing contacts they had with local adventure providers. The corporate adventure market formed the basis of 180° Adventures' early success, and included organizing adventure events, client entertainment, incentive travel, and team-building and personal development products. With this success in KwaZulu Natal, the business quickly expanded into the more lucrative markets of Johannesburg and Pretoria in the province of Gauteng. As new opportunities evolved in the domestic retail market, the company diversified from purely concentrating on the corporate market and moved into the adventure sports events arena. The company then began to pursue investment in order to take the business to the next stage of growth, and this came from the Halcyon Hotel Group in April 2001. For their cash injection of R500 000 (£50 000), Halcyon took 50 per cent equity and worked with 180° Adventures to develop adventure tours based around their hotels, mostly located in Tanzania and South Africa.

180° Adventures – present day

180° Adventures now has a presence in all three of South Africa's major centres, with offices based in Durban, Johannesburg and Cape Town. Its staffing structure reflects the company's expansion activities (see Exhibit 13).

Exhibit 14 illustrates the product categories offered by 180° Adventures, and the current stage of business development in both the domestic Southern African and foreign inbound tourism markets.

Exhibit 13   180° Adventures – organizational structure.

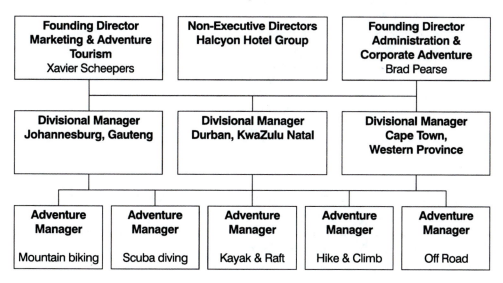

Exhibit 14 180° Adventures' product categories and market development.

Product categories	Southern African domestic market	UK & other inbound tourism markets
Corporate products: ■ Team development ■ Incentive travel ■ Destination management ■ Adventure entertainment ■ Product launches ■ Events management	■ Successful product development within all categories listed ■ Constant development of skills and expertise in corporate training in the outdoors	■ Hoping to attract corporate adventure markets
Adventure tourism: ■ Mountain biking ■ Scuba ■ Kayak and raft ■ Hike and climb ■ Off-road activities	■ Strong push in this category with appointment of managers in each division ■ Strong in South Africa, Tanzania and Zanzibar	■ Entered market in second half of 2001 ■ Leveraging off Halcyon Marketing Network UK, company is attracting adventure tourism from the UK and other foreign destinations
Event management: ■ Adventure-based competitions and expeditions	■ Adventure sports competitions are being developed in exotic destinations (e.g. Zanzibar and Tanzania) for such events as triathlons	■ Once the domestic product has been proven and refined, the foreign inbound market will be actively pushed

In their quest to build a powerful brand, 180° Adventures are pursuing the idea of an Adventure Centre that will cater for all the needs of the adventurer. The Centre will provide the ideal one-stop channel for adventure seekers, whether tourists, corporate clients or local people looking for leisure activities. Facilities will be available for booking trips from a number of tour operators, for purchasing equipment from a range of retail shops, and for 'tasting' adventure from simulated adventure environments. The new centre will also provide adventure guide training and set standards for operators based in Southern Africa and working within the adventure tourism industry.

This case study documents the evolution and expansion of the successful South African-based company 180° Adventures. It illustrates the broad scope of the company's product range and the markets in which it operates at both domestic and international levels. One of the major factors that has clearly facilitated the growth and success of 180° Adventures is the dedication of its founding directors and staff, all of whom are ardent adventurers not only in the workplace but outside it as well.

Case study 13   Space tourism

In 2001 the first space tourist, Denis Tito, a sixty-year-old Californian businessman, paid the Russian Space Agency around $20 million to take him on a ten-day mission that involved an eight-day sojourn at the International Space Station. In May 2002, Mark Shuttleworth, who made his fortune out of the Internet, undertook the same adventure. A media company planned to sponsor Lance Bass, a member of a internationally famous boy band, to visit the International Space Station in November 2002, hoping to base a television special around his experiences. Although this plan has fallen through, it indicates the level of anticipated interest and curiosity in space travel. NASA, the American space administration, originally treated the idea of space tourism with some disdain and claimed civilians were a safety hazard and a waste of valuable research time and space, especially in the International Space Station. However, they have recently been reviewing their policy on space tourism, which can provide a source of money to subsidize the rest of the expedition. Currently, only the Russian Soyuz spacecraft and the American Space Shuttle have the proven capability of being suitable for human travel. However, many other spacecraft have reached the development stage before withdrawal of funding or political support prevented them from becoming operational, or they are currently used for unmanned flight and have the potential to be modified for passengers.

The Russian space programme, which has been progressively starved of cash since the collapse of communism, quickly realized that tourism income is one way of generating revenue. The Russians are marching ahead of the Americans in terms of exploitation of space for tourism, and are currently looking at opportunities for sub-orbital space tourism too.

The Russians unveiled a full-sized model of their new spacecraft, the C-21, in Moscow in 2002, and intend to begin testing the three-man sub-orbital spacecraft in 2004. The C-21 is a re-usable pod that will take two tourists beyond the Earth's atmosphere. It piggybacks on a carrier aircraft up to an altitude of 20 km, and the spacecraft separates from the carrier aircraft at a trajectory angle of 40–60 degrees to the horizon. At the top of the trajectory, at around 100 km altitude, the crew experience a few minutes of weightlessness and the blackness of space, and the C-21 then glides back into the atmosphere to make a parachute-assisted touchdown. The short trip, lasting only an hour or two, with five minutes in space, costs US $98 000 per person (*The Guardian*, 2 April 2002), but 250 people have already paid their deposits through Space Adventures, the US firm that brokered Tito's trip. This development looks like being the first concrete move towards commercial leisure travel in space.

Projections suggest such leisure space travel will become affordable for the general public in twenty to thirty years' time. Frank Sietzen, president of the Space Transportation Association, foresees an eventual space-tourism income of US $10–20 billion per year (*The Guardian*, 2002). The potential for big business is there – the race is on to realize that potential.

The X-prize is a privately funded competition that aims to encourage the development of an economically viable tourist spacecraft. It requires the building of a vehicle capable of taking three passengers to an altitude of 100 km, and of repeating the trip within two weeks. Once the barrier of a re-usable launch vehicle is overcome, the absence of the high development cost and associated risk will make the market much more attractive for related industries such as resort companies, travel agencies, and airlines. It is the economic potential of the tourism market that is driving the development of a re-usable vehicle, as this single factor will contribute significantly to bring down the price of a ticket.

The Californian company InterOrbital Systems is a potential contender for the X-prize, and *The Independent* (13 April 2002) notes that the company is planning to launch its first passenger flights in 2005. The government of the South Pacific State of Tonga has reached agreement with InterOrbital to allow one of its islands to be used as a base for rocket launches. The commercial flight will take two astronauts and four paying passengers. The trip involves orbiting around earth for seven days, and is preceded by a 60-day training programme in a 'resort setting'. Proposed prices for this adventure tourism package are US $2million. InterOrbital's catchline is, 'Why pay high prices for a five-minute suborbital flight at the present going rate of US $20 000 per minute when you can spend up to seven days on an orbital vacation at a cost of less than US $200 per minute?'. The spacecraft has yet to be designed and tested, but this hasn't stopped one Texan woman booking her place.

The proposed 60-day training programme is a reminder that there is much more to space tourism than the flight itself. Although only a few have enjoyed the ultimate thrill of actually being in space, preparations for this adventure are part of the total tourism experience. On-the-ground space activities are big business. The space shuttle launch site at Cape Canaveral in Florida and the Kennedy Space Centre in Houston are already massive visitor attractions, and there are many smaller-scale attractions based on the space theme scattered all over the world. Star City is the Russian equivalent of the Kennedy Space Centre, but it is doing much more to raise revenue from potential space adventure tourists. US $200 000 buys a two-week intensive cosmonaut training course, which includes learning how to fly the Soyuz spacecraft (used for the current space tourism missions), experiencing varying G-forces (similar to those experienced during lift off and re-entry) using centrifuge training, and playing with weightlessness in a neutral buoyancy hydro lab. Mintel (2002) says that over 10 million people visit a space museum, a space camp, a rocket launch-recovery site or a government space R&D centre – a business worth over US $1 billion a year.

There are also space-related possibilities that do not involve such high altitudes, and might be termed 'near-space' options. One potential development is the use of high altitude balloons, which could carry a pressurized capsule containing three people to the stratosphere at around 40–50 km (ISU, 2001). This altitude would give a black sky, and views of the stars and of the curvature of the earth below. Existing activities include 'Edge of Space' flights in Russian MIG 25 jets, which take tourists to the outer limits of the Earth's atmosphere (around 25 km). They fly at two-and-a-half times the speed of sound, and from this altitude the curvature of the earth and the blackness of space can be seen. Flying jet aircraft in loops can also create sensations of microgravity for about 30 seconds.

In terms of destination development, some locations will trade on their links with the space industry and develop space tourism facilities, becoming gateways for this particular form of adventure tourism. Tonga must be anticipating an economic benefit of this kind, in addition to any other inducements offered.

Returning to future developments in orbital space tourism, there are a number of options for the way tourists are delivered into orbit and returned to Earth. Tourists can either lift off in a vehicle that then goes into orbit and returns to Earth, or they can be transported to a separate orbital facility for their stay, and returned at the end. Tourist amenities would be located within the spacecraft in the first option, or in the orbiting facility in the latter option. There are pros and cons to each option, with key factors being the expense per launch versus the size of payload (ISU, 2001). Consideration of 'tourist requirements' suggests that more private space than is currently allowed for astronauts, recreation facilities, client-oriented hygienic facilities, and a greater window area will be needed.

Some people are thinking ahead; the famous American astronaut Buzz Aldrin has ambitious plans for orbiting hotels between Mars and Earth. He is planning for around 2018, and whilst the timing may be optimistic, if space tourism takes off there will almost certainly be opportunities for this kind of space station and infrastructure. More futuristically, interplanetary flight and space trips further afield will depend on inventions that attack the practical problem of covering vast distances at great speed. Solar sails, wormholes, or plasma propulsion systems could hold the answer; the solution is not clear at this stage. Whilst health issues are not a major concern for current short space flights, where anyone in reasonable health can withstand the physical demands of the trip, developing ways of dealing with the effects of microgravity, zero gravity and radiation on human systems on long trips will be important.

Naturally, there are arguments that suggest space tourism might not take off in the way that Buzz Aldrin envisages. There are even arguments that low earth orbital (LEO) space tourism of the kind currently taking place right now will remain beyond the reach of the general public.

Finance is an issue. ISU (2001) suggests that a ticket price in the order of US $50 000 is necessary for space tourism to sustain itself. Achieving such a low ticket price will not simply depend on technological developments in vehicle design and propulsion systems, but also on low operational and maintenance costs.

Developing technology that meets these requirements is costly, risky and long term, and ISU (2001) suggest these conditions do not present an appealing opportunity for private sector investment under normal market conditions. Whilst the expansion of space tourism is not explicitly supported by governments, ISU (2001) argues that governments have a duty to contribute to the funding of essential technological developments. This would be a defensible argument where there is a proven market demand for space tourism, as the benefits of a successful space tourism industry would support businesses, governments, space agencies and the scientific community.

Regulatory and legislative challenges will also have to be overcome in order to create a favourable environment for the development of space tourism. Liability arrangements for loss of life, injury and damage to property will need to be negotiated, perhaps based on current arrangements for the commercial aviation sector. Certification, licensing, traffic control regulations, environmental law and criminal law will also need attention. Ultimately, politics will clearly very much influence the speed and direction of the development of space tourism. The ISU (2001: 139) states:

> The challenge of a space tourism policy is to establish the technological and regulatory environment that will encourage private companies to invest in space tourism and allow commercial ventures to prosper.

The other major influence will be the level and strength of demand from the market. Is this form of adventure just too adventurous? Will people be prepared to pay for it? It appears that the demand is there. A 1998 survey of the general public carried out by NASA concluded that 42.2 per cent were interested in a space holiday, and a recent Harris poll in the USA and Canada found that more than 10 000 people per year would purchase a sub-orbital space experience at a price of US $100 000 (Mintel 2002). Early targeting of the market could focus on the corporate incentive sector, which could afford to fund the ultimate performance reward, or 'corporate jolly'.

Affluent individuals with a keen sense of adventure provide another sector potential. The first space tourist proved that it is possible at 60, so age is no barrier (in fact it may be a spur!).

Case study 14 Adventure travel writing today

Until recently most travel writing fell into one of several classic types, such as the epic adventure, the travels of urbane men, the adventures of intrepid women travellers, and the memoirs of the colonial classes. However, today travel writing has mirrored the growth and democratization of international tourism. Not only has the volume of such writing grown, but it has also become a much more diverse field as authors seek to differentiate their manuscript from the thousands of others that publishers are offered every year.

Most travel writing can be viewed as adventure travel writing, as the travel represents an adventure for the author, and mundane travel tends to make for very dull literature!

The following list provides a typology of such writing, to illustrate this diversity:

- Books about journeys to remote and/or exotic destinations
- Books about visits to dangerous destinations, whether the danger is caused by the terrain, climate, disease or war
- Books that include collections of stories by intrepid backpackers and independent travellers, like those now being published by Lonely Planet
- Books in which the author uses a novel form of transport, from a bicycle to a canoe, an elephant to a microlight aeroplane
- Books about expeditions and epic adventures
- Books in which the focus is on humorous incidents
- Books where the author offers 'alternative views' of well-known places
- Books where the journey is a therapeutic activity for the writer because of some problem or crisis in his or her life
- Books written by women making journeys to places where women would not normally be seen travelling on their own
- Books where travellers recount stories of love and life from their travels
- Books by famous travellers that are autobiographies of their lifetime of travelling
- Books by authors who have observed hedonistic travel at first hand
- Books by people who have worked in the front line in the tourism industry
- Books that combine travel writing with travel guides
- Books in which people seek to discover the dark side of their home country
- Books reliving the world of pioneering forms of transport of yesterday, such as the flying boats
- Books in which authors retrace the steps of famous travellers of the past
- Books about virtual rather than 'real' travels.

Case study 15   Adventure travel as television entertainment

Adventure travel experiences have in recent years become a common topic for television programmes designed to entertain viewers. This point can be illustrated by several examples drawn from the UK.

1 *Castaway*. This programme involved selecting a group of strangers who were left alone on a remote Scottish island together for 12 months, as a social experiment. These people were cut off from their friends, workplaces and everyday lives. The temporary residents of the island had to be largely self-sufficient on this island, which had been uninhabited for a quarter of a century before their arrival. Viewers were invited to tune in several times a week to view their progress, listen to their arguments, and watch new romances blossom. This $3.8 million project was a modest success in terms of ratings.

2 *Temptation Island*. Here, a group of men and women were taken to an idyllic island in the ocean. There, their faithfulness to their partners was tested as they were tempted by other participants.

3 *Survivor*. This is one of a series of popular shows where participants are taken to an unfamiliar and hostile environment. They have to survive by working as a team, but eventually one of them emerges as a winner and enjoys a cash prize.

4 *Ibiza Uncovered* is a voyeuristic programme in which the viewer watches the exploits of young hedonistic tourists on the island of Ibiza, providing a salacious opportunity for viewers to be both excited and disgusted by the spectacle.

5 *Weird Weekend* with Louis Theroux, where the presenter travels to meet 'unusual' people, such as white supremacists in the USA and South Africa, and 'Swingers' in California.

6 A series of shows that put celebrities in adventurous situations, including footballer Ian Wright meeting Kalahari bushmen in Africa and TV star Joanna Lumley being stranded on a desert island.

7 Charity telethons, where celebrities travel to other countries to see how the income from an appeal may be spent. Many of these programmes involve British celebrities travelling to Africa.

8 Wildlife programmes, where presenters travel to remote areas in search of unusual wildlife – a subject of great interest to UK viewers.

9 Programmes such as those featuring Michael Palin, where he undertakes epic journeys with his own gentle sense of humour, like a latter-day Phileas Fogg. These programmes are always towards the top of the ratings.

These few examples show that adventure travel is a popular but diverse, subject for television programmes in the UK.

Case study 16   Personal adventures and the holiday postcard

Adventures and vacations come in all shapes and sizes, and are seen in different ways by different tourists. For over a century postcards have recorded people's adventures as tourists, and the variety of adventures they can have is illustrated by the examples in Exhibit 15, which are taken at random from John Swarbrooke's personal collection.

Exhibit 15   A selection of adventures recorded on postcards 1906–1999.

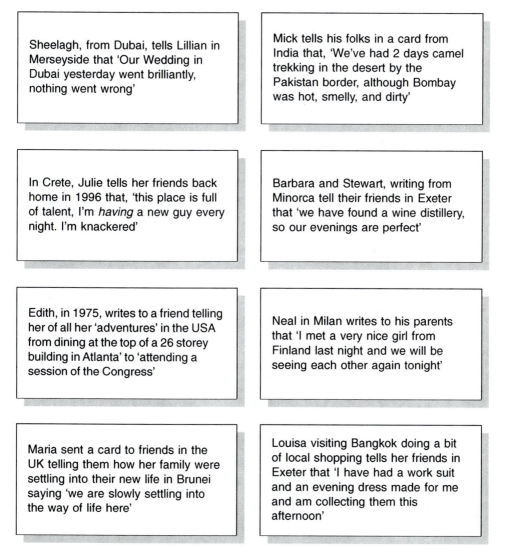

Sheelagh, from Dubai, tells Lillian in Merseyside that 'Our Wedding in Dubai yesterday went brilliantly, nothing went wrong'

Mick tells his folks in a card from India that, 'We've had 2 days camel trekking in the desert by the Pakistan border, although Bombay was hot, smelly, and dirty'

In Crete, Julie tells her friends back home in 1996 that, 'this place is full of talent, I'm *having* a new guy every night. I'm knackered'

Barbara and Stewart, writing from Minorca tell their friends in Exeter that 'we have found a wine distillery, so our evenings are perfect'

Edith, in 1975, writes to a friend telling her of all her 'adventures' in the USA from dining at the top of a 26 storey building in Atlanta' to 'attending a session of the Congress'

Neal in Milan writes to his parents that 'I met a very nice girl from Finland last night and we will be seeing each other again tonight'

Maria sent a card to friends in the UK telling them how her family were settling into their new life in Brunei saying 'we are slowly settling into the way of life here'

Louisa visiting Bangkok doing a bit of local shopping tells her friends in Exeter that 'I have had a work suit and an evening dress made for me and am collecting them this afternoon'

Judy tells her parents that 'we are on a Thomson bargain break and had no idea were we would be staying until we arrived'

Billy has clearly gone to Florida for medical treatment. His Mum writes that 'Thank you for helping make this trip possible. Billy is doing well. Week 2 should really give us some great results. The therapy is intensive but it's working'

Joyce, on a cruise around Madeira and the Canaries writes, 'It has been rough at sea, and smelly, with everyone sick. One lady was very ill. I hope to get some seasick pills'

Josie tells her parents from San Diego, that 'arrived after delays due to fog and snow, and missing my flight due to a mix-up in Chicago'

A woman writes from Athens to her daughter, and says 'We took a taxi . . . it was quite an experience . . . all the drivers are mad . . . I am lucky to still be alive!'

Tom tells his friends in the UK about his trip on an old freighter, 'we are on our way to Panama, Ecuador, Columbia, Ireland and Antwerp, then they sell the ship'

Then Kerry and Pam write to friends in England, 'Tonight we are going on a night jeep safari, . . . it should be very exciting'

Liz, writing from Ecuador is obviously suffering romantically. She writes, 'After 3 years, Colin and I have finally reached something real . . . first two months was very difficult . . . I have not seen Carlos for 2 months'

Anne writes to her friend that on his first trip abroad since he was born 'Neil is such a contented baby, coping well with his travels, while we worry about him'

Mark tells his parents 'Life below the waves is most spectacular . . . with brightly coloured fish, electric eels and sharks!'

In 1916, Sergeant Bacon tells his family in a card from Arras 'I have signed on for the duration of the war'

Lizette tells her friends at work 'I am learning to scuba dive and, of course, the instructor is gorgeous . . . I'm hoping for some private lessons!'

Mary, in 1951, tells friends that she was 'delighted to report that she was relieved to have visited the Empire State Building and get down again safely, although I was scared stiff!'

Beverley, from Dubai, tells her parents 'we are off into the desert in a 4 wheel drive vehicle and then into the Indian Ocean on a catamaran'

Jane, from Corfu, tells her friends 'we just gave the travel agent £200, he gave us tickets and we ended up here. We had no idea where we were going'

Maurice tells his family 'I arrived in Marseilles after a 13 hour journey . . . saw lots of floods on the way . . . will cross to Algiers tomorrow'

Miss Smith writes to Mrs Opperman in Bournemouth telling her that 'It is a lovely pilgrimage, here in Lourdes'

Auntie writes to her nieces from California in 1938 telling them that, 'we have visited the homes of all the great theatrical stars and the top studios'

Dorothy tells her friends that 'Geoff has caught his first ever salmon here [in Ireland] . . . he is so excited'

Alison writes to her grandparents from the French Riviera to tell them that 'on the way to Paris we had a car crash although we are not hurt'

Jane tells her colleagues at work from the Costa Brava that, 'Today, I went topless for the first time . . . nobody seemed to care'

Anne and John tell her father-in-law that he should go to Amsterdam, 'to find that blonde you always wanted . . . you can window shop to choose the one you want'

Lucian, an aid worker sent a friend a card showing land mines, from Afghanistan, saying '50% of Kabul looks like this'

Doug and Susan tell their friends from Greece that, 'this is our first ever holiday without the children'

Alison, an exchange student in France, tells her parents 'It is a real struggle . . . my French is not up to it and the work is really hard'

Bibliography

Addison, G. (1999). Adventure tourism and ecotourism. In *Adventure Programming*, 2nd edn (J. C. Miles and S. Priest, eds) pp. 415–430, Venture Publishing.

Agyeman, J. (1990). A positive image. *Options, Countryside Commission News*, **45(3)**.

Association of Independent Tour Operators (2001). *The Independent Holiday Directory*. AITO.

Atkinson, J.W. (1974). Strength of motivation and efficiency of performance. In *Motivation and Achievement* (J.W. Atkinson and J.O. Raynor, eds), Hemisphere.

Attarian, A. (1999). Artificial climbing environments. In *Adventure Programming*, 2nd edn (J.C. Miles and S. Priest, eds) pp. 341–345, Venture Publishing.

Beard, C.M. (2000). A brave new environmental vision for the millenium. Euro Environment 2000: Visions, strategies and actions towards sustainable industries. Aalborg Congress and Culture Centre, Denmark, 18–20 October 2000.

Beard, C.M. (in press). Constructed adventure: exploring some trends in artificially constructed adventure environments. *Journal of Adventure Education and Outdoor Learning*.

Beard, C. and Egan, D. (1998). Investing in sustainability – an exploration of how firms can adopt a balance sheet approach to achieving sustainable production. *Proceedings of the 1998 International Sustainable Development Research Conference, 3–4 April, Leeds*, pp. 19–24.

Beard, C. and Hartman, R. (1997a). Sustainable design: re-thinking future business products. *Journal of Sustainable Product Design*, **3**, 18–27.

Beard, C. and Hartman, R. (1997b). Naturally enterprising – eco-design, creative thinking and the greening of business products. *European Business Review*, **97(5)**, 237–243.

Beard, C. and Wilson, J.P. (2002). *The Power of Experiential Learning: a handbook for trainers and educators*. Kogan Page.

Bentley, T., Page, S., Meyer, D. *et al.* (2001). How safe is adventure tourism in New Zealand? An exploratory analysis. *Applied Ergonomics*, **32**, 327–338.

Berno, T., Moore, K., Simmons, D. and Hart, V. (1996). The nature of the adventure tourism experience in Queenstown, New Zealand. *Australian Leisure*, **8**, 21–25.

Birkin, F. and Woodward, D. (1997). Accounting for the sustainable corporation. *Environmental Management and Health*, **8/2**, 67–72.

Bleasdale, S. (2000). Charity challenges and adventure tourism in developing countries – who dares wins? In *Motivations, Behaviour and Tourism Types* (M. Robinson, P. Long, N. Evans *et al.*, eds) pp. 15–25, Centre for Travel and Tourism in association with Business Education Publishers Limited.

Boulding, K.E. (1996). The economics of the coming spaceship Earth. In *Environmental Quality in a Growing Economy* (H. Jarrett, ed.), Johns Hopkins University Press.

Bouter, L.M., Knipschild, P.G., Feij, J.A. and Volorics, A. (1998). Sensation seeking and injury risk in downhill skiing. *Personality and Individual Differences*, **9**, 667–673.

Breivik, G. (1996). Personality, sensation seeking and risk taking among Everest climbers. *International Journal of Sport Psychology*, **27**, 308–320.

Brown, T. J. (1999). Adventure risk management. In *Adventure* Programming (J. C. Miles and S. Priest, eds) pp. 273–284. Venture Publishing.

Brown and Williams (1997). *Journal of Sustainable Product Design*, **1**, 28–35.

Browne, A. (2002). Botanists become explorers to claim a place in history. *The Times*, 29 June.

Buckley, R. (2000). Neat trends: current issues in nature, eco- and adventure tourism. *International Journal of Tourism Research*, **2**, 437–444.

Burkeman, O. (2002). Tonga opens a gateway to space tourism. *The Guardian*, 26 March.

Cai, L.A., O'Leary, J. and Boger, C. (2000). Chinese travellers to the United States: an emerging market. *Journal of Vacation Marketing*, **6**(2), 131–144.

Canadian Tourism Commission (1995). Cited in Fennell, D. A., *Ecotourism: An Introduction*. Routledge.

Cater, C. (2000). Can I play too? Inclusion and exclusion in adventure tourism. *The North West Geographer*, **3**, 49–59.

Celsi, R. L., Rose, R. L. and Leigh, T. W. (1993). An exploration of high-risk leisure consumption through skydiving. *Journal of Consumer Research*, **20(1)**, 1–23.

Charlton, C. (1992). Developing Leaders Using the Outdoors. In *Frontiers of Leadership: an essential reader* (M. Syrett and C. Hogg (1992), Chapter 17, 454–461). Blackwell.

Cheron, E.J. and Ritchie, J.R. (1982). Leisure activities and perceived risk. *Journal of Leisure Research*, **14**, 139–154.

Chua Ee Kiam (2000). *Pulau Ubin – Ours to Treasure*. Simply Green Publishing.

Cloke, P. and Perkins, H.C. (1998). 'Cracking the canyon with the awesome foursome': Representations of adventure tourism in New Zealand. *Environment and Planning D: Society and Space*, **16**, 185–218.

Cloutier, K.R. (1998a) The Business of Adventure. Kamloops, BC: Budhak Consultants.

Cloutier, K.R. (2000). Legal liability and risk management in adventure tourism. Kamloops, BC: Bhudak Consultants.

Colinvaux, P. (1980). *Why Big Fierce Animals are Rare*. Penguin Books.

Consalvo, C. (1995). *Outdoor Games for Trainers*. Gower.

Cooper, A. (1998). *Sacred Nature: Ancient Wisdom and Modern Meanings*. Capall Bann Publishing.

Costanza, R. *et al.* (1997). The value of the world's ecosystem services and natural capital. *Nature*, **387**, 253–260.

Countryside Commission (1998). 'UK Day Visits Survey: Summary of 1996 findings', CCX 45FL, Countryside Commission.

Cox, D.F. and Stuart, R.J. (1964). Perceived risk and consumer decision making. *Journal of Marketing Research*, **10**, 113–125

Craggs, C. (1997). *Costa Blanca Rock*, 2nd edn. Cicerone Press.

Craggs, C. (2001). personal communication.

Crompton, J.L. (1979). Why people go on pleasure vacation. *Annals of Tourism Research*, **6(4)**, 408–424.

Csikszentmihalyi, M. (1992). *The Psychology of Happiness*. Rider.

Dankelman, I. and Davidson, J. (1988). *Woman and Environment in the Third World – Alliance for the Future*. Earthscan Publications Ltd.

Dann, G. (1977). Anomie, ego-enhancement and tourism. *Annals of Tourism Research*, **4**, 184–194.

Davies, M. and Longrigg, L. (eds) (1986). *Half the Earth: Women's Experience of Travel Worldwide*, Harper Collins.

Davies, W. (1997). *One River: Science, Adventure and Hallucinogenics in the Amazon Basin*. Simon & Schuster Ltd.

Diamantis, D. (1999). The characteristics of UK's ecotourists. *Tourism Recreation Research*, **24(2)**, 99–102.

Dickinson, M. (1998). *The Death Zone*. Arrow Books.

Dodd, V. (1999). Adrenaline sport's fatal attraction. *The Guardian*, 28 July.

Dowling, R. (1993). An environmentally-based planning model for regional tourism development. *Journal of Sustainable Tourism*, **1(1)**, 17–37.

Duff, J. (1998). Death of a porter. *Summit*, **11**.

Eagles, P.J.F. (1992). The travel motivations of Canadian ecotourists. *Journal of Travel Research*, **31**, 3–7.

Eagles, P.F.J. and Cascagnette, J.W. (1995). Canadian ecotourists: who are they? *Tourism Recreation Research*, **20(1)**, 22–28.

Economic Intelligence Unit (1992). The UK adventure travel market. *Travel and Tourism Analyst*, **3**, 37–51.

Ewert, A. (1989). *Outdoor Adventure Pursuits: Foundation, Models and Theories*. Publishing Horizons.

Ewert, A. and Hollenhorst, S. (1989). Testing the adventure model: empirical support for a model of risk recreation participation. *Journal of Leisure Research*, **21(2)**, 124–139.

Ewert, A. and Shultis, J. (1987). Resource-based tourism: an emerging trend in tourism experiences. *Parks and Recreation*, **32(9)**, 94–104.

Faulkner, B. (2001). Towards a framework for tourism disaster management. *Tourism Management*, **22(2)**, 135–147.

Fennell, D.A. (1999). *Ecotourism: An Introduction*. Routledge.

Fennell, D.A. and Eagles, P.F.J. (1990). Ecotourism in Costa Rica: a conceptual framework. *Journal of Parks and Recreation Research*, **8(1)**, 23–34.

Fennell, D.A. and Smale, B.J.A. (1992). Ecotourism and natural resource protection: implications of an alternative form of tourism for host nations. *Tourism Recreation Research*, **17(1)**, 21–32.

Fickling, D. (2001). Iron men let off steam. *Metro*, 20 July.

Fillion, F.L., Foley, J.P. and Jacquemot, A.J. (1992). The Economics of Global Ecotourism. Fourth World Congress on National Parks and Protected Areas, Caracas, Venezuela, February 10–21, 1992.

Fisher, M. (1986). *The Bright Face of Danger – An Exploration of the Adventure Story*. Hodder and Stoughton.

Fluker, M.R. and Turner, L.W. (2000). Needs, motivations, and expectations of a commercial whitewater rafting experience. *Journal of Travel Research*, **38(4)**, 380–389.

Fox, A. (2000a). Fear – Part 1: The courage myth. *On The Edge*, **102**, 34–39.

Fox, A. (2000b). Fear – Part 2: The death wish myth. *On The Edge*, **103**, 38–40.

Gilchrist, H. (1994). Adventure travel: what is it, who participates in it and why? A questionnaire and interview study with marketing implications. Unpublished Masters' thesis, Sheffield Hallam University.

Gilchrist, H., Povey, R., Dickenson, A. and Povey, R. (1995). The Sensation Seeking Scale: its use in a study of characteristics of people choosing 'adventure holidays'. *Personality and Individual Differences*, **19(4)**, 513–516.

Goodwin, H. (1996). In Pursuit of Ecotourism, Biodiversity and Conservation, **5(3)**, 277–291.

Grant D. (2001). Invited viewpoint – adventure tourism: a journey of the mind. Cited in Roberts, L. and Hall, D., *Rural Tourism and Recreation: Principles to Practice*, pp. 166–170. CABI Publishing.

Greenaway, R. (1996). Thrilling not killing: managing the risk tourism business. *Management*, **May**, 46–49.

Greenaway, P. (1999). The Mongolian scramble. In *Lonely Planet Unpacked* (T. Wheeler, ed.), pp. 117–122, Lonely Planet Publications.

GREENFORCE (1998). *GREENFORCE: A New Approach to Conservation Aid*. GREENFORCE.

Greenpeach (1996). Greenpeach & the Brent Spar Conference. *Greenpeace Business Conference Proceedings*, London, 25 September.

Guardian (1993). Whose new lease on life? *Environment Guardian*, 21 May.

Hall, C.M. (1992). Adventure, sport and health tourism. In *Special Interest Tourism* (B. Weiler and C.M. Hall, eds), pp. 141–158, Belhaven Press.

Handy, C. (1997). *Economist Yearbook*. London.

Hanley, N. and Spash, C. (1993). *Cost Benefit Analysis and the Environment*. Aldershot Edward Elgar Publishing Ltd.

Hanson, E. (2001). *Orchid Fever: A Horticultural Tale of Love, Lust and Lunacy*. Methuen.

Hardin, G. (1968). Tragedy of the commons. *Science*, **162**, 1243–1248.

Hawks, T. (2000). *Playing the Moldovans at Tennis*. Ebury Press.

Hemming, J. (1978). *Red Gold*. Macmillan.

Herold, E., Garcia, R. and De Moya, T. (2001). Female tourists and beach boys: romance or sex tourism? *Annals of Tourism Research*, **28**(4), 978–997.

Hibbert, F. (2001). Risk management: operationalizing the concept in the context of mountain adventure tourism. Unpublished Masters dissertation thesis, Sheffield Hallam University.

Hill, B. J. (1995). A Guide to Adventure Travel. *Parks and Recreation*, September, 56–65.

Hollman, K. W. and Forrest, J. E. (1991). Risk management in a service business. *International Journal of Service Industry Management*, **2**(2), 49–65.

Holmberg, J. (1992). *Policies for a Small Planet*. Earthscan Publications Ltd.

Hopkins, D. and Putnam, R. (1993). *Personal Growth Through Adventure*. Fulton.

Hunt, J. (ed.) (1989). *In Search Of Adventure*. Talbot Adair Press.

Iso-Ahola, S.E., LaVerde, D. and Graefe, A.R (1988). Perceived competence as a mediator of the relationship between high-risk sports participation and self-esteem. *Journal of Leisure Research*, **21**(1), 32–39.

ISU (2001). *Space Policy 17: Dreams and Realities: The Challenges of Facing Development of Space Tourism*, pp. 133–140. Elsevier Science Ltd © 2001.

IUCN (1980). *World Conservation Strategy*. Gland, Switzerland, IUCN.

Jack, S.J. and Ronan, K.R. (1999). Sensation seeking among high and low risk sports participants. *Journal of Personality and Individual Differences*, **25**(6), 1063–1083.

James, T. (2000). Can the mountains speak for themselves? *Scisco Conscientia*, **2**(2), 1–4.

Johnston, M. E. (1992). Case study. Facing the challenges: adventure in the mountains of New Zealand. In *Special Interest Tourism* (B. Weiler and C.M. Hall, eds), pp. 159–169. Belhaven Press.

Judd, T. (2001). Man-made reef to form building block for sea-life. *The Independent*, 19 May.

Kellert (1993). The Biological Basis for Human Values of Nature. In *The Biophilia Hypothesis* (S.R. Kellert and E.O. Wilson, eds). Island Press.

Krakaeur, J. (1997). *Into Thin Air: A Personal Account of the Everest Disaster*. Pan Books.

Krippendorf, J. (1987). *The Holiday Makers*. Heinemann.

Laarman, J.G. and Durst, P.B. (1987). Nature Travel and Tropical forests. *FPEI Working Paper Series*. Southeastern Center for Forest Economics research, North Carolina State University.

Laarman, J.G. and Durst, P.B. (1993). Nature Tourism as a tool for economic development and conservation of natural resources. In *Nature Tourism in Asia: Opportunities and Constraints for Conservation and Economic Development* (J. Nenon and P.B. Durst eds). US Forest Service.

Leiper, N. (1995). Cited in Pigram, J. and Jenkin, J. M. (1999), *Outdoor Recreation Management*, p. 227. Routledge.

Lipscombe, N. (1995). Appropriate adventure: participation for the aged. *Australian Parks & Recreation*, **31(2)**, 41–45.

Loverseed, H. (1997). The adventure travel industry in North America. *Travel & Tourism Analyst*, **6**, 87–104.

Lutzenburger, J. (1992). The Future of Amazonia. Proceedings of the International Conference, The Royal Geographic Society, London, May 1990. In *The Rainforest Harvest*, Friends of the Earth.

Martin, P. and Priest, S. (1986). Understanding the adventure experience. *Adventure Education*, **3**, 18–21.

Maslow, A.H. (1976). *The Farther Reaches of Human Nature*. Penguin.

McGrath, J.E. (1982). Methodological problems in research on stress. In *Achievement, Stress and Anxiety* (H.W. Krohne and L. Laux, eds), Hemisphere.

McKercher, B. (1993). Some fundamental truths about tourism: understanding tourism's social and environmental impacts. *Journal of Sustainable Tourism*, **1(1)**, 6–16.

Meadows, D.H., Meadows, D.L., Randers, J. and Brehens, W. (1972). *The Limits to Growth*. Earth Island.

Meier, J. (1978). Is the risk worth taking? *Leisure Today*, **49(4)**, 7–9.

Middleton, V. (1998). *Sustainable Tourism – A Marketing Perspective*. Butterworth-Heinemann.

Mies, M. (1993). *Ecofeminism*. Zed Books.

Miles, J.C. and Priest, S. (eds) (1999). *Adventure Programming*. Venture Publishing.

Millington, K., Locke, T. and Locke, A. (2001). Occasional studies: adventure travel. *Travel and Tourism Analyst*, **4**, pp. 65–97.

Ministry of Environment and Tourism (Namibia) (1997).

Mintel International Group Limited (2000a). *2020 Vision: Tomorrow's Consumer* (also online). Mintel Marketing Intelligence.

Mintel International Group Limited (2000b). *Family Lifestyles and the Effect of Work – Family Leisure* (also online). Mintel Marketing Intelligence.

Mintel International Group Limited (2001a). *Extreme Sports* (also online). Mintel Marketing Intelligence.

Mintel International Group Limited (2001b). *Overland Expeditions* (also online). Mintel Marketing Intelligence.

Mintel (2002).

Mitchell, R.G. (1983). *Mountain Experience: The Psychology and Sociology Of Adventure*. The University of Chicago Press.

Morgan, D. (2000). Adventure tourism activities in New Zealand: perceptions and management of client risk. *Tourism Recreation Research*, **25(3)**, 79–89.

Mortlock, C. (1984). *The Adventure Alternative*, Cicerone Press.

Muller, T.E. and Cleaver, M. (2000). Targeting the CANZUS baby boomer explorer and adventurer segments. *Journal of Vacation Marketing*, **6(2)**, 154–169.

Murphy, D. (1994). *In Ethiopia with a Mule*. Flamingo.

Murphy, D. (1995). *On a Shoestring to Coorg*. Flamingo.

Murphy, D. (1995). *Eight Feet in the Andes*. Flamingo.

Myers, N. (1992). Genetic Materials and the Climate Connection. Proceedings of the International Conference, The Royal Geographic Society, London, May 1990. In *The Rainforest Harvest*, Friends of the Earth.

Newsome, D., Moore, S. and Dowling, R.K. (2002). *Natural Area Tourism: Ecology, Impacts and Management*. Channel View Publications.

O'Connell, D. (2002). Innovations 100: Travel: why getting away from it all has never been easier – and cheaper – for you and your dog. *The Observer*, 31 March.

Oddie, B. (1995). *Bill Oddie's Little Black Bird Book*. Robson Books Ltd.

O'Donnell, M. (ed.) (2001). Extreme sports: what, where and how; Observer Sport Monthly's detailed guide to taking up extreme sports. *The Observer*, 5 August.

O'Riordan, T. (1981). *Environmentalism*, 2nd edn. Pion.

Palacio, V. and McCool, S. F. (1997). Identifying ecotourists in Belize through benefit segmentation: a preliminary analysis. *Journal of Sustainable Tourism*, **5(3)**, 234–243.

Park, M., Yang, X., Lee, B., Jang, H C. and Stokowski, P.A. (2002). Segmenting casino gamblers by involvement profiles: a Colorado example. *Tourism Management*, **23**(1), 55–66.

Patmore, J.A. (1983). *Recreation and Resources; Leisure Patterns and Leisure Places*. Basil Blackwell.

Pearce, D. (1987). *Tourism Today: A Geographical Analysis*. Longman Scientific and Technical.

Pearce, D.W., Markandya, A. and Barbier, E.B. (1980). *Blueprint for a Green Economy*. Earthscan.

Pearce, D.W., Turner, R.K. and Bateman, I. (1994). *Environmental Economics*. Harvester Wheatsheaf.

Pearce, P.L. (1988). *The Ulysses Factor: Evaluating Visitors in Tourist Settings*. Springer-Verlag.

Pearce, P.L. (1996). Recent research in tourist behaviour. *Asia-Pacific Journal of Tourism Research*, **1(1)**, 7–17.

Peard, G. (1999). Spirit of the Earth – Chief Seathl's Speech. *Horizons*. UK Institute for Outdoor Learning, Issue No. 4.

Pelton, R.Y., Aral, C. and Dulles, W. (1997). *The World's Most Dangerous Places*. Fielding Worldwide.

Pigram, J. and Jenkin, J.M. (1999). *Outdoor Recreation Management*. Routledge.

Poon, A. (1993). *Tourism, Technology and Competitive Strategies*. CAB International.

Prance, G. (1992). *Rainforest Harvest: An Overview*. Friends of the Earth.

Price, T. (1974). Adventure by numbers, 'Mountain' 38 (1974). Reproduced in Wilson, K., *Games Climbers Play*. Baton Wicks.

Priest, S. (2001). The semantics of adventure programming. Chapter 14 in *Adventure Programming* (J. Miles and S. Priest, eds), Venture Publishing.

Priest, S. and Gass, M.A. (1997). *Effective Leadership in Adventure Programming*. Human Kinetics.

Pringle, H. and Thompson, M. (1999). *Brand Spirit: How cause related marketing builds brands*. Wiley.

Pritchard, P. (2000). *The Totem Pole*. Constable and Robinson Ltd.

Proudman, S. (1999). Urban adventure in 1989 and reflections ten years after. In *Adventure Programming* (J. Miles and S. Priest, eds), Venture Publishing.

Rayment, M. (1997). *Working with Nature in Britain: Case studies of nature conservation and local economies*. RSPB.

Rayment, M. and Dickie, I. (2001). *Conservation works ... for the local economies of the UK*. RSPB.

Reason, J. (1990). *Human Error*. Cambridge University Press.

Redclift and Benton (1994). *Social Theory and the Global Environment*. Routledge.

Reed, C. (1999). A weekend in the country – the outdoors, the earth and drama therapy. *Horizons*, **3**.

Roberts, L. and Hall, D. (2001). *Rural tourism and Recreation: Principles to Practice*. CABI Publishing.

Robinson, D. (1985). Stress seeking: selected behavioural characteristics of elite rock climbers. *Journal of Sport Psychology*, **7**, 400–404.

Robinson, D.W. (1992). A descriptive model of enduring risk recreation involvement. *Journal of Leisure Research*, **24(1)**, 52–63.

Robinson, N. (2001). Booby prize. *The Guardian*, 27 January.

Robinson, M., Long, P., Evans, N., Sharpley, R. and Swarbrooke, J. (eds) (2000). Reflections on International Tourism: motivations, behaviour and tourist types. Centre for Travel and Tourism in association with Business Education Publishers Ltd.

Roe, D., Leader-Williams, N. and Dalal-Clayton, B. (1997). *Take Only Photographs, Leave Only Footprints: The environmental impacts of wildlife tourism*. Wildlife and Development Series No. 10, International Institute for Environment and Development.

Ross, B. (2002). It's rocket science: The complete guide to outer space; the final frontier has been breached and space tourism is now a reality (for the rich). But package holidays to the Moon are a long way off. Or are they? *The Independent*, 13 April.

Rossi, B. and Cereatti, L. (1993). The sensation seeking in mountain athletes as assessed by Zuckerman's Sensation Seeking Scale. *International Journal of Sports Psychology*, **24**, 417–431.

Rough Guide (1991). *Nothing Ventured – Disabled People Travel the World*. Rough Guides.

Rowland, G.L., Franken, R.E. and Harrison, K. (1986). Sensation seeking and participation in sporting activities. *Journal of Sport Psychology*, **8**, 212–220.

Ryan, C. (1998). The travel career ladder: an appraisal. *Annals of Tourism Research*, **25(4)**, 936–957.

Schanzel, H.A. and McIntosh, A. (2000). An insight into the personal and emotive context of wildlife viewing at the Penguin Place, Otago Peninsula, New Zealand. *Journal of Sustainable Tourism*, **8(1)**, 36–52.

Scherl, L.M. (1989). Self in wilderness: understanding the psychological benefits of individual-wilderness interaction through self-control. *Leisure Sciences*, **11**, 123–135.

Schoon, N. (1997). What Price Nature? At £20 trillion a year it is truly our most precious asset. *The Independent*. 15 May.

Schueller, G.H. (2000). Thrill or chill. *New Scientist*, **29 April**, 20–24.

Schuett, M.A. (1993). Refining measures of adventure recreation involvement. *Leisure Sciences*, **15**, 205–216.

Schumacher, E.F. (1973). *Small is Beautiful: A Study of Economics as if People Mattered*. Harper Collins.

Scott and Asikoglu (2001). Gambling with paradise? Casino tourism development in northern Cyprus. *Tourism Recreation Research*, **26**.

Shackley, M. (1996). *Wildlife Tourism*. International Thomson Business Press.

Shaw, G. and Williams, A.M. (1994). *Critical Issues in Tourism: A Geographical Perspective*. Blackwell Publishers.

Shoham, A., Rose, G. and Kayle, L.R. (2000). Practitioners of risky sports: a quantitative examination. *Journal of Business Research*, **47**, 237–251.

Simmonite, D. (1999). Mallorca. *High Mountain Sports*, **February**, 10–13.

Skidelsky, R. (1983). *John Maynard Keynes, Volume 1. Hopes Betrayed 1883–1920*.

Macmillan WCED (World Commission on Environment and Development) (1992). Our Common Future (The Brundtland Report), London. Oxford University Press.

Smith, C. and Jenner, P. (1999). The adventure travel market in Europe. *Travel and Tourism Analyst*, **4**, 43–64.

Speciality Travel Index – Fall/Winter (1992). San Francisco.

Sung, H.H., Morrison, A.M. and O'Leary, J.T. (1997). Definition of adventure travel: Conceptual framework for empirical application from the provider's perspective. *Asia-Pacific Journal of Tourism Research*, **1(2)**, 47–67.

Tate, P. (2002). Alternative destinations. *Travel and Tourism Analyst*, Feb 2002, Mintel International Group Limited.

The Economic Intelligence Unit (1992). The UK adventure travel market. *Travel and Tourism Analyst*, **3**, 37–51.

Tourism Concern (2002). Beyond green backslapping. *Focus*, **42**, 9–10.

Trailblazer Publication (1998). *Asia Overland*.

Travel and Tourism Intelligence (2000).

Travel and Tourism Intelligence (2002).

Trimpop, R.M., Kerr, J.H. and Kircaldy, B. (1998). Comparing personality constructs of risk-taking behaviour. *Personality and Individual Differences*, **26(2)**, 237–254.

Tubbs, C. (1974). *The Buzzards*. David and Charles.

Turner, B.A. (1979). *Man-made Disasters*. Taylor & Francis.

Turner, B.A. (1994). Causes of disaster: sloppy management. *British Journal of Management*, **5**, 215–219.

Turner, S. (2001). Natural wonders of the world. *The Observer*, 18 February.

Tuson, M. (1994). *Outdoor Training for Employee Effectiveness*. CIPD.

UK Day Visits Survey (1998).

Ulrich (1974). Aesthetic and effective responses to natural environments. In *Behaviour and the Natural Environment* (I. Altman and J. Wohlwill, eds). Plenum Press.

Van der Smissen, B. (1990). Legal liability and risk management in public and private entities. In *Effective Leadership in Adventure Programming* (S. Priest and M.A. Gass, eds), Human Kinetics.

Vester, H.G. (1987). Adventure as a form of leisure. *Leisure Studies*, **6**, 237–249.

Voase, R. (1995). *Tourism: The Human Perspective*. Hodder and Stoughton.

Wearing, S. and Neal, J. (1999). *Ecotourism: Impacts, Potentials and Possibilities*. Butterworth-Heinemann.

Weaver, D.B. (1998). *Ecotourism in the Less Developed World*. CAB International.

Weiler, B. and Hall, C.M. (eds) (1992). *Special Interest Tourism*. Belhaven Press.

Weizsacker, E., von Lovins, A.B. and Lovins, L.H. (1997). *Factor Four – Doubling Wealth, Halving Resources. The New Report to the Club of Rome*. Earthscan.

Wheeler, T. (ed) (1999). *Lonely Planet Unpacked*. Lonely Planet Publications.

Wickens, E. (1994). Consumption of the authentic: the hedonistic.

Wickers, D. and Ryan, R. (2002). What are you doing this weekend? *Sunday Times*, 20 January.

Wight, P.A. (1996). North American ecotourists: market profile and trip characteristics. *Journal of Travel Research*, **35(1)**, 2–10.

Wilks, J. and Davis, R. (2000). Risk management for scuba diving operators on Australia's Great Barrier Reef. *Tourism Management*, **21**, 591–599.

Winch, D. (1971). *Analytical Welfare Economics*. Middlesex Penguin Education.

World Tourism Organization (1997). *Tourism 2020 Vision: Executive Summary*. WTO.

Wright, G. (1996). *National Parks and Protected Areas: Their Role in Environmental Protection*. Blackwells.

Yerkes, R. (1985). High adventure recreation in organized camping. *Trends*, **22(3)**, 10–11.

Young, J. (2000). Don't feed the animals. *Sunday Telegraph*, 24 December.

Zuckerman, M. (1979). *Sensation Seeking: Beyond The Optimal Level Of Arousal*. Erlbaum.

Zuckerman, M. (1994). Behavioural Expressions And Biosocial Basis Of Sensation Seeking. Cambridge University Press.

Brochures

Activities Abroad Holiday Brochure, UK Edition, 2002
Exodus Multi-Activity Holiday Brochure 2001–2002

Explore Worldwide Holiday Brochure 2001–2002
Foundry Mountain Activities (2001) 'Great Adventures' holiday brochure.

Websites

British Mountaineering Council (2001)
URL: http://thebmc.co.uk/indoor/walls
Centre Standards Board (2002): Approval Scheme
URL: http://www.adventuresports.ie/
Climb Catalunya (2002) General information.
URL: http://www.njday.com/host/climbcatalunya/info.html
Climb Catalunya (2002) Montserrat Massif.
URL: http://www.njday.com/host/climbcatalunya/mont.jtml
Climbing Media (2001) Microguide: climbing in Mallorca.
URL: http://www.com/mallorca/
Compass West International School of Rock Climbing, Spain
URL: http://www.compasswest.co.uk/files/spain/
Exodus (2002) Company information
URL: http://www.exodus.co.uk
First Choice (2002) Company information
URL: http://www.firstchoice.co.uk/
GREENFORCE (2001)
URL: http://www.greenforce.org/
High Places (2001) Trek grades
URL: http://www.highplaces.co.uk/
Mintel International Group Limited (1999)
www.activefamilyvacations.com
Plas-y-Brenin National Mountain Centre (2001)
URL: http://www.pyb.co.uk/course/rock.htm
ROCKFAX (2001)
URL: http://rockfax.com
www.spaceadventures.com
Thomas Cook (2002) Company history
URL: http://cms.thomascookag.com/

Index

CPSIA information can be obtained at www.ICGtesting.com
Printed in the USA
LVOW032048271211

261266LV00002B/3/P